Campaigns on the Cutting Edge

Campaigns on the Cutting Edge

Edited by
Richard J. Semiatin
American University

CQ PRESS

A Division of Congressional Quarterly Inc.
Washington, D.C.

CQ Press
2300 N Street, NW, Suite 800
Washington, DC 20037

Phone: 202-729-1900; toll-free, 1-866-4CQ-PRESS (1-866-427-7737)

Web: www.cqpress.com

Cover design by McGaughy Design, Centreville, VA
Typesetting by MacPS, LLC, Indianapolis, IN

⊗ The paper used in this publication exceeds the requirements of the American National Standard for Information Sciences—Permanence of Paper for Printed Library Materials, ANSI Z39.48-1992.

Printed and bound in the United States of America

12 11 10 09 08   1 2 3 4 5

LIBRARY OF CONGRESS CATALOGING-IN-PUBLICATION DATA

Campaigns on the cutting edge / edited by Richard J. Semiatin.
    p. cm.
  Includes bibliographical references and index.
  ISBN 978-0-87289-579-9 (pbk. : alk. paper) 1. Political campaigns—United States—History—21st century. 2. Elections—United States—History—21st century. 3. United States—Politics and government—21st century. I. Semiatin, Richard J.
JK2281.C37 2008
324.70973—dc22

                                                                  2007051575

To our families and friends,

to whom we owe so much

Contents

Preface

Campaigns on the Cutting Edge marks the beginning of a new era in campaigns, as the job of managing candidacies moves toward a new frontier. The new frontier represents both change from and continuity with the past. As new technology enables campaigns to reach voters through a virtual medium, it does not mean that campaigns will eschew the techniques of the past. The personal campaign politics that dominate the first presidential precinct caucus (Iowa) and presidential primary (New Hampshire) remain critical. However, with the Internet and responsive media, major campaigns for national political office are virtually or actually alive twenty-four hours a day. The pressure on candidates, consultants, campaign organizations, political parties, interest groups, and the press is unceasing. The election cycle for presidential races is now two years and for major Senate races, in many cases, eighteen months. Books and articles have been written on the permanent campaign. Today we have the *ever-present* campaign—that is exciting and challenging to both the campaign consultant and the armchair political analyst.

The book you are about to read captures the transformation that is taking place in campaigns today and where they are headed in the future. The book's scope goes beyond the 2008 elections and looks toward the next decade of campaign politics. The authors have been asked to make informed speculations on the next wave of political change, so that the book remains as relevant in 2010 or 2012 as it is today. These authors include not only skilled political scientists but also participants—including Tad Devine (media consultant and chief strategist for Al Gore), Tari Renner (congressional candidate in 2004), and Dick Simpson (congressional candidate in 1992 and 1994). Almost all the contributors have lived and worked in the cauldron of Washington, D.C., politics and policy. The book is written to give students, faculty, and political observers a keen sense of the reality of national political campaigns from an insider's perspective. In that light, the book is written without a lot of jargon.

Even as the book is being prepared for publication, changes are taking place in the political environment. For example, in January 2008 the U.S. Supreme Court heard a case from the state of Indiana regarding a law that requires voters to present a photo ID at the balloting station. Do such laws discriminate against nondrivers, or poor voters who may lack a photo ID? The Court will decide. Its decision can certainly affect how voters are contacted, registered, persuaded, and motivated to vote. We cannot account for all the changes that may take place over the next five or ten years, but we look through the lens of contemporary politics to see what cutting-edge changes are on the horizon. The import of those changes is expressed eloquently in the book's conclusion on the implications for the democratic process.

I would like to thank my colleagues who have written chapters on such short notice—particularly Mark Rozell, who has been my chief sounding board for the project. The contributors to this volume collectively have written and edited over fifty scholarly books. It is an honor to work with such a group of thoughtful and active scholars.

The editors and other staff at CQ Press deserve great thanks for the skill and speed with which they prepared this manuscript. I would particularly like to thank Charisse Kiino, who worked with me diligently to conceptualize the process and is exceptionally intelligent; Brenda Carter, the director of CQ Press's College division, who gave an enthusiastic thumbs-up for the project; and Allie McKay, who works efficiently and cheerfully on a daily basis with difficult people (a.k.a., authors) and can multitask with the best! Steve Pazdan and Gwenda Larsen deserve kudos for shepherding an expedited production process—no easy task and no small thank you. Erin Snow is a delight to work with because she understands how to market political science books and has a can-do attitude that inspires. For colleagues, please note that Nancy Geltman did an excellent job copyediting the book under pressure. She edits in the voice of the author and not her own. What a pleasure, and I cannot thank her enough.

I would also like to thank my dean, David C. Brown, who provided me with a course reduction to work on this project in the spring of 2007; that was very thoughtful and helpful. And I thank my long-term colleagues at American University for their moral support: Donna Chapman, Candy Nelson, Christian Maisch, Bea Siman-Zakhari, Katharine Kravetz, Jack Rossotti, Sue Headlee, Iris Krasnow, John Calabrese, Diane Lowenthal, and Barb Palmer. My oldest D.C. politics colleague, Tari Renner, who wrote a chapter in this book, has been a valuable sounding board, as well, because he is a thoroughly grounded person and a true friend. I would like to thank my great friend Max Cleland, who is one of the most kindhearted, thoughtful, and inspirational people you could ever meet. A special thank you to my students, especially the perceptive ones, from whom I have learned that just because someone is twenty does not mean he or she cannot teach you. Finally, I want to thank my wonderful parents, siblings, nephews, and nieces for putting up with me for the last half-century. What a supportive family I have, and what an honor it is to be one of them.

Now, I want to welcome the reader into the exciting and provocative world of campaigns.

Contributors

About the Editor

Richard J. Semiatin, PhD, American University, assistant professor of government, is a current faculty member of the Washington Semester Program at American University. He was one of twenty-one professors selected in a national search by the Carnegie Foundation for the Advancement of Teaching to participate in its Political Engagement Project (PEP). Semiatin specializes in campaigns and elections. He is the author of *Campaigns in the 21st Century* (2005), five monographs on elections, book chapters, and articles. He is also a contributing editor of *NetPulse,* the global e-journal of online politics.

About the Contributors

Robert G. Boatright is an assistant professor of government at Clark University. He is the author of *Expressive Politics: Issue Strategies of Congressional Challengers* (2004) and several articles on campaign finance and congressional politics. Prior to joining the faculty at Clark, he was a research analyst at the Campaign Finance Institute and an American Political Science Association Congressional Fellow. Boatright is coauthor of a forthcoming Campaign Finance Institute study of interest group adaptations to the Bipartisan Campaign Reform Act, and he is currently preparing a book manuscript comparing American and Canadian interest group responses to campaign finance reform.

Tad Devine is a Democratic media consultant who has produced political ads for candidates in the United States and around the world. He is president of Devine Mulvey, a media and strategic consulting firm in Washington, D.C. He has created media in seventeen winning U.S. Senate campaigns and dozens of winning races for governor, local and statewide elective office, and the House of Representatives. He has extensive experience at the highest levels of presidential campaigning in the United States and has worked on nine winning campaigns for president or prime minister around the world. Devine has taught courses on campaigns and media at Boston University and at The George Washington University Graduate School of Political Management.

Peter L. Francia is an assistant professor in the department of political science at East Carolina University. He is the author of *The Future of Organized Labor in American Politics* (2006) and coauthor of *Conventional Wisdom and American Elections: Exploding Myths, Exploring Misconceptions* (2008) and *The Financiers of Congressional Elections: Investors, Ideologues, and Intimates* (2003). Francia has published more than thirty articles and book chapters on subjects such as American national elections, campaign finance, election reform, political parties, political action committees, and interest groups. He holds a PhD in government and politics from the University of Maryland, College Park.

Joseph Graf is assistant professor in the school of communication at American University. He is a former newspaper reporter and the former research director for the Institute for Politics, Democracy & the Internet at The George Washington University. He has published on political communication and online politics and focuses on the intersection of civic involvement and new media.

Wesley Y. Joe is a research scholar/policy analyst at the Campaign Finance Institute. He has published several articles and book chapters on the efficacy of campaign finance regulations, major individual contributors to congressional campaigns, and other topics. He received his PhD in government from Georgetown University, where he has also taught as an adjunct assistant professor of government.

Nina Therese Kasniunas is a visiting assistant professor at Allegheny College, where she teaches courses on American institutions, interest groups, and women in politics. Her current research is examining congressional committee hearings and influence that interest groups may exert on policy by participating as witnesses. Other projects include looking at the potential democratizing effect of Internet technology on the mobilization activities of interest groups.

Jeremy D. Mayer is an associate professor at the George Mason University School of Public Policy who specializes in presidential elections, public opinion, racial politics, and foreign policy. He has published widely on American politics, and his book *Running on Race: Racial Politics in Presidential Campaigns 1960–2000* (2002) was selected by *Washington Monthly* as one of the best political books of 2002. His other books include *American Media Politics in Transition* (2008), and he has just completed a coauthored book on politics in higher education.

Candice J. Nelson is an associate professor and chair of the department of government at American University. She is the coauthor of *Vital Signs: Perspectives on the Health of American Campaigning* (2005); *The Myth of the Independent Voter* (1992); and *The Money Chase: Congressional Campaign Finance Reform* (1990) and coeditor of *Campaigns and Elections American Style* (2004); *Shades of Gray: Perspectives on Campaign Ethics* (2002); *Campaign Warriors: Political Consultants in Elections* (2000); and *Crowded Airwaves: Campaign Advertising in Elections* (2000). A former American Political Science Association Congressional Fellow, Nelson received her BA from Wheaton College (Massachusetts), her MA from UCLA, and her PhD from the University of California at Berkeley.

Tari Renner is a professor and chair of the political science department at Illinois Wesleyan University in Bloomington. He has served three terms as an elected member of the McLean County (Bloomington area) legislature. In 2004, Renner was the Democratic nominee for U.S. Congress in Illinois' Eleventh Congressional District. His research interests include American electoral behavior and local government structures. Renner received his PhD from American University in 1985.

Mark J. Rozell is a professor of public policy at George Mason University. He is the author or coauthor of nine books on American politics, including *Interest Groups in American Campaigns* (2nd edition, 2006), *Power and Prudence: The Presidency of George H.W. Bush* (2004), and *Executive Privilege: Presidential Power, Secrecy, and Accountability* (2nd edition, 2002).

Ronald G. Shaiko is a senior fellow and associate director for curricular and research programs at the Nelson A. Rockefeller Center for Public Policy and the Social Sciences, at Dartmouth College. He was recently named the Gridley Faculty Fellow at Dartmouth College for 2007–2008. He has served as the Fulbright Distinguished Chair in American Politics at Warsaw University, Poland (2000–2001); as a Democracy Fellow in the Center for Democracy and Governance at the U.S. Agency for International Development (1997–1999); and as the William A. Steiger APSA Congressional Fellow in the U.S. House of Representatives (1993–1994).

Dick Simpson has uniquely combined a distinguished academic career with public service in government. He began his academic career in 1967 at the University of Illinois at Chicago, where he has taught for forty years and where he currently serves as department head and professor of political science. Simpson was alderman for

Chicago's 44th ward and leader of the opposition bloc from 1971 to 1979. He ran for Congress in 1992 and 1994 against Congressman Dan Rostenkowsi. Simpson has published more than ninety professional journal articles, magazine articles, book chapters, documentary films, and book reviews. He is the author or coauthor of sixteen books on political action, elections, ethics, and politics, including *Inside Urban Politics* (2004); *Rogues, Rebels, and Rubber Stamps* (2001); and *Winning Elections* (1996).

Clyde Wilcox is professor of government at Georgetown University. He worked for the Federal Election Commission in the 1980s and is the author of numerous books and articles on campaign finance, religion and politics, gender politics, and the politics of science fiction. His most recent books include *New Boundaries of Political Science Fiction* (2008), *The Politics of Same-Sex Marriage* (2007), *Onward Christian Soldiers? The Religious Right in American Politics* (3rd edition, 2006), and *The Financiers of Congressional Elections: Investors, Ideologues, and Intimates* (2003).

Campaigns on the Cutting Edge

Part I:

The New Political Campaign

CHAPTER 1

Introduction — Campaigns on the Cutting Edge

Richard J. Semiatin

"YOU SAY SOMETHING TODAY, and it will be on the air in eight or nine minutes." [1] Fifty years ago, an offhand comment by a politician might never be on the air, or at least it would have been vetted for hours, or even a day, before it was aired or published. The world of political campaigns has changed, and some of that change is irrevocable. Every aspect of a campaign is public today. In fact, starting in 2008 some presidential campaigns have their own online television networks, showing the candidate at events, campaign surrogates speaking on the candidate's behalf, or live action at the campaign's headquarters.

Campaigns are becoming more individualized and tailored to *you,* the voter. For the first 150 years, U.S. campaigns were largely the domain of party organizations. The birth of television and the advent of advertising spawned personality-driven campaigns. Today we see the next revolution: that campaigns are attempting to reach each voter individually. The campaigns of the future (and to some extent the future is now) can target each household. Campaigns used to be about parties and candidates. Increasingly, campaigns will be about you, the voter, or as Madison Avenue would say, the customer. This book is neither a review of the political science literature nor a discourse on the democratic implications of elections and campaigns, although that latter discussion remains valuable and important (and is addressed in the book's conclusion). The book focuses instead on evaluating current trends and assessing how national campaigns are changing. We look at the changes on the presidential, congressional, and gubernatorial levels.

We explore the most important facets of campaigns (fundraising, paid advertising, new media, polling, and voter mobilization); the institutions that work in campaigns (parties and interest groups) and report on them (the press); and those that govern the process of campaigns (campaign finance and election administration). The authors examine the current place of politics within each of those realms and what the future may hold. Given the pace at which new technology is entering the political arena, it is often difficult to capture every possible trend on the horizon—a decade ago we could not have foreseen iPhones and the new ways that campaigns might be able to communicate to voters. We also note that changes and trends will develop in the interim between the book's completion and publication. Given that, we still prepare to examine and evaluate, even if imperfectly, what the future holds in store for campaigns.

Readers should note that some of our themes weave together. Campaigns of the future will involve more overlapping functions. For example, drawing a distinct line between what the paid advertising consultant does and what the campaign's Internet consultant does is not always possible. Some videos produced by ad makers appear on the Internet and not on television; some appear on both. Consultants work together to determine the best venue for disseminating particular information. Problems can arise when the Internet consultant seeks to edit, for space and production, the ad makers' work. The division of labor in campaigns is less neat than in the past, and that could spell trouble. For if the campaign manager allows those lines to become too blurred, turf fighting within a campaign can be all-consuming.

Yet the changes that are taking place are breathtaking and empowering. Campaigns we passively watched on our living room televisions twenty years ago are now in our hands because of new technologies, including the new wave of handheld devices that work as phones, computers, and personal assistants. We have greater control over how we receive information. Yet information coming to us can be manipulated, for better or worse, as addressed in the book's conclusion. Campaigns that fail to adapt to the new world of politics will not succeed. But technology's reach is not limitless; it complements many of the traditional aspects of campaigns. Technology can never supplant a personal appearance on behalf of a candidate that stirs you personally. Imagine what it would have been like to attend one of Lincoln's speeches in person or to watch Lincoln and Douglas debate slavery at Knox College, Illinois, in 1858. The power would not be the same if one watched it on television or cnn.com. Technology is a facilitator but not a substitute. Traditional campaign techniques that worked a hundred years ago (such as volunteers knocking on neighbors' doors to get out the vote on election day) still work today. Campaigns just have new tools to complement the old ones.[2] That makes the process of running campaigns more complex, and time becomes a more precious commodity.

The New Political Campaign

The new political campaign demonstrates the importance of contact, communications, and feedback with voters. Part I of this book, "The New Political Campaign," discusses the various facets of campaigns, from raising money and communicating through paid and new media, to targeting messages to mobilize citizens to vote. Campaigns are not only incorporating new technological changes into the tactics of campaigns, but also must make them work seamlessly with the techniques of the past. Chapters examine what has worked in the past and present and, most important, speculate what the future may hold.

"Money is the mother's milk of politics"—when California state legislator Jesse Unruh (D) uttered those words two generations ago, it was important.[3] Given the high cost of national campaigns today—presidential campaigns or even congressional—Unruh's words are more than important; they are prophetic. Money helps facilitate speech and amplify a candidate's message to a mass audience. Money helps to identify voters and to target them for mobilization.

Robert G. Boatright's chapter 2, on fundraising, illuminates the various techniques of traditional fundraising (direct mail, events, telemarketing) and then ventures into the new world of fundraising using targeted lists and e-mail and online solicitations. Boatright shows how campaigns seek repeat visitors to candidate Web sites. The more often they come, the more often they will donate. Boatright shows the distinction between presidential and congressional campaigns online. Because presidential races have substantially more resources, and the candidates are much better known, attracting visitors to those Web sites is much easier. He wisely points out that the Internet by itself is not enough and that candidates will not get by in the foreseeable future without understanding that they still must reach potential donors in traditional ways. Technology adds more dimensions to fundraising, but it does not supplant traditional techniques.

Most of the money expended in major campaigns goes to advertising. The percentage can range from 50 percent up to more than 80 percent of the total budget in a presidential race. Tad Devine, one of the nation's leading campaign media consultants, discusses the role of paid advertising in political campaigns in the third chapter. Devine covers the role of media consultants as ad makers and strategists. Ads are research-based for message development. He draws on well-known campaigns he has worked on, including John Edwards's successful bid for North Carolina senator in 1998, Sen. Bill Nelson's reelection race in Florida in 2006, Bernie Sanders's successful Senate campaign in Vermont, and Chris Carney's election to the U.S. House from Pennsylvania, to illustrate biographical, accomplishment/vision, issue, and negative ads. Devine points out that digitization has improved the visual quality of commercials far beyond what was seen in the past. Visual cues, sound, and script must work together to produce a convincing ad. Devine shows that paid advertising in the future will incorporate television, the Internet, and phones. The challenge for media consultants in the future is using them together effectively.

In chapter 4 Joseph Graf addresses the brave new world of "new media" and how campaigns try to harness the changes that are transforming communications daily. Online social networks (such as Facebook), political e-mail, video, and blogs enable citizens to interact with campaigns. On the one hand, they create greater social interaction. On the other hand, even the most financially well off campaigns do not have the resources to patrol what bloggers write daily. The task is simply too great, and the priorities are with the actual business of day-to-day campaign operations. For example, Anne Marcotte, who was a blogger for the John Edwards presidential campaign, resigned in February 2007 after making disparaging comments that were interpreted to be anti-Catholic by some in that community.[4]

Graf also finds that given the amount of interaction, and modes of interface from desktop to cell phones to iPhones, the audience that campaigns engage is the faithful or the interested. Technology is a facilitator that, when managed properly, enables a campaign to communicate with its base and enlist their support.

When campaigns communicate, as noted earlier, they do so on the basis of research. That includes examining past voting behavior in states and localities, the demography of the electorate, and their attitudes and behavior. It is that last skill that is the most sensitive to measure, for it involves surveying voters. The cutting edge of change in technology sometimes results in problems for pollsters, as Candice J. Nelson explains in the fifth chapter. Nelson shows that cell phone users who do not have landlines are a growing proportion of the population. It means pollsters reach fewer voters, given that mobile telephone numbers are not widely available, and that it is becoming more difficult for researchers to reach individuals under the age of thirty. Furthermore, the cost of campaign polling is greater and obtaining a truly random sample of a population to survey is more difficult. While that might seem like a good invitation to do online surveys, perhaps it is not. Reaching voters online is fraught with problems, too, as Nelson explains. Nelson has surveyed many of the nation's top survey research experts to provide the reader with insight into the difficulties of polling today and the reasons why online solutions have not yet appeared.

The new voter mobilization to get people to the polls merges traditional demographic and voting information with information about people's lifestyle and patterns of consumption. The result is that campaigns, which in the past targeted down to the neighborhood and block levels, can now target individual homes on almost every street. These activities, which were the province of party organizations several decades ago, are today the work of the campaigns, as I describe in the sixth chapter. In 2004 the Bush/Cheney campaign, and not the Republican National Committee, supervised the party's major get-out-the-vote (GOTV) effort. Campaigns are now using lifestyle targeting that melds consumer information with traditional voting and polling data. These customer-centered techniques have invaded from the business world and now are a permanent part of campaigns. This author argues that in 2008 and beyond, the major-party presidential campaigns will be spending hundreds of millions, and together about a billion dollars. As they soak up so much of the available contribution money, the presidential campaigns increasingly are running the major GOTV operations, supplanting the parties in that traditional role in White House election years.

The Evolving Campaign—Adaptation by Political Institutions and Implications for Democracy

Part II, "The Evolving Campaign," features political parties, interest groups, and press coverage in the campaign process. The administrative institutions that govern campaign finance and elections administration are also coping with new technologies, with changes coming at rapid pace. Parties and interest groups have benefited from what that small rectangular box—the computer—can do for them to raise money and awareness among constituents. Press coverage has mushroomed through the proliferation of citizen reporters who monitor the *virtual* campaign on the Internet and blogs, as well as the *real* campaign.

Congress sought to restrict the unregulated contributions known as "soft money" through the Bipartisan Campaign Reform Act of 2002 (BCRA—better known as "McCain/Feingold"). Campaign reform is part of the populist effort to regulate the $4 billion campaign industry, which continues to grow and adapt to the political marketplace. Another major controversy concerns the process of counting votes; that became a preeminent issue when the Supreme Court adjudicated the end to the 2000 presidential elections. The changing roles of campaigns, parties, interest groups, and the press and the reform issues of campaign finance and election administration leave us to consider their impact on democracy.

For years, political scientists and politicos bemoaned the declining party system. But Ronald G. Shaiko's seventh chapter finds that parties are now more vigorous than a generation ago because they have become revitalized as campaign service organizations—recruiting candidates, training them, and raising hundreds of millions of dollars. Shaiko's analysis includes an interview with Democratic National Committee chairman Howard Dean. He shows that the Republicans were the pioneers in modernizing the campaign organization. That modernization, as we know, paid dividends during the 1980s and 1990s, as Republicans slowly reemerged as the majority, first in the U.S. Senate and later in the House, while the Democratic Party organization floundered. Shaiko demonstrates that since the 2000 election the Democrats have not only caught up to Republicans as innovators, but have recently surpassed them. In fundraising they have more than caught up with Republicans; recently they have surpassed them. The parties are now using customer relationship management (CRM) techniques (the aforementioned lifestyle targeting), just as campaigns do, for GOTV operations. National party committee organizations are structured similarly to major national political campaigns.

Interest groups are taking a similar route, according to Nina Therese Kasniunas and Mark J. Rozell, acting more like campaign organizations and using new technologies such as podcasting and online videos in addition to the standard techniques of group contact. The purpose, the authors explain in the eighth chapter, is to keep in continuous contact with their members. Given that interest groups members are more closely associated with their group than a random campaign supporter is with a candidate, Web sites are particularly important for contributions and mobilization, especially those of the giant interest groups such as the National Rifle Association and the Sierra Club. Interest groups now have more tools at their disposal to maximize their influence by serving as a third force between two campaigns. Kasniunas and Rozell also take a somewhat different perspective on the changes in campaigning, arguing that the change is toward group-centered politics. Vive la différence!

Nowhere has new technology concerning campaigns had more effect institutionally than with the press. Jeremy D. Mayer especially focuses on the Internet as a new medium in the campaign world. Mayer's ninth chapter demonstrates a disturbing trend in which the line between campaign activist and reporter becomes blurred. "News" reporting on the Internet lacks the filter of traditional journalistic review for confirmation, making the net a haven for innuendo and rumor. While that is not new to journalism, it is more harmful today because candidates have little time to squelch rumors. Moreover, with newspaper readership and broadcast news viewing in decline, the mainstream news media must compete in this new marketplace. Because of competition from the Internet, political news coverage is often a search for the lowest common denominator, in the effort to attract readers and viewers. Mayer points out that bloggers as reporters have no editors to edit them. The consequences are profoundly distressing, especially if bloggers present themselves as journalists, when in fact they are partisans.

Although the future promises much change in political campaigns, political institutions, and parties and how they raise money and spend it, there is little evidence that major reform to limit the role of money in politics is likely to happen. McCain/Feingold brought more accountability to campaign finance but left a loophole for independent political groups, known as "527s." Peter Francia, Wesley Joe, and Clyde Wilcox explain in the book's tenth chapter that the chances of major campaign finance reform in the near future are slim. Instead, campaign reform may result from thinking "outside the box"; what may emerge are cutting-edge ideas to attract donors who do not give large contributions. As discussed near the close of chapter 10, such new modes of thinking may eventually enable Republicans who support campaign finance deregulation and Democrats who support contribution limits once again to work together in a bipartisan way. However, that does not appear to be on the immediate political horizon.

Election administration ties the ends of the campaigns and elections process together. Federalism governs election administration—although the federal government has a role in governing voter participation and access, ultimately the elections process is administered in the states, as explained in chapter 11. The cutting edge of change in elections administration is in the new computer technology that has been enabled by the Help America Vote Act (HAVA) after the 2000 election debacle of counting chads in Florida. Tari Renner shows that whereas computer technology facilitates voting at the polling booth, concerns remain not only about security but also about the verification process. Internet voting, by and large, is still a work in progress.

The conscience of the book is in its conclusion. Technology increases participation, but does it not also increase the ability to manipulate voters? Author Dick Simpson, who has politicked in the wards of Chicago, wants us to consider that the wonderful, cutting-edge changes discussed in the book, no matter how inviting and exciting, have the potential for great harm as well as hope—that democracy is fragile. Technology should be monitored so that it does not endanger rights that we hold dear. Consultants, citizens, and officeholders should understand that longtime rituals in politics are still virtuous. If they do, there is hope, and if not, the seeds of destructive politics will be sown for the future. But the present does offer great possibilities for the future, and the future is increasingly becoming the present, as we journey into the world of campaigns.

Notes

1. Tim Crawford, consultant, New Models, personal interview, August 9, 2007.
2. Rob Engel, former executive director, Democratic National Committee, currently directing the Foundation for the Future redistricting project for 2011–2012, personal interview, July 9, 2007.
3. "The New Jess Unruh," *Time,* September 14, 1970 (accessed September 6, 2007, from time.com).
4. Howard Kurtz, "A Blogger for Edwards Resigns after Complaints," *Washington Post,* February 13, 2007, A4.

CHAPTER 2

Fundraising — Present and Future
Robert G. Boatright

IN THE FIRST SIX MONTHS OF 2007, 258,000 people contributed to Sen. Barack Obama's (D-Ill.) presidential campaign.[1] This was an unprecedented number of contributors, especially for so early in the campaign season. The Obama campaign's achievement, however, is just the newest step in the drive by candidates—and presidential candidates in particular—to harness new technology to communicate with contributors and attract more of them.

Few politicians will openly admit that they enjoy raising money. Although some excel at it, most find it at least a little bit humiliating to call strangers, or even close friends, to ask for contributions. One successful candidate, Rep. David Price (D-N.C.), has written that in his first campaign he and his wife had to "shed their inhibitions," sending solicitations to "our Christmas card lists from years past, our professional colleagues at home and across the country, and far-flung family members." [2] Yet the ability to raise large sums of money quickly—to win the "money primary"—is one of the most important factors in congressional and presidential elections. Candidates must be equally skilled at courting people who have given to them in the past and at identifying new contributors. The fundraising techniques of the next several years will be those that can bring in large amounts of money cheaply and quickly, while at the same time establishing an ongoing relationship (or at least the illusion of one) between candidates and donors. The most promising of those techniques is Internet fundraising.

It is unclear whether money raised on the Internet is really "new" money or is money that candidates would have raised anyway through other means, such as direct mail or telephone. Techniques such as phone banking, direct mail, and face-to-face fundraising entail significant costs to candidates, however. The Internet yields a much greater return for the fundraising dollar than other means of fundraising, and the yield is almost instantaneous.

Internet fundraising has the potential to bring different types of donors into the political system and to improve the effectiveness of different types of appeals. Online donors are different from traditional donors demographically and ideologically, although they are becoming less so every election cycle.[3] Because of this, many traditional assumptions about how to raise money for campaigns have been called into question. Candidates who use the Web to raise money can raise larger sums from small donors than has traditionally been the case in campaigns; they can effectively give donors an idea of how their money will be used; and they can more easily resolicit donors throughout the campaign. Although building an early base of large donors can send a signal to political elites about the viability of one's campaign, candidates and interest groups showed in 2004 and 2006 that "viral" campaigning—meaning using social networks to contact people whose names the candidates and groups do not already have—can help candidates raise money quickly to respond to their opponents, to mount advertising campaigns, or to meet fundraising benchmarks.

I begin this chapter by summarizing what we know about campaign contributors and then describe how fundraising has traditionally worked in congressional and presidential elections and how it has changed in the past three election cycles. Finally I turn to how fundraising will evolve in the future.

Where the Donors Are

Unlike other forms of political participation, the ability to contribute money to political campaigns is highly dependent on how much money you have. It costs a person nothing other than his or her time to attend campaign rallies or to campaign actively for a candidate, but it is not possible to make a thousand-dollar contribution if one does not have that kind of money to give. Not surprisingly, studies of campaign contributors in the past have consistently shown that the majority are wealthy, well educated, white, and male.

One of the most common misperceptions about campaign contributors, however, is that donations to political causes are a form of "checkbook participation," a substitute for other forms of political activism. Peter Francia and his coauthors have shown, to the contrary, that contributors to congressional candidates are people who are ensconced in political networks.[4] Seventy-eight percent of those who give to congressional candidates are habitual donors, 60 percent are involved in soliciting contributions from others, and nearly half have worked for candidates in another capacity. Contributors also are more likely than nondonors to belong to professional or business groups, fraternal or civic associations, or issue-oriented political groups.[5] Contributions are best seen as an extension of political activism, not a substitute for it. People give because they are part of a community.

Successful candidates may have an active list of friends or longtime supporters, but the costs of campaigning are now so high that such a list is rarely enough. Today candidates are finding that not only must they encourage potential donors to give, they must court people who have given to other candidates and persuade them to give to them, and they have to encourage donors to go out and recruit friends or colleagues to give.

Highly ideological candidates of both the left and the right have been notably successful at this in the past. In the 1990s, for instance, liberal senator Paul Wellstone (D-Minn.) and conservative Senate candidate Oliver North (R-Va.) excelled at raising contributions in amounts of $20 or $50 from citizens around the country. Similarly, former representative Bob Dornan (R-Calif.) was known for his effective direct-mail program, through which he was able raise substantial amounts of money, again in very small individual contributions.[6] But while it may look good for a candidate to raise money in small amounts, it is not very efficient to do so. One estimate from the 1990s is that fundraising costs a campaign fifty cents for each dollar raised in amounts under $50, whereas it costs only twenty cents for each dollar raised in amounts above $50.[7]

There is little evidence, however, that donors are more extreme than the general public in their ideology. The 2004 and 2006 elections attracted many new donors into the political process. According to one estimate, virtually all younger donors gave via the Internet. In those elections, small donors and Internet donors were disproportionately younger, more politically active, and more liberal than prior donors.[8] This may be a temporary shift, or it may reflect the fact that Internet users in general tend to display those traits more than the general public. A study by the Institute for Politics, Democracy, and the Internet discusses what its authors describe as "Online Political Citizens," individuals who engage in political discussions and activism on the Internet. Such individuals, again, are disproportionately younger, better educated, and more Democratic than the general public and other Internet users.[9] These individuals are not, however, veteran political activists; the study found that 44 percent had never worked for a campaign, attended a campaign event, or made a campaign donation before 2004.

There is some evidence, then, that the universe of donors is changing. Although it is difficult at this point to argue that donors have changed enough for candidates to completely jettison successful fundraising strategies of the past, several recent campaigns have shown that the Internet has changed the process of political fundraising. Twenty years ago, most Americans gathered political information from the TV network news; today, many Internet users report gathering the bulk of their political news from political news sites, blogs, e-mail listservs, and even from news satire programs such as *The Daily Show*.[10] Well-placed campaign advertisements on heavily trafficked sites can lead Internet users straight to a campaign donation page. In recent elections fundraisers have had far less idea who their contributors or potential contributors were than was the case in the past.

Traditional Fundraising Practices

Candidates for the House, the Senate, and the presidency expend tremendous effort to raise money. For incumbents, the volume of money they raise can deter potentially strong challengers. For open-seat candidates and challengers, prolific fundraising can provide instant credibility. Campaign organizations have the daunting task of determining the trade-off between time spent raising money and time spent campaigning. A successful campaign can have it both ways, using fundraising techniques that actively employ the candidate, such as fundraising events, to complement those with little direct candidate participation, such as direct mail.

Setting the Stage for Fundraising

Political communications consultant Marty Stone advises potential candidates for Congress to make a list of everyone they know and then contact each individual for a donation.[11] For aspiring candidates, it is never too early to start compiling lists. Former governor Jimmy Carter (D-Ga.) built a list of contacts when he chaired the Democratic National Committee's campaign for congressional and gubernatorial races in the 1974 midterm elections. Those contacts helped Carter build an organizational and fundraising network for his 1976 presidential campaign, even though he had little national exposure. The national party organizations want to know whether a candidate, at any level, has the potential to raise a substantial amount of money—anywhere from several hundred thousand dollars for a congressional candidate to over one million for a senatorial candidate—on his or her own before they are willing to take a serious role promoting that candidate's election.

Phone Banks

Telemarketing remains one of the mainstays of fundraising. For years, Republican candidates built their donor base through extensive telemarketing efforts. The Republican National Committee (RNC) had a tremendous advantage in fundraising over the Democratic National Committee (DNC) during the 1980s and 1990s, largely because of its extensive telemarketing database. Much of the Republican advantage was built through the close links between the Ronald Reagan campaigns of 1980 and 1984 and the RNC, which was staffed during the 1980s by Reagan administration loyalists. In 1984, Linda Cherry, deputy director of voter programs for the Reagan reelection campaign, launched what has been dubbed "the first nationwide presidential campaign telemarketing operation."[12] Telemarketing enabled the Reagan campaign, and others that followed the model, to reach potential supporters for two purposes—fundraising and voter mobilization. Ultimately the strategy contributed significantly to expanding the database of contributors to the party and to Republican candidates.

The scripts that phone solicitors read are generally based less on partisanship and more on "gut" issues such as gun control, abortion, and the environment. The scripts also can connect candidates to an issue. Having someone to run against can be particularly useful. During the 1980s, opposition to Sen. Ted Kennedy (D-Mass.) caused many people to donate to the Republicans, and Sen. Jesse Helms (R-N.C.) did a similar service for the Democrats. During the 1990s, Bill and Hillary Clinton and House Speaker Newt Gingrich (R-Ga.) were also highly effective as generators of opposition fundraising.

Fundraising Events

Events are another long-standing means of raising money in campaigns. Among the best known are the Jefferson-Jackson Day dinners for Democrats and Lincoln Day dinners for Republicans. From the traditional "rubber chicken" fundraiser at $100-per-head to the $2,300-per-head dinners that presidential candidates hold at posh vacation resorts, events remain a critical part of candidate fundraising because there is no substitute for the opportunity to meet and converse with other like-minded supporters (and even the candidate).[13]

Candidates often bring in political "superstars" to help them raise money. According to ABC News, Sen. Hillary Clinton (D-N.Y.) set a goal of raising $5 million for Democratic congressional and senatorial candidates while running for her own reelection in 2006. Moreover, that $5 million goal, from start to finish, was reached between late September and late October. The senator appeared at individual campaign and fundraising events for others, such as Senate candidate Jim Webb (D-Va.) on October 3, Senate candidate Sherrod Brown (D-Ohio) on October 7, and House candidate Diane Farrell (D-Conn.) on October 8.[14]

Direct Mail

Direct mail has been a staple of campaign fundraising since the 1970s, when conservative activist Richard Viguerie raised tens of millions of dollars for Republican candidates. In House races, direct-mail solicitations tend to be sent within the district, but in many high-profile Senate contests (such as the Jim Webb–George Allen contest in Virginia in 2006) solicitations are sent throughout the nation.

The quality of the lists candidates obtain has much to do with the success of their fundraising effort. Many recent campaigns have exhibited depth and sophistication that easily surpass Viguerie's techniques. Lists of past contributors, contributors to other candidates, and interest group supporters are mined for data and then geocoded to target potential contributors.[15] Geocoding is a process in which neighborhoods are identified by type (for instance, in terms of their economic circumstances); it allows the direct-mail consultant to mine for names down to the street level. That level of microtargeting saves campaigns money up front and reduces the amount of mail sent to incorrect addresses. Such steps are critical for congressional campaigns, which have smaller budgets and must be more cost-effective. In the future, technology and more refined microtargeting will likely bring down the costs of direct mail even more.

Bundling

The Federal Election Commission (FEC) defines bundling as a process in which an intermediary earmarks a contribution toward a specific candidate.[16] There are three parties involved: an interest group, a contributor, and a candidate. One of the first groups to bundle money was EMILY's List ("Early Money Is Like Yeast"), which began bundling contributions for female, Democratic pro-choice candidates during the 1980s. By 2006, the group claimed to have bundled $11 million for its endorsed candidates.[17] EMILY's List provides biographical information on candidates it endorses, and contributors can receive a brochure of information or read it online. EMILY's List then "bundles" all the checks from contributors to its endorsed candidates. Other groups have begun to operate similarly, including WISH List, which bundles money to female pro-choice Republican candidates, and the Club for Growth, which bundles for business-oriented Republican candidates, often in primaries. Bundling is not limited to groups, however. As the discussion below shows, candidates have encouraged their individual supporters to recruit friends and colleagues to donate, in a process similar to bundling. Although it is nothing new for candidates to compete for the support of interest groups, the groups' ability to bundle donations can make them a pivotal part of fundraising and enable them to help candidates well above and beyond contributions made by the group itself.

Recent Trends in Campaign Fundraising

The complexity and diversity of fundraising are evident in congressional and presidential campaigns over the last several election cycles. Congressional or statewide races, particularly those of incumbents, often rely on established means of fundraising. However, innovations do occur. In presidential campaigns, the scale of fundraising initiatives is far bigger, and because budgets are larger, presidential campaigns can build on innovations to a greater extent than congressional campaigns.

Congressional Campaign Fundraising

One might expect congressional elections to be a major source of innovation in fundraising. On the one hand, the average age of incoming members of Congress (forty-nine years) is low enough that new members may be conversant in the language of younger donors or more in tune with new types of media.[18] On the other hand, however, turnover in Congress has declined sharply in the past decade, and incumbent members of Congress may be reluctant to tamper with electoral strategies that have worked in the past. To take one example, approximately 40 percent of the funds raised by congressional candidates in the past four elections have come from political action committees (PACs). Not only is raising money from PACs easier than raising money from individuals, but it is a strategy that has served incumbents well for decades. As the cost of congressional campaigns has increased, however, members of Congress have needed to diversify their fundraising strategies.

The cost of congressional elections has increased for a number of reasons. The narrow majorities the Republican Party held between 1994 and 2006 led the campaign committees of both parties to focus on the small number of seats considered vulnerable. That in turn has fueled record levels of candidate, party, and interest group spending in competitive races, while leaving challengers in other races struggling for funds. This focus is likely to continue in future elections. It does not, however, mean that political elites have had perfect foresight. The Republican wave in 1994 brought with it several candidates who raised paltry sums of money; likewise, the Democratic wave in 2006 swept into office several candidates who spent far less than the average competitive challenger. Although thirty Democratic challengers raised over $1 million in 2006, a handful of the victors raised substantially less than that, including Nancy Boyda (D-Kan.), who raised $710,000; Dave Loebsack (D-Iowa), who raised $522,000; and Carol Shea-Porter (D-N.H.), who raised less than $360,000. However, the average incumbent typically outspends the average challenger by a six-to-one margin.

Challengers and open-seat candidates are the congressional candidates to whom one should look for innovations in campaign fundraising. That is not to say that most challengers are skilled fundraisers. But challengers who have held lower-level elected positions have some lists to start with, and many others have experience in business positions where individual initiative in raising money or meeting with people is prized. Realtors, for instance, are unlikely to approach former clients, but they can draw on experience in making individual sales pitches. Challengers have to try harder and have to be more creative in their fundraising. Challengers and open-seat candidates have taken the lead in developing interactive Web sites, in creative placement of fundraising ads, and in other innovative fundraising schemes.

Presidential Campaign Fundraising

Spending by all presidential candidates increased from $671 million in 2000 to $1.23 billion in 2004.[19] This increase took place despite the passage of the Bipartisan

Campaign Reform Act (BCRA), which was designed, if not to decrease spending, at least to control it somewhat.

In part the increase in spending may be a consequence of temporary factors, such as the number of candidates running, whether there is an incumbent running, or the popularity of the incumbent. But an enduring legacy of the 2004 campaign was the maturation of Internet campaigning. Although Sen. John McCain (R-Ariz.) raised $2.2 million for his campaign online in a single week during 2000, the 2004 campaign featured far more sophisticated online fundraising techniques. Those techniques, mostly pioneered by the Howard Dean presidential campaign, have served as a template for others.[20] Barack Obama raised $10.3 million in the second quarter of 2007 through Internet fundraising.

The Dean campaign raised $20 million, or 40 percent of its total receipts, through the Internet.[21] According to members of the campaign, Dean's successful fundraising strategy rested on four major components: First, the Dean campaign ceded much of its organizing to volunteers and contributors. In this so-called hub-to-hub model, activists can develop strategies for fundraising and organizing independent of the national campaign,[22] and that ensures that a variety of techniques are in place at any given time. Second, the Dean campaign emphasized repeated small donations, often by initiating challenges (of the sort common to charity fundraising drives) or by describing current financial needs (e.g., what sorts of advertisements Dean's opponents were running, or how much money the campaign needed to run a new advertisement). Third, communications from the campaign about contributions were supplemented by ongoing updates about the campaign or requests for advice. And fourth, the campaign sought to use social networking sites such as Meetup.com to "take the online campaign offline." This strategy provided social and networking opportunities for volunteers, particularly in areas where there was limited campaign or Democratic Party infrastructure. In sum, Dean contributors, even those who gave only token amounts, were made to feel as if they were a vital part of the campaign.

The George W. Bush campaign's bundling strategy also sought to make donors feel that they were an important part of the campaign. In 2000, the Bush campaign kept careful track of "Pioneers," supporters who raised at least $100,000. Each Pioneer was assigned a tracking number, and donors who were solicited by a Pioneer would provide the tracking number to the Bush campaign when making their donation. The Pioneer program, according to political scientists John Green and Nathan Bigelow, "tapped into the competitive drive of business executives, lawyers, and politicians." [23] Of 551 people who pledged to become Pioneers, 241 met the $100,000 goal.[24] In 2004, the Bush campaign added a second tier, "Rangers," for individuals who pledged to raise $200,000 for the campaign and also created a category for "Mavericks," supporters under forty years of age who committed to raising $50,000. There were ultimately 221 Rangers and 327 Pioneers in 2004, accounting for at least $76.9 million, or roughly 26 percent of the money that the Bush campaign raised.

In 2004, the John Kerry campaign followed suit, creating special categories for individuals who raised $50,000 and $100,000; these bundlers raised an estimated 23 percent of the Kerry campaign's total funds. These bundling strategies gave special status to influential contributors but also sought to give them the sense that they were integrated into the campaign. The Kerry campaign went on to raise far more money online than the Dean campaign ($82 million, or 33 percent of total receipts).[25] This shows that the Dean model might benefit insurgent candidates, but that more risk-averse candidates can also raise large sums online simply because the Internet is, particularly for younger voters and Democrats, where people go to contribute money. The Bush campaign expanded its online fundraising in 2004 but still raised only $14 million, or 5 percent of total receipts, online.[26] Some have argued that this difference merely reflects the fact that the Bush campaign already had a successful fundraising strategy and donor base from the 2000 campaign; others claim that Internet users and Internet political activists tend to be disproportionately Democratic.[27]

Emerging Fundraising Techniques

Fundraising in future years will be a matter of developing new ways of finding potential donors and raising money from them quickly. As effective as many of the direct-mail campaigns of the 1970s and 1980s were, there was often a significant lag between the time an appeal was sent and when funds were received. Successful grassroots campaigners thus had to make their pitch early and were less able to respond to sudden events in the campaign. In the 2006 and 2008 campaigns, candidates clearly sought to capitalize on events that took place during the campaign for fundraising purposes. For instance, following the second Republican presidential candidate debate in 2008, Governor Mike Huckabee (R-Ark.) placed a barber's pole on his Website to measure donations; the barber's pole was based on a well-received joke Huckabee had made during the debate about John Edwards's haircuts.

Early fundraising will continue to be crucial, but the possibility that relatively underfunded candidates might raise enough money to become competitive in a short period of time has the potential to change the dynamics of elections. Moreover, the ease and cost-effectiveness of raising money online have democratized fundraising. Direct mail costs at least forty cents for every dollar raised. On the Internet, solicitations are essentially free. These developments may have profound effects on candidates in 2010 and beyond.

Encouraging Repeat Contributions through Blogs and Meetups

The Internet is a powerful tool for many aspects of campaigning, but its greatest strength is the way it facilitates fundraising. According to Alan Locke, publisher of *Winning Campaigns* magazine, candidate Web sites have "become a credit card collector" for candidates: "The Internet facilitates collection. It's a bank." [28] Web sites are set up to attract political activists, as groups such as MoveOn.org, which used its opposition to the Iraq war to build a base of 3.3 million donors by 2005, have shown.[29]

The purpose of candidate Web sites is not just to attract visitors but to make viewers repeat contributors. The more often they come to a Web site, the more often they are willing to give. According to several political consultants, blogs and meetups are not used for persuasion. Rather, their purpose is to heighten interest in the candidate among volunteers and supporters. The reason is that the Internet is not a passive medium; it requires someone to search for a particular candidate's or party's Web site. By having bloggers and meetups, candidates seek to establish an online community that can be used for two purposes: fundraising and voter mobilization (the latter is discussed by Richard Semiatin in the "Voter Mobilization" chapter of this book).

E-mail fundraising appeals enable campaigns to keep in touch with viewers who express an interest in the campaign. E-mail often serves as a method to encourage viewers to return to a home page for updated information on the candidate or provides them with new reasons to contribute (in an appeal similar to direct mail, but faster). Moreover, e-mail appeals can focus attention on a timely issue or debate. For instance, the Republican and Democratic National Committees have frequently coupled appeals for contributions with updates on congressional votes on appropriations to keep American troops in Iraq beyond 2007.

Web Site Fundraising in Presidential Campaigns and Other High-Profile Races

In general, successful Internet fundraising strategies follow the advice given by members of the Dean campaign. Successful campaign Web sites tend to feature buttons that take viewers directly to a donation form, but they also provide viewers with options other than simply contributing. For example, Democratic presidential candidate Barack Obama's Web site, "Obama for America," features various links on the home page for "blog," "state," and "issues." The largest button is the red "donate" button.[30] Republican presidential candidate Mitt Romney is more aggressive about pushing fundraising on his Web site. The Romney campaign has buttons on the home page for "contribute," "donate," and "fundraising tools." The "fundraising tools" link gives viewers a way to join "Team Mitt," in which each individual commits to building a contribution network for the candidate.[31] In the past, candidates have built large fundraising networks by getting commitments from leading donors to attract donations of from $10,000 (in congressional races) to millions (in presidential races). Now such fundraising networks are visible to anyone; the hope of candidates is that contributors will see the networks as a sort of competition and will strive to create a network that looks as good as the ones they see on the Web site.

Most campaigns now accept that the Howard Dean campaign was noteworthy because it provided a different package of benefits for campaign contributors than is the norm in presidential campaigns. Whereas large donations are traditionally solicited in social contexts, such as a fundraising dinner, creating a social context for small donors increased the social benefits for that group and made campaign contributions one component of political engagement. Consultants parsing the lessons of the Dean campaign have even emphasized the importance of timing e-mails to reach supporters when they are in a more social mode; for instance, pitches received on a Thursday afternoon may reach supporters just as they are starting to focus more on their weekend and less on their work activities.[32] One guide to fundraising notes the importance of spacing out fundraising pitches so that the e-mail conversation between candidate and supporters consists of far more than simply asking for money. Fundraisers are advised to carefully monitor "unsubscribe" requests to see whether they are related to repeated requests for money.[33]

There are two caveats to this strategy, however. First, creating this sort of community can mean that the candidate and the campaign organization lose some control over how money is raised. In 2004, the Howard Dean campaign encouraged supporters to design their own fundraising pitches, but the John Kerry campaign kept a much tighter rein on the fundraising pitches that supporters developed.[34] In 2008, most of the major candidates gave supporters the ability to send customized fundraising e-mails that made reference to recent events. There are risks to giving supporters too much ability to define the campaign, however. Pitches by overzealous supporters can embarrass a campaign or pull a campaign off-message. Two Internet videos made by supporters of Barack Obama may have distracted his campaign organization as much as they helped: the "Obama Girl" video, in which a young woman sings of her crush on Obama, and the "Vote Different" video, which compared Hillary Clinton to the totalitarian rulers in George Orwell's dystopia *1984*. These videos were not directly linked to fundraising, but both illustrated the pitfalls of encouraging supporters to make pitches independent of the campaign organization. In future elections, candidates will need to find ways to encourage their supporters to be creative, while at the same time exerting some control over their activities.

Second, the Internet remains the domain of candidates with high name recognition. Well-known presidential, senatorial, and gubernatorial candidates benefit from Internet fundraising. The majority of House members, to say nothing of challengers and open-seat candidates, will have to create different means of raising money on the Internet.

Challenges for Congressional Candidates in Future Elections

Congressional candidates have lagged behind presidential candidates in their online activities. That will change in upcoming elections. Nevertheless, as noted above, congressional candidates face several limitations that presidential candidates do not face. They are less visible than presidential candidates. The successes of the McCain, Dean, and Obama campaigns could not have happened had those candidates not been highly visible and well known throughout the country. Few congressional candidates can generate traffic on their Web sites the way the Dean campaign did. The establishment and maintenance of a good campaign Web site is itself an expense, so the best ones usually belong to candidates who were strong to begin with. Many successful candidates in 2006, such as Christopher Murphy (D-Conn.) and Joe Donnelly (D-Ind.), benefited from the combination of Internet appeals and offline fundraising and campaigning conducted by the interest group MoveOn.org. In such cases, Internet campaigning by outside groups can generate the "buzz" that candidates would struggle to create on their own.[35]

During the 2006 campaign, it became evident that online advertising had become a crucial component of fundraising. Such advertisements are necessary to direct people to the candidate Web site. In the past some candidates, such as California's Loretta Sanchez (D), had used cable television to raise money, but for the most part, advertising has been more about attracting votes than attracting money.[36] A successful Internet advertisement, on the other hand, directs people to the campaign Web site, where they might take the time to make a contribution. In instances where a candidate posts video clips on his or her own site or on YouTube, the content can often, again, be both highly partisan and highly entertaining; the goal is to encourage supporters to donate (or to donate again) or to recommend the clips to their friends.

The expanded use of niche advertising could attract more donations over the next decade. Niche advertising is aimed at inducing highly motivated base voters to give money through dramatic appeals or humor. For example, in 2006 the Sherrod Brown Senate campaign distributed video clips via its Web site poking fun at Brown's opponent; these were ads clearly designed for supporters, not for television. Some candidates who cannot afford to run ads on television can create ads for the Web. Primary candidate Jennifer Lawless (D-R.I.) distributed video clips of her own door-to-door campaigning, in an effort to emphasize the grassroots nature of the campaign.

Traditional advertisements have often steered clear of controversial issues, but many successful Internet appeals in 2006, particularly those of challengers, were both edgier and riskier. For instance, in the North Carolina race between incumbent Republican representative Charles Taylor and his Democratic challenger, Heath Shuler, which Shuler eventually won, the Taylor campaign provided a Web site that consisted mostly of text and did not give viewers the option of donating through the Web site. The Shuler site provided links for viewers to contribute, volunteer for the campaign, view advertisements, or register to vote. In addition, several fake news reports highly critical of Taylor were distributed via YouTube. Many 2006 campaign Web sites included blogs, but the degree to which the blogs actually featured open dialogue, as opposed to simply descriptions of campaign events, varied from one campaign to the next. Incumbents tended to play it safe, while some nonincumbents provided much more dialogue and often encouraged viewers to take part.

The lessons for Internet campaigning in congressional races, then, are the ones learned from presidential races: Donors are more likely to feel appreciated, and hence to give again, if communications from the campaign are somewhat personalized, if they are not limited to requests for money, and if feedback from donors is encouraged. Congressional campaigns face greater challenges than presidential campaigns in generating traffic on their Web sites, and that may lead to far more creative Web site ad placement. It may well be that politically savvy Internet users are willing to be convinced to pay attention to a congressional candidate they have never heard of, and thus to click on an ad, even though they may be less persuadable in a presidential race. One popular Internet advertising company, Blogads.com, touts on its Web site the ability of advertisers to target blogs that fit their campaigns and use do-it-yourself software to develop effective advertisements and manage an advertising campaign.[37] Users of its site can also view what Blogads deems to be successful ads and emulate them.

Why Internet Fundraising Is Not Enough—Challenges for the Future

Internet fundraising will always be somewhat limited insofar as candidates cannot know whom they are soliciting. They may target particular audiences, but they cannot target individuals. Thus, an enduring concern is the importance of lists. At the most basic level, a "house list" of prior contributors, or contributors to one's predecessors for a first-time candidate, can provide a starting point for any type of fundraising strategy. Parties and interest groups have invested substantial resources over the past several election cycles in developing lists of supporters or potential supporters, which can benefit candidates. Studies from the 1980s contended that a house list can have a 10 percent to 20 percent yield, whereas lists drawn from commercial or interest group databases often have no more than a 1 percent to 2 percent yield.[38] In the era of direct mail, that made such "prospecting" lists costly. In an era when Internet communication limits the expense of solicitations, and when computer techniques enable much more precise data to be collected on individuals, using such lists becomes more affordable.

Many such lists already exist. For instance, between 2002 and 2004, the advocacy group America Coming Together developed extensive lists of sympathetic voters. Following the group's dissolution in early 2005, much of the data from its lists became the property of a new corporation, Data Warehouse, which made the list available to candidates for fundraising purposes.[39] The Democratic National Committee has developed its own list, named "Demzilla," to enable fundraising appeals to be tailored to the interests or habits of the potential donors on the list.[40] In 2005, the DNC began providing access to the list to the congressional campaign committees. The Republican Party also maintains a similar list, Voter Vault, which is shared by the three party committees and has been used for fundraising purposes.[41] This list allegedly includes individuals whose purchasing habits, tastes in food and drink, or favorite sports or hobbies correlate with a preference for Republican candidates. Beyond 2008, it is probable that parties and candidates will continue to refine this approach to fundraising, which merges consumer preferences with demographics, polling data, and election data.

In the future campaigns may employ artificial intelligence (AI) or other technological self-learning systems to help them identify effective appeals to new donors as well as ways to attract previous donors back to campaigns. Such techniques may rely on the Internet, but compiling effective lists can help improve direct mail, phone banking, and face-to-face fundraising as well.

Conclusions

These developments show that campaigns have sought to use new technologies to better integrate donors into their campaigns, but their effect should not be overstated. In the right circumstances, Internet appeals can raise money quickly, and they increase the possibility of sudden financial windfalls for candidates. Yet they are hardly a reliable source for veteran candidates. Most candidates are "rational prospectors" and will continue to concentrate on proven donors through whatever medium seems most promising. A candidate with a successful offline fundraising operation may be reluctant to experiment with new techniques. Online fundraising strategies and bundling are thus best seen as supplements to proven tactics rather than as entirely new means of raising money. Most money in congressional and presidential elections is raised the old-fashioned way—through fundraisers in Washington or in a candidate's district, through direct mail or phone banking to one's proven supporters, from PACs, or from the candidates' own pockets.

Innovative fundraising techniques tend to use technology to maintain a personal touch, or at least to create the illusion of one.

Meanwhile, the limits of older fundraising techniques are becoming clear: The increased volume of telephone solicitations and the increasing number of citizens who screen their phone calls or rely on cell phones limit the effectiveness of phone banking. The increase in direct-mail appeals limits the likelihood that citizens will open letters from a campaign. As the Dean campaign's Zephyr Teachout asserts, a properly conducted Internet campaign can overcome the barriers faced by direct mail or telephone banking: Recipients of an e-mail message can read the message at a convenient moment; they can receive forwarded messages from a trusted friend and may find the messages less intrusive than a telephone call or less disposable than a mailed solicitation.[42]

These changes have not necessarily been either the sole cause, or a clear consequence, of increasing campaign costs, but they clearly go hand in hand. The past two elections have shown that unsolicited donors can become an important part of a campaign. The process of contributing is far less cumbersome than it once was. Today, it is easier for citizens to discover how to contribute to a candidate than it was in the past, and in many instances, citizens reading a news story online can simply click on an advertisement to go straight to a candidate's donation page.

These changes make it hard to tell whether online fundraising can be any sort of a substitute for traditional fundraising practices. The cost of campaigns had been increasing before the Internet became a part of them, and the current polarization of American politics provides many citizens with the motivation to open their checkbooks. Much of the money raised online in these elections cycles might well have been raised by other means had the Internet not existed.

It is also hard to tell whether online donors are different from past donors. Online donors have tended to be slightly more liberal than the average voter and average donor, but that may primarily reflect the types of candidates who have engaged in this sort of fundraising and the fact that Democrats had a greater need to come up with new ways of raising money. Republicans, after all, were the pioneers in fundraising during the years when they were out of power. What has changed in campaigns is not that new techniques have supplanted old ones but that competition has produced additional means—for everyone from obscure House challengers to major presidential candidates—to raise money. In some ways raising money has become easier, but it has not become less time-consuming. With fundraising strategies very much in flux, candidates and parties will need to invest substantial time and resources in ensuring that they are, and remain, on the cutting edge in their fundraising practices.

Notes

Thank you to the students in my Campaigns and Elections course, particularly Jim Callahan, Julie Cariglia, Maryann Christensen, Kenyon Hayes, Derek Lundquist, and Jonathan Webb, for their comments on the fundraising strategies of congressional candidates in 2006.

1. All fundraising figures in this chapter are drawn from the Center for Responsive Politics, www.opensecrets.org.
2. David Price, *The Congressional Experience,* 3rd ed. (Washington, D.C.: CQ Press, 2004), 16.
3. Pew Internet and American Life Project, *Election 2004 Online* (Washington, D.C.: Pew Internet and American Life Project, 2005); Pew Internet and American Life Project, *Election 2006 Online* (Washington, D.C.: Pew Internet and American Life Project, 2007).
4. Peter L. Francia, John C. Green, Paul S. Herrnson, Lynda W. Powell, and Clyde Wilcox, *The Financiers of Congressional Elections: Investors, Ideologues, and Intimates* (New York: Columbia University Press, 2003), 24–26.
5. Ibid., 34.
6. Michael John Burton and Daniel M. Shea, *Campaign Mode: Strategic Vision in Congressional Elections* (Washington, D.C.: CQ Press, 2003), 105.
7. Dennis J. McGrath and Dane Smith, *Professor Wellstone Goes to Washington* (Minneapolis: University of Minnesota Press, 1995), 183.
8. Pew Internet and American Life Project, *Election 2004 Online*; Pew Internet and American Life Project, *Election 2006 Online.*
9. Institute for Politics, Democracy, and the Internet, *Political Influentials Online in the 2004 Presidential Campaigns* (Washington, D.C.: Institute for Politics, Democracy, and the Internet, 2004).
10. Pew Internet and American Life Project, *Election 2004 Online,* iii.
11. Richard J. Semiatin, *Campaigns in the 21st Century: The Changing Mosaic of American Politics* (Boston: McGraw-Hill, 2005), 75.
12. Ann Bunting, "Telemarketing Like There's No Tomorrow: Predictive Dialing for the Political Arena," *Telemarketing,* September 1994, findarticles.com (accessed July 9, 2007).
13. Michael D. Shear and Nathaniel Vaughn Kelso, "Fundraising in Vacationland," *Washington Post,* August 22, 2007.
14. "Political Radar," ABC News blog posting, September 28, 2006, blogs.abcnews.com/politicalradar/2006 (accessed July 9, 2007).
15. Data Productions Inc., dataproductions.com (accessed July 9, 2007).
16. "Bundling by Individuals," *FEC Record,* August 1996, 2.
17. See www.emilyslist.org/about/where-from.html (accessed August 29, 2007).
18. Andrew Taylor, "Democrats to Regain Power in Congress on Thursday, Elect First Female House Speaker," Associated Press, January 4, 2007.
19. Kelly D. Patterson, "Spending in the 2004 Election," in *Financing the 2004 Election,* ed. David B. Magleby, Anthony Corrado, and Kelly D. Patterson (Washington, D.C.: Brookings Institution Press, 2006), 71.
20. Campaign Finance Institute, *Small Donors and Online Giving: A Study of Donors to the 2004 Presidential Campaigns* (Washington, D.C.: Campaign Finance Institute, 2006).
21. Pew Internet and American Life Project, *Election 2004 Online,* 1.

22. Zephyr Teachout, "Powering Up Internet Campaigns," in *Get This Party Started: How Progressives Can Fight Back and Win,* ed. Matthew R. Kerbel (Lanham, Md.: Rowman and Littlefield, 2006).

23. John C. Green and Nathan S. Bigelow, "The 2000 Presidential Nominations: The Costs of Innovation," in *Financing the 2000 Election,* ed. David B. Magleby (Washington, D.C.: Brookings Institution Press, 2001).

24. Michael J. Malbin, "A Public Financing System in Jeopardy: Lessons from the Presidential Nomination Contests of 2004," in *The Election After Reform: Money, Politics, and the Bipartisan Campaign Reform Act,* ed. Michael J. Malbin (Lanham, Md.: Rowman and Littlefield, 2006), 224.

25. Pew Internet and American Life Project, *Election 2004 Online.*

26. Ibid.

27. Institute for Politics, Democracy, and the Internet, *Political Influentials Online in the 2004 Presidential Campaigns.*

28. Personal interview with Alan Locke, publisher, *Winning Campaigns,* July 12, 2007.

29. Moveon.org, "About Moveon.org," http://moveon.org/about.html (accessed August 18, 2007).

30. Barack Obama for President, www.barackobama.com (accessed July 18, 2007).

31. Mitt Romney for President, www.mittromney.com (accessed July 18, 2007).

32. Institute for Politics, Democracy, and the Internet, *The Political Consultants' Online Fundraising Primer* (Washington, D.C.: Institute for Politics, Democracy, and the Internet, 2004).

33. Ibid.

34. Teachout, "Powering Up Internet Campaigns."

35. Carl M. Cannon, "Movin' On," *National Journal,* December 5, 2006.

36. Burton and Shea, *Campaign Mode: Strategic Vision in Congressional Elections,* 104.

37. See www.blogads.com (accessed August 29, 2007).

38. R. Kenneth Godwin, *One Billion Dollars of Influence: The Direct Marketing of Politics* (Chatham, N.J.: Chatham House, 1988).

39. Thomas Edsall, "Democrats' Data Mining Stirs an Intra-party Battle," *Washington Post,* March 8, 2006, A1.

40. Chris Cillizza, "Critics Slam 'Demzilla,' " *Roll Call,* June 5, 2003; Anthony Corrado, "Party Finance in the Wake of BCRA: An Overview," in *The Election After Reform: Money, Politics, and the Bipartisan Campaign Reform Act.*

41. Hans Nichols, "Hill Dems Get into Demzilla," *The Hill,* February 17, 2005.

42. Zephyr Teachout, comments at the Campaign Institute Pre Super Tuesday Forum: Money and Politics in the 2004 Primaries, February 27, 2004, www.cfinst.org/transcripts/022704.html #goldstein (accessed February 22, 2007).

CHAPTER 3

Paid Media — In an Era of Revolutionary Change

Tad Devine

PAID POLITICAL ADVERTISING, which has been the centerpiece of campaign communication in the United States for decades, has entered a period of potentially revolutionary change. For more than four decades political advertising has been the most powerful vehicle for a candidate to deliver an unfettered message directly to voters. From the landmark "Daisy" ad in 1964 (to which I will return later in the chapter) to the high-definition ads of tomorrow, mass advertising is changing, particularly in presidential campaigns. Advances in research technology and in the sophistication of targeting are leading ad makers to develop increasingly individualized advertising tailored to niche audiences.

The purpose of this chapter is to review paid media in political campaigns, to show how it became powerful and how it is changing. I first examine the role of media consultants and then look at the way research-based message development works in the context of ad making. Then the chapter reviews message development by looking at specific campaigns and ads by way of example. Finally the chapter looks ahead at the cutting edge of campaign advertising, focusing on the way digital technology, the Internet, conversion technology, and media targeting are affecting the way political ad makers work and deliver messages to voters on behalf of campaigns and candidates.

Most of the examples and all of the case studies appearing here are ads that I have worked on with my past and present partners and ads that I have made. My perspective is that of a practitioner spending the last decade and a half writing, directing, and producing television ads here in the United States and around the world.

That perspective is undoubtedly biased toward the power of television advertising. But until campaigns—from presidential races to statewide and even local elections—begin to concentrate their resources on paid communication other than television advertising, TV's primacy as a means of communicating with voters will remain obvious. And while rapidly evolving technologies may soon fundamentally change this calculation—as the first screen of television is rivaled, and perhaps someday eclipsed, by the second and third screens of the computer and the cell phone, today at least, television advertising is still king.

Paid Television Advertising

Campaign television ads are the most powerful tool in modern American politics.[1] That is why major statewide and national campaigns spend more on paid media than on anything else.[2] Some may dispute that statement, and with the emergence of the Internet and other means of communication it is a legitimate topic for debate. But until statewide and national campaigns start spending up to half or more of their resources in areas other than television advertising, it is difficult to dispute that paid ads are more powerful than any other tool they have.[3]

Paid advertising can have an impact that ripples throughout a campaign. In the 2006 Tennessee race for the U.S. Senate, Democrat Harold Ford Jr. was attacked by an ad that referred to a visit Ford once made to a party at the Playboy Mansion.[4] The fact that the reference came from a young white woman led to charges that Republicans were "playing the race card" against the African American Democrat. But the provocative paid media led to a groundswell of free (i.e., "earned") media coverage, and Ford's was one of the handful of targeted races that Democrats lost in that election.

Given the power of television advertising and the need of a campaign to reach many people in a short time, television advertising—at least in the United States and other countries that accommodate ubiquitous advertising—will likely remain the dominant paid communications device in campaigns at least through the next decade. And in many ways, alternative media will enhance the power of television advertising.

First, increased Internet fundraising is already providing campaigns lots of money to buy more television time. Second, there is now the possibility of inter-activity between television advertising and campaigns, as ads drive viewers to campaign Web sites to do everything from contributing to fact-checking the allegations in an opponent's negative ads. Finally, as more and more people have access to faster and faster Internet connections, and as those connections extend to handheld devices, not just computers, the likelihood increases that voters will one day watch ads or even longer-format pieces as they commute to work on a train or sit in the doctor's waiting room. Perhaps one day truly undecided voters will make up their minds while standing in line at a crowded polling place and watching an ad. Sound far-fetched? It is perhaps not as far-fetched as was the very idea of the Internet only a generation ago.

The Role of Media Consultants

Media consultants have two main roles in campaigns: First as creators of television ads, we write, direct, produce, and deliver campaign advertising. We work with other skilled professionals, such as film crews, producers, editors, and media time buyers. These production specialists typically work not only on political campaigns but on other kinds of advertising as well. They bring their skills in editing and filmmaking, as well as media placement and time buying, to political campaigns under the direction of media consultants, who are typically the people who work directly with the candidates and campaigns. Successful media consultants need two very different skills: (1) They need the political know-how to do such things as read and interpret polls, understand demographics, and assimilate voting patterns. Consultants also need (2) the artistic and people skills to create ads and communicate personally to voters with substance, passion, and/or humor.

The second principal role of media consultants is as campaign strategists. In that capacity consultants are among the architects of a campaign's message. Media consultants collaborate with pollsters, campaign managers, candidates, and others to develop a message. For example, the slogan of the 2006 U.S. Senate campaign of Democrat Sheldon Whitehouse (R.I.) was, "Finally, a Whitehouse in Washington we can trust." The "Whitehouse" from Rhode Island decided to run against the "White House" in Washington, not against Sen. Lincoln Chafee, his Republican opponent. By sticking to his message—that reelecting Chafee would strengthen Bush—Sheldon Whitehouse was able to defeat an incumbent senator who had a 63 percent job approval rating. Strict message discipline made possible the defeat of the only Republican senator who voted against the Iraq war, in a campaign where the challenger continually invoked Iraq. The lesson was that a winning message must be amplified not only in paid advertising but in free media communications, from press releases to interviews, from candidate town hall meetings to debates.

In addition to using research, media consultants use their experience in campaigns to anticipate likely lines of attack and to react quickly to changing circumstances. After many years and many campaigns, circumstances that have occurred previously inevitably reemerge. Experience can be useful in making the quick decisions necessary in the short time frame of a typical campaign. For example, in 2006 my firm worked on a number of U.S. Senate races, among them Bernie Sanders's race in Vermont and the Democratic Senate Campaign Committee Independent Expenditure in New Jersey. Having worked previously in both states, my partner and I could advise our clients about the tone and tenor of the advertising, not just the issues in the ads. That experience led us to produce entirely positive ads in Vermont and tough, negative ones in New Jersey. This kind of battle-tested experience is particularly useful because campaigns frequently involve changing circumstances: Decisions have to be made quickly and decisively for candidates to win or to deal with fast-unfolding events.[5]

Writing Campaign Ads

Writing is the essential starting point of almost all television and radio advertising. Political consultants write scripts that typically are made into thirty- or sixty-second ads that are read by a narrator, a third party (such as a person who knows the candidate), or the candidate.[6]

Scripts provide a focal point at which strategy and research converge to create a deliverable message. Scripts also embody the reality that television ads are typically limited to a very short format—in the United States, almost always thirty seconds. They may then be shortened by the visual and oral disclaimers required in federal races.

Sometimes ads are not scripted and are the result of a "cinéma vérité" technique of filming the candidate. These ads are typically made by filming a live event such as a speech or by simply following the candidate around as he or she campaigns, interviewing the candidate, and using their live responses to questions that the interviewer asks. They provide a way of communicating with voters that tends to depict the candidate in a more realistic and less formal or scripted light. The message discipline required for making these ads usually is applied not at the front end (as when the candidate would read a script in the thirty-second format), but at the back end, when the consultant must cut and assemble the candidate's (or third party's) words and phrases in the studio. The ad maker then uses the tools of editing to ensure that the spot makes the intended point in the short time allotted.

Ad makers now have less than thirty seconds or sixty seconds because the Bipartisan Campaign Reform Act (BCRA) of 2002 requires that federal candidates "stand by their ads." That means that four seconds of each ad are taken up by a candidate saying something like, "I am Jane Jones and I approve this message." The consequence of this law is that ads have less time to present persuasive information and content to voters, truncating not only the visual aspects of the ads but the written aspects as well. Whether the principle of "standing by the ad" is right or wrong, the law constrains the media consultant in the task of presenting a coherent and substantive message.

The Importance of Audio and Video

Other powerful tools of media consultants are the images and sounds that are the heart of television advertising. Television is primarily a visual medium, and television ad makers look for strong visuals and credible sources of authority to make their case visually. Television and radio are also audio media, in which everything from the sound of the candidate's voice to the soundtrack behind an ad can have a powerful impact with voters. In many ways, music is the secret weapon of television political advertising, since it can evoke a mood or underline the message being delivered through words and images.

Research for Message Development

One of the keys to media production in political campaigns is the use of research to develop a message. Campaigns and consultants review the research, and based on that research they develop concepts for television, radio, and other forms of advertising.[7] Typically this takes the form of converting short narrative statements about a candidate or set of issues into an ad. The statements are road tested before they are developed in text for broadcast ads.[8] Successful political campaigns almost always emanate from a disciplined regime of research, where tools such as polls, focus groups, people-metered ad- or event-viewing sessions, opposition research, and issues or candidate-record research provide the basis for a message.

For example, in the 2004 Kerry for President campaign, every ad that was ultimately broadcast was subjected to both pre- and post-production research. Research included the polling that would occur prior to the development of scripts and detailed focus group testing of ads after preliminary versions had been produced. The campaign also used online media testing of ads; discussion focus groups saw the advertising and were asked to comment on its impact. In almost every major U.S. campaign today at the statewide level, campaign advertising is tested in one way or another prior to broadcast. Although there are exceptions to the rule, pre- and post-production testing is the industry standard. By gauging the impact of messages on voters in preproduction polls, or by showing preliminary versions of a commercial to focus groups, ad makers can get a good sense of the impact on potential voters before making the costly commitment to broadcasting the spot.

Projective Research

Perhaps the most important development in the last-quarter century in U.S. political campaigns is the use of "projective research" in the production of television advertising and in message development. This technique, pioneered in the United States and used extensively in political campaigns, allows researchers to push and probe respondents with a variety of questions to gauge how voters will respond to issues and arguments. By determining whether voters are affected, either positively or negatively, by a particular argument, projective research can inform media consultants about what ads are likely to be most powerful in moving the voters who emerge as the primary targets of campaign communication strategies. If the research is well conceived and executed, campaigns can avoid the costly mistake of putting enormous resources behind messages that do not have a good chance of succeeding with voters.

Developing winning messages in a poll and successfully testing the depictions of those messages in a qualitative focus group setting (as discussed below) are the best way to ensure success in the real world of elections.

Quantitative and Qualitative Research

Polling is the form of quantitative research that campaigns use the most (see chapter 5 for more analysis on survey research). Polls—either a random survey of respondents or a discrete panel back survey of a previously identified group who are contacted more than once—are at the heart of modern research.[9] Campaigns essentially play out the election in polls, testing to see not just where the electorate is today but how voters will be affected by issues and information.

Focus groups and other forms of qualitative research are the other key tools that media consultants use to determine which ads will work and why. Focus group research typically occurs after production, when at least a preliminary version of an ad has been made. By letting a selected group of target voters evaluate an ad prior to broadcast, campaigns can avoid running an ad that may not produce the desired effect.

Communicating the Message through Different Ads

The skills and tools of experience, writing, and research enable the media adviser to craft a message (or messages) for a campaign. Political ads communicate that message to voters in a number of forms: biographical, issue, accomplishment/vision, and negative ads. The appendix at the end of this chapter provides case studies for all four types of advertisements.

Typically in a campaign, candidates introduce themselves to the voting public in terms of their biography. One of the most important qualities that they can communicate is shared values. Biographical advertising opens a window into the lives of candidates so that voters can better understand and relate to them on the basis of shared values. Biographical ads help to frame the narrative of a campaign. Sometimes the biographical ads are deeply personal, and sometimes the narrative is directed towards accomplishment, agenda, or vision. Democrat John Edwards's personal story of his American dream, in his 1998 U.S. Senate race against incumbent Lauch Faircloth (R), set against the backdrop of a water tower in his hometown of Robbins, N.C., made the case that he shared the values of North Carolinians (illustrated in the first case study).

Issue ads tend to be more about policies than people. The issues may be important to a particular place or demographic group. These ads are typically informational, supplying voters with facts and a candidate's position on issues that he or she is putting at the center of the campaign. For example, Bernie Sanders, a Democratic Socialist elected to the Senate from Vermont in 2006, used job outsourcing as a successful issue against his opponent, millionaire Republican businessman Rich Tarrant (as seen in the second case study).

Another category of advertising focuses on the accomplishments of candidates and looks ahead to future achievements. Almost every campaign is really about the future. It is critical for candidates, particularly incumbents seeking reelection, to remind voters of what they have done and of the bonds that exist between the candidate and the electorate; but also to focus on the fights that lie ahead. This formula of accomplishment and vision is a winning one that ad makers try to capture and apply in campaigns here in the United States and around the world. Incumbents seeking reelection typically use accomplishment-and-vision ads laying out their record of accomplishment and their vision for the future. Campaigns are well aware that in politics, the future can come in sixty years or sixty hours. Given the rapidity of events and the necessity to respond to them, accomplishment-and-vision ads are critical to inoculating incumbents against attacks from challengers, which are endemic in modern campaigns. Sen. Bill Nelson's (D-Fla.) role as an innovator and forward thinker (as seen in the third case study), from his experience as a NASA astronaut to his work on energy issues, exemplifies how accomplishment and vision contributed to his 2006 landslide reelection.

The final category of political ads is the most famous (or infamous): negative ads. If TV ads are the most powerful force in politics, then negative ads may be the most powerful force within the most powerful force. The most famous negative ad was, and still is, the "Daisy" spot televised on September 7, 1964.[10] In that ad, President Johnson's campaign showed a young girl plucking petals from a daisy and juxtaposed that picture with a countdown to a nuclear explosion. The spot left the impression with viewers that if Johnson's opponent, Sen. Barry Goldwater (R-Ariz.), was elected president, he might actually lead America into a nuclear confrontation with the Soviet Union. Even though the ad was only aired once during the 1964 presidential race, it had a tremendous impact, which is felt even to this day. Indeed, some advocacy groups are still using remakes of that ad to make points on issues such as the war in Iraq.[11] The fourth case study recounts Chris Carney's (D) successful campaign for the House of Representatives in Pennsylvania's tenth district, which employed negative ads against his scandal-plagued opponent.

Cutting-Edge Changes in Advertising

Technological changes that will affect paid advertising in 2008 will transform the way candidates communicate with voters in the following decade. Not only is the digital process changing the quality of the product, but the means of communicating information are becoming more and more diverse. Media consultants no longer make ads just for television and radio; they make them also for the new small screen—the Internet. And they make them for particular audiences of potential supporters and persuadable voters.

Digital Technology

Advances in digital technology have fundamentally changed the political consulting business in recent years. In the last decade political ad makers have moved from producing television ads in either videotape or film to using high-definition video (HD) for most production. HD video allows media consultants to have high-quality, clear images and also is much more convenient for producing and editing ads. Instead of shooting in film, where there is a time-consuming physical demand of changing the film cartridge after only several minutes of filming, an HD camera will usually run for an hour of continuous filming. And the image quality of HD is superior to lower grades of video. That is important when you consider that political ads must compete not only against other political ads for audience attention, but also against the more expensive production values of ads for financial institutions, auto companies, and other high-end consumer marketers. Those ads run before and after political ads in front of the same audience, and a drop in production quality can adversely affect the way viewers perceive the lower-quality ad.

HD gives quick and easy access for editing; with the right equipment it can be edited without development or film transfer. This technological change has enabled campaigns to broadcast higher-quality images to the public. Political advertisers can produce more interesting and potentially powerful images faster and at less expense. There is no more waiting for film to be developed and transferred to a format that is used for editing and post-production purposes. All of this contributes to the quickening pace of campaign advertising, which can move from shoot to broadcast even faster with the advent of high-definition video.

In the past when political ads, typically costing about $10,000–$15,000 to produce and deliver to a station, had to compete in the same airspace with a nationwide car commercial that cost over half a million dollars to produce, it amounted to an unfair fight. This may be part of the reason why people generally hate political advertising. It wasn't just the content of the ads; it was their inferior production qualities compared to the superior and much more costly commercial advertising that dominates most television today. HD technology makes it a fairer fight. Even though political ads still cost a fraction of what Madison Avenue advertisers are charging big corporate clients, they will increasingly look better at almost every level.

The change in editing in recent years has been as dramatic as the change in filming. Political ad makers moved from large-scale online editing, which typically occurred in big studios, to PC/Avid digital editing, which can be done on hardware as small as a laptop computer. Similarly, ads can now be delivered to television and radio stations anywhere almost instantly using digital transfers. An ad can go from concept to execution, to delivery to broadcast, all in the same day. And in many senatorial or gubernatorial campaigns today, particularly at the end of a closely fought race, that is precisely what happens.

Technology is also making big changes in the content of advertising. Ads can direct viewers to campaign Web sites and create the potential for interactive communication driven by the power of paid media. Once this interactivity occurs—when a viewer responds to a call to action by going to a Web site as directed in an ad, campaigns can capture the e-mail addresses of people who are interested in candidates or particular issues, allowing them to continue to speak directly to those voters at will and for almost no cost.[12]

As digital technology changes the way ads are filmed, edited, and delivered to voters, media consultants and campaigns must adjust to this faster and more efficient process. As more and more people have access to editing technology, the process of making political ads may even become more homegrown. We've already seen competitions in which ad makers working at home have sent in ads for various causes.[13] This is happening in Web venues like johnkerry.com and elsewhere. It is not surprising that Madison Avenue is following suit, with ads made by amateurs on their home computers featured in the Super Bowl broadcast. In the future, the media consultant in some campaigns may become the volunteer with a laptop, a creative young person who has the ability to edit images either captured by personal digital video cameras or selected from the vast expanse of imagery available now to almost anyone, anywhere, at the click of a mouse.

The Internet and Advertising

The powerful connection between the Internet and campaign advertising has been established in modern campaigns, and that connection is only likely to be enhanced in the future. The connection was demonstrated vividly in the 2006 Senate election in Virginia. In that race, an offhand comment by the incumbent senator, George Allen, was captured by videotape and ultimately displayed on the Web site YouTube. This "YouTube moment," in which Allen ridiculed a young staffer from the campaign of his opponent, Jim Webb, and referred to the young man, an Indian American student at the University of Virginia, as a "macaca," spiraled through the viral world of the Internet. Ultimately, the "moment" made its way into paid television advertising produced by the Democratic Senate Campaign Committee Independent Expenditure group. Here technology showed its power, both in the Internet exposure of the incident and ultimately in the ubiquitous broadcast of it in the paid and free media, where Virginia voters were likely to see it many times in their homes across the state.

Reaching Niche Markets

As the delivery of television advertising and the research behind campaigns become more and more sophisticated, the demand to reach niche voters in niche markets will grow. As campaigns identify voters and categorize them in various ways, it has become easier to reach them with television advertising, just as direct mail has been delivered to voters on a highly segmented basis for many years. In the future more campaigns will use niche marketing for advertising on television and the Internet.

Cable channels, with their multitude of format and geographical options, are already giving political advertisers ways of getting to different groups of people. For example, an ad can be delivered on a cable system that only reaches a specific geographic area. This type of geographic niche advertising is important in campaigns where media markets spill over from large states to smaller states. For campaigns in New Hampshire, where so much advertising occurs every four years in presidential races, the Boston media market (of which it is a part) is much more expensive than the Manchester market. As cable systems become pervasive, political ad makers can use them to deliver messages to voters who live in places like New Hampshire or southern Vermont at a fraction of that larger market's cost. The ability to penetrate only New Hampshire counties, instead of paying for Massachusetts voters to see an ad in a New Hampshire primary, saves enormous amounts of money for campaigns.

Likewise, groups of voters may congregate around certain television shows or television channels. If the research for a campaign shows that a certain demographic of voters lines up with particular TV venues, then the campaign not only can deliver messages to them through the broader advertising on network television, but also can tailor discrete messages to be delivered to a target audience via cable. So, if suburban voters living near a metropolitan area are concerned about development, for example, an antidevelopment ad can be delivered in a specific county, targeting a specific candidate's opponent in a race. That way, campaigns can communicate aggressively with voters who care about particular issues, causes, or concerns, even in paid television advertising, without spending enormous sums to communicate with groups of voters who have no interest.

The Next Wave: The Future of Media Advertising

Television advertising in the future will have to adjust to a more rapid pace of delivery. It's simply a faster world, in which ads on TV compete with other forms of communication, such as the Internet, direct mail, and paid telephone banks, to deliver and amplify the message of a campaign. Perhaps the biggest adjustment that television advertising will have to make will be the move to "convergence technology." Advertising in future political campaigns is not likely to be limited to the single screen of television, but is just as likely to appear on the second screen (the computer) and more and more likely to appear on the third screen (the telephone).

The iPhone as a Precursor?

The Apple iPhone is a precursor to what may become an everyday means of first-hand communication with voters. Now that voters can easily view videos through their telephones, and the images are so clear that they may have the kind of powerful impact that television advertising first had thirty-five years ago, political ad makers may decide they need to move to the second and third screens even more. If so, it will create an interesting new way of communicating with voters. Campaigns used to go door to door with candidates and ground troops; now they may go hand to hand with video images and sound bites.

YouTube and Beyond

It is not just the advent of convergence technology that is likely to influence ad making. In the age of YouTube, not only has the delivery of advertising been democratized, but so have the means of production. For example, when MoveOn.org held a contest in the 2004 presidential campaign in which individuals were invited to make ads attacking President Bush, hundreds of entries were produced by people who had little more than laptop editing systems at their disposal.[14]

The democratization of the means of production, through the ready availability of editing software and laptop computers, and the democratization of the means of delivery through the Internet mean that a person sitting in a room almost anywhere in the world, who has access to a computer, appropriate software, and a high-speed connection, could produce political advertising. Even better, they can deliver it to anyone with a Web connection anywhere in the world. And through such platforms as YouTube, that ad could be viewed by a huge audience. This is a breakthrough that political ad makers are only beginning to understand and exploit. As we see more of it in the 2008 presidential campaign, from the "Obama girl" ads to the next "macaca moment" (which will likely be captured by someone's cell phone out on the campaign trail), it's clear that in many ways "the revolution" in political advertising "will be televised." [15] This revolution is happening today, and the people who are likely to win the next wave of campaigns are the campaigners and consultants who understand what is happening and exploit the many opportunities that are available as a result of rapid technological change.

Independent Expenditures

One of the most important developments in political advertising in recent years has been the growth of "independent-expenditure" advertising in political campaigns. This phenomenon has existed for many years but was first recognized by the national news media in the 1988 presidential campaign. In that campaign, groups supporting George H. W. Bush broadcast ads about Willie Horton, an escaped Massachusetts criminal who, while on a weekend "furlough" from a Massachusetts prison, committed a heinous crime in the state of Maryland. The Willie Horton ad caused a sensation and helped bring about the defeat of Bush's opponent, Democrat Michael Dukakis, who was governor of Massachusetts. The ad became notorious for its use of race in the presidential campaign, and although many of its aspects were so roundly criticized that they were never repeated, fundamentally the same thing happened to another Massachusetts Democratic nominee for president sixteen years later. Sen. John Kerry's presidential campaign was attacked by an independent group organized under Section 527 of the Internal Revenue Code. The so-called Swift Boat ads harshly attacked Kerry's service during the Vietnam War. The group spent millions broadcasting ads paid for by individuals supporting the reelection of George W. Bush.

It is ironic that two of the most notorious independent-expenditure ads would be bookended by the campaigns of the two presidents named Bush. However, independent-expenditure advertising, on both ends of the political spectrum, has proliferated like the nuclear arms race during the Cold War.

Now, independent expenditure advertising is something engaged in not only by groups distinct from campaigns, but by political parties and by the political party committees established at a national level to support candidates for the House and Senate. At the heart of this independent-expenditure advertising are firm rules and laws that forbid the independent groups and committees from coordinating, or even communicating in most cases, with political campaigns. This division between campaigns and the independent actions of groups choosing to exercise their right to political free speech in American constitutional democracy is making it more difficult for political campaigns to control the message being delivered to voters.

Voters naturally attribute any political advertising that they see (whether or not it contains a legal disclaimer) to a particular campaign and not to an independent-expenditure group to which it has no connection. Thus, a campaign that may have decided strategically to pursue positive advertising to introduce a candidate may have to engage in a battle over that tone, and the content of the campaign's message may be undermined by groups mounting their own highly negative campaigns. Unfortunately the campaign, and not the independent-expenditure group, may pay the price because many voters will believe that candidates control everything that is being said by their side. Unless the laws governing independent-expenditure advertising are changed in a significant way, we are only likely to see more of these ads in the years ahead.

Conclusion

Political advertising remains the most powerful tool in the campaign manager's arsenal of communication weapons, but it will change in the years ahead, as technology changes the way we communicate. Soon negative political ads may be popping up on your cell phone or may be downloaded with a newscast to your iPod. Whatever the future holds, one thing is certain—as long as we have political campaigns, we are likely to have political ads of one form or another. Others will debate the impact of that reality on American democracy. For now, those who want to win campaigns will try to understand and exploit the power of political ads.

The future of political campaigns is not just on the Internet; the Internet requires motivation by the user to seek out information. Such voters tend to have much higher political interest, awareness, and participation. Campaigns, however, must still reach that enormous segment of voters who are less involved than activists but still believe that the act of voting and the choices made for political offices are critical. For the foreseeable future, the single best way to reach those voters is through television advertising. To those who posit that old-fashioned political ads don't matter, that the future of political persuasion lies on the Internet and elsewhere on the technology highway, perhaps the best rejoinder is the ancient chant: "The King is dead. Long live the King."

Appendix to Chapter 3 begins on the next page.

Appendix to Chapter 3: Contemporary Case Studies of Paid Advertising

Biographical Ad

Case Study: John Edwards for U.S. Senate, North Carolina, 1998

John Edwards speaks from his hometown of Robbins, North Carolina, in "Tell You."

When John Edwards ran for the U.S. Senate in North Carolina in 1998, hardly anyone knew who he was. His career as a trial lawyer had been enormously successful, but he had never before sought public office. Running as a Democrat in a southern state—first in a Democratic primary against more-experienced politicians, and then in a general election against an incumbent Republican—achieving victory was a tall order. But Edwards had a number of assets, including his compelling life story. Raised in the small town of Robbins, N.C., Edwards exuded the mainstream values that were at the heart of the rural parts of his state.

To tell Edwards's story, the campaign used a biographical ad. The ad ran heavily at the beginning of the primary campaign in the spring and continued to be broadcast right up until election day in November. The only change in the ad between the initial primary version and the one that ran in the general election was the inclusion of a scene with Edwards's new daughter, Emma Claire, who was born during the summer of 1998. The Edwards biographical ad was scripted, and Edwards himself narrated. Forty years ago, ads would never have been voiced-over by candidates. Today (and in the future) candidates voicing-over their own ads creates greater authenticity.

The ad began with Edwards walking down the flag-draped street of his small town, introducing himself to voters in a straightforward manner, in a voice and accent that would become famous later but were unfamiliar when voters first saw him. He spoke directly to the camera while walking down the street: "I'm John Edwards; I'm running for the United States Senate. I want to tell you about where I come from, and what I believe." The story of the ad continued, describing his youth and growing up in Robbins, in the middle of North Carolina; his father, who worked in a mill for thirty years; the public high school he attended, where he played football; the church where he and his family went to services every Sunday. Edwards talked about loading UPS trucks as he worked his way through North Carolina State University. He talked about the "good people" he grew up with in Robbins and how he learned from them "to treat people right and take responsibility" for his actions. He introduced his wife, Elizabeth, and told people that they had just celebrated their twentieth wedding anniversary.

Then a narrator interjected a critical piece of biographical information about Edwards. Even though the campaign knew that one of the later attacks against Edwards would be that he was a "trial lawyer," a profession subject to constant attack by Republicans, the campaign decided to plead guilty to Edwards's being a lawyer. At that point in the ad, a scene of Edwards arguing to a mock jury, which was filmed during the commercial shoot, appeared. The narrator proceeded to introduce an important credential: the fact that John Edwards had been "named one of the six best trial lawyers in the nation." Edwards then appeared on camera and spoke directly to voters about the heart of his case in the Senate campaign, saying, "I've had a lot of practice taking on powerful interests, and that's what I plan to do in the Senate." The spot then moved to an Edwards voice-over in which he said, "The only test I plan to use is the one I learned in Robbins: to do what's right and fight for people."

The ad culminated with a scene that had a powerful visual and symbolic impact: Edwards stood in front of the water tower with the name of the town of Robbins written across its front, and the narrator delivered the tagline of the campaign: "John Edwards. The People's Senator." That image—John Edwards standing in front of the water tower in the small town he grew up in—would become the iconic image of Edwards's long-shot Senate campaign. In one image, in one ad, everything that his campaign wanted voters to know about this political newcomer's values was expressed and delivered to the voters of North Carolina.

Issue Ad

Case Study: Bernie Sanders for U.S. Senate, Vermont, 2006

An ad from Bernie Sanders's campaign highlighted his commitment to protecting American workers.

Bernie Sanders occupies a unique position in American politics. Elected as an independent, he is the only "Democratic Socialist" in the U.S. Senate. He replaced another independent, James Jeffords, who had switched from the Republican Party to become an independent and, after deciding to caucus with the Democrats, had swung control of the narrowly divided senate from the Republican Party to the Democratic Party. Sanders had been the long-serving, popular representative from a state that has only one seat in the U.S. House. He began his campaign well ahead of his opponent, who was a newcomer to politics but who had ample resources to introduce himself and make his case to the Vermont electorate. Indeed, Rich Tarrant went on to spend more money ($7,315,854) than anyone has ever spent in Vermont's electoral history. Real differences existed between Sanders and Tarrant, and while the Sanders ads were never negative and hardly even mentioned his opponent, they set forth the enormous substantive differences between the two candidates.

Rich Tarrant, a successful businessman who had made a fortune in high tech, believed that globalization in general was good for America's economy. He argued that the loss of some manufacturing jobs had to be looked at in the context of what good could come from America's competing and winning in the larger scheme of free trade and global competition. Sanders believed that trade policies that encouraged shipping American jobs overseas, particularly the jobs of hardworking Vermonters, were bad for Vermont and America, and he talked passionately about his opposition to policies that led to the outsourcing of American jobs.

This debate between the two positions, Tarrant's support of globalization and Sanders's opposition to outsourcing, took the form of a political ad (which had thirty- and sixty-second versions) that addressed the plight of Vermonters whose jobs had been outsourced to foreign countries. The ad then highlighted the work that Bernie Sanders had done in the Congress to try to protect the workers and businesses that were hurt by policies that encourage outsourcing, his fight to protect American jobs and American workers.[16]

The Sanders ad focused on a potent issue on which there were real differences between the candidates. And whereas the ad was hardly negative, in a small state, where an engaged electorate follows substantive differences between the candidates closely, it made the point that Bernie Sanders's priority would be standing up for American workers. Meanwhile, his opponent—unnamed in the spot but positioned on the other side of the issue in many widely published press reports—would not fight for Vermonters as Bernie had in the past and would in the future. The ad may not have been the least bit negative in tone or content, but it conveyed a central difference between the two candidates in a powerful way that voters remembered and acted on by giving Sanders nearly two-thirds of the vote on election day.

The Sanders ad has one important similarity to the Edwards bio ad: authenticity. Candidates who are viewed as authentic have a tremendous advantage today, when their every word and nuance is scrutinized by the traditional press, the electronic press, and the blogs that represent the new frontier of political reporting.

Accomplishment and Vision Ad

Case Study: Sen. Bill Nelson Reelection Campaign, Florida, 2006

An ad from Sen. Bill Nelson's 2006 Florida campaign for reelection to the Senate is a good example of accomplishment-and-vision advertising. Nelson was seeking reelection to the Senate in a campaign that began as one of the closest races, targeted by the Republicans for a pickup of a Democratic seat. Instead, the result was a lopsided victory for the incumbent.

In every one of Nelson's four statewide elections, campaign ads have made reference to the fact that he was a crew member on the space shuttle. Nelson's association with NASA and the space program is obviously a powerful connection to his home state of Florida. But beyond that connection, the space program evokes a sense of the future and a sense of innovation, which can help a candidate speak to the future. In an ad titled "Innovation," the Nelson campaign both reminded voters

"Innovation," an ad from Bill Nelson's 2006 Florida Senate race, showcases Nelson's space shuttle crew member experience and his plans to harness the power of innovation to build a stronger future.

of his flight aboard the space shuttle and connected the theme of innovation to a pressing concern of 2006—the spiraling cost of energy and the fact that U.S. dependence on Middle Eastern oil was affecting the nation's security as well as its economy.

The Nelson ad began with footage of the space shuttle liftoff, with Nelson entering the launch pad in the background. In the foreground, the incumbent senator said, "When I flew in space I saw firsthand that American innovation could conquer any challenge." Scenes evoking energy independence, from solar panels to fields of corn, appeared on the screen, as Nelson continued, "Now we need to use the power of American innovation to make our country independent of foreign oil. We need to commit ourselves to producing alternative fuel from sources like ethanol." As the senator reappeared on the full screen he concluded by saying, with a sense of optimism reminiscent of Ronald Reagan, "We can do it. And we will."

This ad had the virtue of using several elements of advertising in one compact, thirty-second format. An important part of Nelson's biography is his training and flight as a crew member aboard the shuttle. The issue of energy independence was a pressing concern in the 2006 election and is likely to be a growing concern among American voters in the years ahead. By laying out an optimistic, can-do vision for the future, Nelson was able to demonstrate to voters that he believed that even the toughest problems the country faces can be solved if we have the right leadership.

The ad combined these elements in one short format and contributed to Nelson's stunning, twenty-point victory in the general election.

Negative Ad

Case Study: Chris Carney for U.S. House of Representatives, Pennsylvania, 2006

PAUL MACKNOSKY
DICKSON CITY, PA

Residents of Pennsylvania's Tenth Congressional District voice their disgust with Don Sherwood's unscrupulous behavior, in this negative ad for Chris Carney.

A recent example of high-impact negative ads is from the 2006 U.S. House of Representatives race in Pennsylvania's tenth district. Two years earlier the Republican incumbent, Don Sherwood, had won a landslide victory. Sherwood's wins had been getting bigger and bigger in election after election, in a heavily Republican district. But as with many incumbents who lose, Sherwood's personal affairs affected and ultimately undermined his reelection.

An incident in which Sherwood had allegedly choked his mistress became front-page news in his district and in Washington. But Sherwood's worst nightmare was not just the bad publicity from that sordid affair, but the emergence of a new, clean-cut, anti-Washington, outsider candidate who embodied the conservative values of Pennsylvania's heartland.

Chris Carney was a navy veteran who had served after 9-11. He was also the father of five children and a devoted family man. His early campaign introduced Carney on the basis of those Pennsylvania values—his family, his service to country in the navy, and his commitment to the well-being of middle-class families, including tax cuts for the middle class.

The heart of his campaign, however, was not the positive message about Carney. Instead, the Democrat's campaign revolved around a series of negative ads directed at Sherwood and his personal life. Negative ads dealing with personal issues are the most sensitive and potentially powerful forms of advertising. In this case, Carney's media consultant, Julian Mulvey, used negative testimonials from voters in the district talking about the Sherwood scandal in their own words. Some of this testimony was backed up by newspaper headlines and other authoritative sources. The series of ads about the Sherwood "incident" let voters express their shock, disgust, and outrage at his actions. Some took the form of individual testimony from single voters, while another in the series featured several voters, all making the same point: that Sherwood had lost touch with Pennsylvania values and betrayed them by his actions in Washington.

In the end these ads helped Carney achieve a stunning victory. Indeed, the net swing of eighty-five points was the largest single shift in vote margin in any congressional district in the 2006 election. The election of Democrat Carney in a heavily Republican district is an example of the power of well-executed negative advertising and the dramatic impact those ads can have if they are properly crafted.

Notes

1. See Edwin Diamond and Stephen Bates, *The Spot: The Rise of Political Advertising on Television* (Cambridge, Mass.: MIT Press, 1992).
2. Federal Election Commission, Campaign Disclosure Reports, cir. 2006, 2004, and 2002, www.fec.gov/finance/disclosure/disclosure_data_search.shtml.
3. Steve LeBlanc, "Campaign Spending Hit All-Time High in 2006," Associated Press, state and local wire, December 5, 2006.
4. See Ed O'Keefe, "Harold Ford Eyes Senate Upset, Denies Being a Playboy," *ABC News,* October 15, 2006.
5. Robert J. Huckshorn and Robert C. Spencer, *The Politics of Defeat: Campaigning for Congress* (Amherst: University of Massachusetts Press, 1971).
6. W. I. Romanow, *Television Advertising in Canadian Elections* (Waterloo, Ont.: Wilfrid Laurier University Press, 2003).
7. For more information about the use of research in campaigns, see Douglas E. Schoen, *The Power of the Vote* (New York: William Morrow, 2007); and Frank Luntz, *Words That Work* (New York: Hyperion, 2007).
8. Ivor Crewe, Brian Gosschalk, and John Bartle, *Political Communications: Why Labour Won the General Election of 1997* (London: Routledge, 1998), 56–57.
9. A panel "back survey" refers to a survey of a discrete group of voters, who are established initially as a random group, and who are subsequently re-contacted by the same pollster and asked to give their opinions on new issues, as well as on previously asked questions such as candidate support. Panel back surveys allow pollsters and campaigns to follow the

dynamic within a discrete group of respondents, which may be different than what is happening at the same time with the electorate at large.

10. See Kathiann M. Kowalski, *Campaign Politics: What's Fair? What's Foul?* (New York: Twenty-first Century Books, 2000).

11. Ian Stewart, "Anti-War Group Revives 'Daisy Ad' Campaign," Associated Press state and local wire, January 16, 2003; see also *CBS News,* October 27, 2000, discussion of "Daisy Girl 2," a Republican ad broadcast before the 2000 election in battleground states, redoing the "Daisy" ad in distinctly Republican terms and saying that "under Republican leadership, the Cold War has ended, securing our children from the threat of nuclear confrontation." It then points to the sale of our security to communist China in exchange for campaign contributions to the Clinton-Gore campaign. The ad features a young girl plucking petals from a daisy and concludes with a countdown and not only the explosion of a nuclear bomb, but a simple narrated text: "Don't take a chance. Please vote Republican." These two examples show how the "Daisy" ad is still alive and well today and being reinvented in new forms by both sides of the political spectrum to advance whatever cause they deem important.

12. Steve Davis, Larry Elin, and Grant Reeher, *Click on Democracy: The Internet's Power to Change Political Apathy into Civic Action* (Boulder: Westview Press, 2004), 30.

13. See MoveOn.Org's "Bush in 30 Seconds Contest" at bushin3oseconds.org.

14. Beth Fouhy, "Ad Showing Kids Laboring to Pay Off Deficit Wins MoveOn Contest," *USA Today,* January 13, 2004.

15. See Joe Trippi, *The Revolution Will Not Be Televised: Democracy, the Internet, and the Overthrow of Everything* (New York: William Morrow, 2004).

16. This ad won the 2006 "Pollie" award for a television ad for an independent candidate. Each year, the American Association of Political Consultants awards "Pollies" to firms for extraordinary work in political advertising in various categories.

CHAPTER 4

New Media—The Cutting Edge of Campaign Communications

Joseph Graf

POLITICAL CAMPAIGNS HAVE ALWAYS EMBRACED new communication technology to reach voters, from partisan newspapers in the 1800s, to Franklin Roosevelt's radio "fireside chats" in the 1930s. Today new communication technology in political campaigns is more widespread and diverse than ever. Not since the first widely televised campaigns, in 1956 and 1960, has new technology taken such a central role in presidential campaigns. Despite that, we do not fully understand the changes taking place today—or which changes will be truly significant—as we move from old media to new.

It is said that new media adopt the forms of the old. When television news arrived it looked like radio news with pictures. It was years before there appeared a television aesthetic, or the fuller realization of the differences in the television experience. We have not yet arrived at an Internet aesthetic. Early online newspapers looked like the paper on your doorstep. Early online radio was just a radio tuner in a different spot on your desk. We do not fully appreciate how online media differ from the communication media that have preceded them. There is no better evidence of this than the frenzy with which we chase after innovations like YouTube, Second Life, or the iPhone. We pore over each new development, unsure which one is truly important.

If our task in this chapter is to imagine the future of new media in political campaigns, we can make our best guess about the future by studying campaigns today. It is a truism, but one we forget: The next political campaign will look pretty similar to the last one. To say that is not to discount the dramatic changes under way in politics. Instead it is a warning that too often we have oversold the potential impact of new media and the pace of change. Consider, for example, online fundraising in presidential politics. In the 2004 presidential election, money raised online, using e-mail and Web sites, had a dramatic impact. Former governor Howard Dean's (D-Vt.) campaign for the Democratic presidential nomination surprised the political establishment with the $7 million it raised online in the summer of 2003. Then Sen. John Kerry (D-Mass.) raised nearly $70 million online in the general election in 2004. A fundraising revolution? Perhaps. But at the same time most money in the presidential campaign was raised by donors writing checks, especially early in the campaign when seed money is critical. Most of the donors were responding to traditional requests for money, usually through direct mail. Most donors got a letter or phone call, not an e-mail. The Democratic National Committee (DNC) sent more direct mail in the first few months of 2004 than the party sent throughout all of the 1990s. More than sixty million pieces of direct mail were sent during the campaign.[1] So although new technology raised about $100 million, the "old" technology shattered previous records with another $500 million. Great change to new technology did not displace the old methods.

Again, the task of this chapter is to imagine the future of new media, or what we will also call "new communication technology," in political campaigns. I will begin by reviewing new communication technology in the past three presidential elections, then examine some of the newest efforts taking place today, with an emphasis on using new communication technology to generate "earned media" for the campaign. Earned media is publicity gained by means other than advertising, such as via the press or communicating directly with constituents. I will try to glean some lessons from the past and imagine future trends. In this task one risks falling into the trap of gee-whiz technology, making revolutionary claims about the future because of the latest gizmo. The history of new media in politics is filled with pie-in-the-sky forecasts. Analysts in the last ten years have predicted the end of traditional methods of campaign fundraising, television political advertising, and the two-party system—all of which remain firmly part of the political landscape.

The World of New Media

The enthusiasm for new communication technology reflects the enthusiasm of the news media and their focus on the new and unfamiliar, as well as our own optimism about the potential for political change. Futurists also have underappreciated the conservative and risk-averse nature of political campaigns. Since 1996, major candidates have rarely been the major innovators online. Third parties were the first to experiment with the Internet as an organizing tool, though their efforts were quickly surpassed by the better-funded major parties. But even among major-party candidates, the most surprising innovations usually came from the candidate who was atypical, not an expected front-runner, but one apart from the political establishment. The archetypical example is the 2004 presidential campaign of Howard Dean, who took great risks with online innovation.

Futurists consistently tend to focus on the producer side of the media equation, while ignoring the needs and habits of the media consumer. In the 2000 presidential election, online video was unveiled with great fanfare, not just as a means for political information but as a way to empower voters and level the playing field among candidates. The trouble was that Internet users, most still with dial-up connections, were unwilling to wait for video to download. For the first time, a mass audience had access to online video libraries of candidates discussing their views, but no one was watching.[2] This is a hard lesson for the future: That communication technologies are available does not ensure that they will be used, or even that they will be used in the ways their designers intended. Indeed, the history of the Internet is filled with examples of innovations that were adopted in ways that were never expected. It seemed far-fetched that people would shoot and edit their own films and then post them online, but tens of thousands of YouTube users do so every day.

We forget how far communication technology has advanced in a short time. The use of new communication technology was only a footnote to political campaigns as recently as 1996. The adoption of new technologies online required reliable and fast Internet access that really was not widely available until the 2004 presidential election. Broadband access encouraged people to remain online longer and do more tasks online.[3] The revolution in search engine technology that occurred with Google's introduction in 1999 made finding Internet sources easier. Before that, Internet users had to work harder to find what they were looking for.

Political New Media in the 1990s

In the span of four presidential election cycles the Internet has become a central part of every national political campaign. President Bill Clinton made technology a priority, and soon after his administration moved into the White House in 1993 it introduced e-mail addresses. E-mail was collected on floppy disks and sent by postal mail or couriered the last mile to the White House. If you wanted a response, you had to include a postal address—the White House would not e-mail you back. The House of Representatives announced an e-mail pilot program the next day. To obtain your representative's e-mail address, you sent him or her a postcard requesting it. Members of Congress feared a deluge of e-mail (which they contend with today).[4]

Candidates in congressional campaigns in California were among the first to build Web sites—Senate candidate Dianne Feinstein (D) in 1994 and House candidate Jerry Estruth (D) in 1995.[5] In February 1995, Republican Lamar Alexander (Tenn.) announced his candidacy for the presidency to a group of supporters in an online chat room. But most campaigns remained offline. Internet penetration remained low: Only about 14 percent of Americans were Internet users in 1995.[6] Access was unreliable, and audio or video could be painfully slow. During the 1996 election cycle—a presidential campaign cycle—candidates began to invest in putting campaign materials online. All the major presidential candidates had built

Web sites by fall 1995, but only about a third of candidates for Congress did so. These sites looked amateurish by today's standards, little more than digital yard signs, and they received little traffic.[7] There were few interactive features and little online communication between the campaign and its supporters.

The number of political Web sites exploded during the 2000 campaign. Every presidential campaign sponsored a Web site. Nearly all major-party Senate candidates and about half the House candidates did the same. Sites were more likely to be found in competitive races: They were a response to innovation online by competitors. In addition to the campaign Web sites, a huge number of other political sites appeared. One search engine counted 5,000 sites, including sites for campaigns and parties, interest groups, news media, and other organizations. That was far more than had ever appeared in an election (but a minute fraction of the political Web sites online today).[8] Most were not affiliated with a party or candidate but instead were founded by independent operators, entrepreneurs, or nonprofit foundations to make political information easily available. These Web sites reflected the philosophy of "cyber-utopians" who saw a new age of direct democracy and power centered in a well-informed citizenry.[9] Citizens would access the unprecedented amount information available and become more engaged in political life. Unfortunately, although information about politics was plentiful, interest in politics was not, or at least it was not so easily fostered. Information easily obtained online did not translate into an informed electorate, and most of the nonpartisan political Web sites closed after the 2000 election.[10]

The Dean Phenomenon and the 2004 Election

In the 2004 presidential election, new media were prominent in the insurgent campaign of Democrat Howard Dean but were also important to the surge of fundraising by the eventual Democratic nominee, John Kerry, and the grassroots organizing of the reelection campaign of George W. Bush. Dean was the first presidential candidate to center his early campaign efforts and cement his early support online. His Web site included blogs by the candidate, campaign workers, and supporters, which remains fairly unusual. A blog (derived from "Web log") is a Web site where writers post comments and links, with the most recent postings displayed at the top. Some blogs, including Dean's, allowed anyone to post a message. Campaigns generally have been loath to hand over control of content to people unaffiliated with the campaign, although we saw more of that among the Democratic candidates in 2008. Several candidates in 2008 allowed supporters to blog or post comments on their sites. Dean's supporters also effectively used Meetup.com, a Web site that helps supporters organize online to gather offline.[11] Thousands of Dean groups gathered regularly during his campaign, and even afterward, reflecting the zeal of his supporters.

More money was raised online in the 2004 campaign than ever before, and Dean was the most successful candidate to that time in raising money online. After Dean's success early in the campaign, online fundraising became critical to the John Kerry campaign, which raised about a third of its donations from individuals online, much of that during spring and summer 2004.[12] (This was partly by necessity, as Kerry needed to catch up in fundraising.)

During the same time, the George W. Bush campaign focused its Web site on organizing grassroots support. The Bush campaign used its Web site to help supporters connect with each other, contact local media, and access campaign materials such as talking points, petitions, and campaign paraphernalia. A Bush volunteer could enter his or her zip code on the site and generate a list of voters in his neighborhood that the party wanted to target. This sort of grassroots organizing was seen as important to the Bush victory and a harbinger of things to come.[13]

Internet Strategy in Campaigns

Internet strategy now plays a central role in presidential political campaigns. In 1996, a campaign's Internet strategy meant having a Web site that by today's standards seems amateurish. Internet strategy was allocated a tiny proportion of the campaign budget and was often carried out by younger campaign staffers or volunteers with technical skill but little political experience. Staffers complained that they could not get their candidates to mention the Web site in speeches or devote any money to site development. Web sites were often little more than "electronic brochure(s)." [14]

Now, however, campaigns have focused Web sites on fundraising and attracting and mobilizing activists. Campaign organizers driven by cost-benefit analyses have realized the extraordinary potential of online fundraising. In February 2000, within two days after Sen. John McCain (R-Ariz.) won the New Hampshire presidential primary, donors pledged more than $1 million to his campaign. McCain's online adviser called it "the splash of cold water" that woke everyone to the potential of Internet fundraising.[15] Four years later, Dean made online fundraising (and the Internet in general) central to his campaign. Raising the most money in summer 2003, Dean overnight became the front-runner (although he ultimately withdrew without winning a primary in February 2004). Almost half of Dean's donations came through his campaign Web site.[16] At the time, no one else was close.

After the 2004 election there was a sentiment among experts in online politics that George W. Bush had won on the back of a strong grassroots effort that was partly organized and driven from the campaign Web site. While John Kerry focused his Web site on fundraising out of necessity, George Bush was able to focus his on grassroots activism. The Bush campaign claimed that its Web site attracted

1.2 million volunteers and more than six million e-mail activists.[17] Kerry's Web site was less effective in that regard.

From 2000 to 2008 the Internet adviser became part of the inner circle of most presidential campaigns, and online campaigns shifted from using the Internet to inform and mobilize the broad electorate to focusing on a smaller group of activists. Those activists would become grassroots volunteers. The lesson from 2004 was that online politics must be complemented with offline politics, and that a strong online campaign—like Howard Dean's—was not enough.

Earned Media through New Technology

"Earned media" is free publicity through the media, as distinct from "paid media," or advertising. Political campaigns rely on both. Earned media generally enjoys a wider audience than paid advertising and is cheaper to obtain. A cheaply produced press release can sometimes lead to enormous media attention, whereas paid media can have trouble breaking through the morass of advertising we encounter every day. Earned media can carry greater influence with the audience. Viewers give greater credence to news stories about the campaign than to campaign advertising. Campaign messages passed from person to person are also earned media, and that means of transmission is especially influential. We are more likely to believe and be persuaded by messages from people we know personally.[18]

What has been termed "social media," or publicity garnered through grassroots action, particularly on the Internet, is especially important. Because social media often consists of user-generated content or campaign content forwarded from one person to another, it can be even more influential with the audience that receives it. If you receive a political e-mail forwarded from a close friend, along with their recommendation, you are far more likely to read it and be open to its message than if that e-mail comes from a political campaign. That is true of any kind of message—videos, letters, or e-mail. It is the core insight of social media and its great value in political campaigns. But earned media and social media also have an enormous drawback in that, by relying on others to communicate their message, campaigns give up control.

Once a journalist leaves a press conference or receives a press release, the campaign has limited influence on what that journalist produces. Once a campaign sends an e-mail or releases a campaign video, it has no influence over who passes along that e-mail or how they edit the video. Campaign e-mail is dissected in political blogs and never completely deleted, sitting in a file somewhere to be used against a candidate twenty years from now. A campaign video, which used to be considered controlled media, can today become part of a "mashup," re-edited and combined with other video for a different purpose and easily broadcast around the world. A video of a speech by Sen. Hillary Clinton (D-N.Y.) was re-edited for the famous "1984" video, which cast her as a futuristic Big Brother (or Sister?), and posted to YouTube. The heroine in the video, a takeoff on an Apple computer ad that ran in 1984, wears a Barack Obama T-shirt and destroys Clinton's image on a huge screen.[19] The video has been seen on YouTube at least four million times. The obvious lesson is that it is much more difficult to control the message in this new media environment.

Earned media focused on the gee-whiz aspect of new technology is short-lived. A news story about new technology will not be a story for long. In 1996 and 1998 the mainstream media wrote news stories about the unveiling of campaign Web sites, something rarely newsworthy today. In 2000, online video was news; today we assume a political Web site will post video. Journalists are obsessed with the new and the unusual, so news coverage of new media in politics takes such an approach. It is much easier to produce news stories about the introduction of a new campaign technology than it is to write about what the technology means. In the 2000 presidential election, all kinds of new political Web sites were launched. They were a phenomenon that had not been seen before, and their unveiling was news. New Web sites offered online debates (DebateAmerica), candidate videos (FreedomChannel), or an online quiz that matched you with a candidate (GoVote).[20] These sites relied on earned media for publicity, but after the novelty waned so did the press. The continuing operation of the sites was not news. The first Web site, campaign blog, online video, or chat room is a story; the second is not. In many cases, nonprofit organizations with small budgets had hoped to rely on earned media to publicize their political Web sites, but that publicity again was short-lived. And as it turns out, so were the Web sites. This sort of earned media is a declining and ultimately losing proposition.[21]

Online Social Networks

New technology is dramatically more effective in fostering a broader sort of earned media through what is called "viral marketing." Viral marketing uses social networks to pass along messages, usually on behalf of a commercial brand. The networks can be personal social networks, in which messages pass by word of mouth, or communication networks in which messages pass via e-mail, blogs, videos, text messages, or even video games. New technology has made this sort of earned media more accessible to political campaigns, which in many cases can sidestep the mainstream media entirely with their campaign messages. Although viral marketing can take place in many different ways, one of the most effective is through online social networks.

College students were among the first to discover online social networks in huge numbers, but there are less well-known networks for businesspeople, ethnic groups, senior citizens, and political groups. A social network is a network of social relations tied together by the individual connections, or links, between each person, or node, on the network. "Online social networks" generally means networks of individuals connected to each other via personal Web sites. Some online social networks offer great flexibility, whereas others only allow users to post responses to questions.

The driver of online social networks is the ease with which anyone can link their information with information from someone else, usually with that person's consent. The first person's network then immediately extends to include all those connected with his or her new contact. Because of this, personal networks can expand at an exponential rate. In some communities, the networks have expanded to include so many participants that at some point it becomes unusual to be *outside* the network. Most of the community's relationships become organized and even defined by the social network. At some universities, that was the case with Facebook, an online social network that enjoys great popularity on college campuses. In mid-2007, Facebook claimed more than thirty million members and an expanding reach beyond college and high school students. Facebook is not the largest social network Web site. At the same time, MySpace claimed that it had more than 100 million registered accounts worldwide and was adding more at the rate of 250,000 a day. The numbers are deceptive, however, because some people have multiple accounts.

These enormous potential audiences are what have attracted political campaigns, which have flocked to set up pages on sites such as MySpace, Facebook, YouTube and Flickr. (Sen. Barack Obama hired one of the founders of Facebook to run his online presidential campaign.) Obama (D-Ill.) and former senator John Edwards (D-N.C.) were early and active users of social networks. Both have social network pages with tens of thousands of "friends" who have chosen to link to the candidate's page and are presumably supporters. Candidates' pages include campaign information—speeches, video, and position statements—but also tools to empower members of the network to campaign for their candidate. Network members can advertise their support for a candidate and can easily help the campaign by, for example, posting on their page a button to raise money or a link to the campaign Web site. As the number of links among pages increases, a candidate's page becomes more likely to be accessed by more members of the network.

Candidates have already highlighted their support on these networks, and candidates with less visibility on them have been criticized for missing the boat. MySpace sponsored an online presidential primary for early 2008, which makes it one of the earliest straw polls of candidate support. Depending on the results, campaigns cast the primary as either an indicator of popular support or an unscientific and unreliable poll. The Web site also sponsored discussions with the candidates.[22]

As campaign organizers work to put social networks to use, foremost in their minds is the failure of the 2004 Dean campaign to translate its online energy and success into votes. Dean had vibrant success in his online campaign operations and appeared to be a strong candidate until the Iowa caucuses showed the weakness of his support. By summer 2004, the Bush campaign was seen as more successful in organizing and empowering its local activists.

Virtual Worlds: Second Life

The most unusual social networks that political campaigns use are virtual worlds such as Second Life. Second Life is an online virtual world in which users who join create "avatars," or computer-generated characters, which they then direct through the Second Life universe. (There are several other examples of virtual worlds, such as There.com and Whyville.) Second Life has attracted several million visitors who have created a dynamic economy that is both online and offline. Some people now make a living in their real life selling goods or trading in "real estate" that exists only as computer bits in Second Life.[23] Many universities and businesses have purchased online real estate for online classrooms, libraries, or product showrooms. Reuters news service and at least fifty other major companies have opened satellite offices in Second Life. Many of the 2008 candidates have offices in Second Life (which are sometimes subject to virtual vandalism), and the yearly convention of progressive political activists called YearlyKos held a Second Life version for those unable to attend in person.

Political E-Mail

Little is known about the effects of political e-mail on its recipients, but it has become a part of every political campaign, especially because it may be the cheapest means of reaching potential voters. Its effectiveness is unclear. Political e-mail is easily deleted and ignored. Most candidates offer subscriptions to e-mail newsletters on their Web sites, and campaigns also collect e-mail addresses at rallies, through social networking Web sites, and when supporters make donations online. E-mail often appears to come straight from the candidate, but campaigns also rely on others as senders. Former president Bill Clinton, political consultant James Carville (D), Vice President Dick Cheney (R), and former House Speaker Dennis Hastert (R-Ill.) have all sent e-mail in the 2008 election season on behalf of a candidate campaign or a party committee. E-mails are immediately credible as information directly from the party or candidate. They are easily forwarded to others, passing along both the message and personal support for it. Because of the power of the personal recommendation, many campaign Web sites and e-mails make it easy to forward their messages and encourage recipients to do so. E-mail allows a quick response, and indeed a great deal of political e-mail is in immediate response to news reports or campaign events. This rapid response online is a big part of a campaign's day-to-day duties. Within hours of an event the campaign can send a video statement by the candidate or some other response to, for example, a political attack.

The 2004 Bush and Kerry presidential campaigns sent hundreds of millions of e-mails to their supporters. E-mail was used extensively to try to recruit volunteers, encourage voter registration, and to a lesser degree, solicit contributions. The Kerry campaign made greater use of e-mail to solicit contributions and was highly successful at collecting money online. (The Bush campaign had less need to solicit money online and focused its fundraising elsewhere.) The Bush campaign segmented its e-mail audience to a great degree, sending out e-mails to more than a thousand different groups during the last ten months of the campaign, including messages that went nationwide and ones sent to a single county. (Similar data from the Kerry campaign were not available.) In the last six months of the campaign, more than a thousand e-mails were sent from the campaigns and party committees.[24] Any single e-mail address would, of course, receive fewer. One researcher received seventy-eight e-mails from the two campaign committees alone in the last month of the campaign. Among Kerry's donors, about 40 percent said in response to a survey question that they received political e-mail "almost every day," and about a third of Bush donors said the same.[25]

In 2004, the presidential campaign organizations also used political e-mail to try to frame their candidates and their opponents. Bush framed himself as a strong war president and Kerry as untrustworthy, unqualified, and deficient on the issues. Kerry framed himself as trustworthy, knowledgeable, and a strong leader, while framing Bush as a failure in foreign policy and on the domestic economy.[26]

Video

Campaigns employ what are called "video stalkers" to record the opposition and to allow their candidate to respond rapidly to an opponent's comments. With a low-priced digital camcorder, campaign staff members or volunteers can shoot fair-quality video on the scene at an opponent's event. They download the video to a laptop computer and transmit it via cellular modem. Campaign strategists can be reviewing an opponent's comments minutes after they are made.

The most influential example of this use of video occurred during the 2006 Virginia race for the U.S. Senate between the incumbent Republican senator, George Allen, and Democratic challenger Jim Webb. Allen was a strong favorite until he was caught on video three months before the election calling a Webb campaign volunteer a "macaca," a demeaning term and in some cultures a racial slur. Allen was speaking before a friendly local crowd when he pointed out the Webb volunteer, a young man of Indian descent who had been assigned to videotape Allen. "Let's give a welcome to macaca here," Allen said. "Welcome to America and the real world of Virginia." [27] Those sixteen words were preserved for posterity on video—they are still available online—and were viewed on YouTube more than half a million times. Perhaps more important, the video provided endless fodder for political bloggers, whose criticism seeped into the mainstream media, even making national news. Blogs offered a place for Allen's critics to gather, and blog comments prompted more news stories, more apologies from Allen, and more online viewers.

Former Massachusetts governor Mitt Romney, a 2008 Republican presidential candidate, was forced to respond quickly when video surfaced on YouTube of comments he had made more than ten years ago when he was a candidate for the U.S. Senate. Romney, whose presidential campaign appealed to conservative Republicans, had said in a debate in 1994 that he supported abortion and the right of homosexuals to be Boy Scout leaders. Within hours after the video surfaced, the Romney campaign responded online with new video of the candidate, saying his statements on those issues had been wrong.[28] For candidates, all of this means that they must be mindful that everything they have said in the past may be recorded and ready for release online, and every moment on the campaign trail could be caught on video.

Blogs

Perhaps none of the new media generated as much notice leading up to the 2008 election as political blogs. The impact of blogs on political campaigns has come, first, through their interplay with journalists and the news media and, second, through the way they have fostered social networks of supporters and communication with the campaigns. The prominence of political blogs in the scramble for the Democratic nomination was illustrated in 2007 at the YearlyKos Convention, a convention of liberal bloggers that was founded the year before. This group is considered so influential among party activists that all the major Democratic candidates appeared, even though the conference only drew about a thousand participants and a few hundred journalists and most of the participants represented the liberal wing of the Democratic Party. There is no similar conference among Republican bloggers; some observers argue that the political right has been less successful in attracting blog audiences and has been more successful with talk radio. Nonetheless, political blogs span the political spectrum.

There are perhaps tens of thousands of political blogs, but their audience is fairly concentrated among a small group. Several dozen prominent political blogs attract a large share of the total audience, and they are heavily linked to by other blogs. Only a fraction of Internet users regularly read political blogs. They are politically active, more partisan than the general public, and deeply distrustful of the mainstream media.[29] Several prominent blogs attract hundreds of thousands of readers each month, as well as submissions from politicians and celebrities. Sen. John Kerry and Democratic Speaker of the House Nancy Pelosi (Calif.) have contributed to Daily Kos, and the Huffington Post has a long roster of celebrity contributors.

The relationship between political blogs and other political media is complex. Many political blogs have a symbiotic relationship with the conventional news media. Interlinking is a key feature of blogs, and some are nothing more than a collection of links. They often link with conventional media accounts and use those accounts as jumping-off points for discussion or criticism of the mainstream media ("MSM" in blog parlance). In the last few years, a few blogs have hired journalists and produced original content, but those examples are rare. For the most part, political blogs rely on the conventional news media as both a source of material and a foil to criticize. Political blogs have helped to shape the media agenda (as in the 2006 Senate race in Virginia, discussed above) and to construct an interpretive frame for the news. For example, in 2002, Senate Majority Leader Trent Lott (R-Miss.) lost his leadership position as a result of news stories that were prompted by political blogs. At Sen. Strom Thurmond's (R-S.C.) hundredth-birthday party, Lott praised Thurmond and his segregationist presidential campaign of 1948 in remarks that journalists who covered the event ignored. Political bloggers paid attention, though, and criticism on the blogs spread to the political establishment. Two weeks later Lott resigned as majority leader.[30]

For the purposes of this chapter and our focus on earned media, the most relevant impact of political blogs is in their facilitating social networks of supporters and communication with the campaign. Since early in the history of online politics people have been wary about the potential of new media for greater communication with the public. When members of Congress first acquired their own e-mail addresses they were reluctant to make them public. Early Web sites in 1996 and 1998 avoided interactive features, and campaigns resisted adding them.[31] Campaigns worried that they would be overwhelmed by e-mail or blog postings, or that a campaign would be held accountable for objectionable postings that others made on its Web site.

Those kinds of considerations made the Howard Dean presidential campaign all the more remarkable. In March 2003, the campaign became the first major campaign to openly encourage political conversation on a blog on the campaign Web site. Other candidates in the 2004 election would later adopt blogs, but the Dean campaign's effort was far more active, energized and enthusiastically promoted by the candidate. Dean's blog received abundant traffic and media attention. Campaign staff and occasionally Dean posted behind-the-scenes stories and campaign strategy. One scholar, however, has called this a "façade of interactivity" because in reality, there was minimal communication between campaign staff and participants. Using the blog in this way was a double-edged sword; the energy and excitement it generated helped to make Dean the front-runner, but people who felt invested in a campaign that they thought would respond to their suggestions left disappointed:

The joy of weblogging is that it energized and seemed to invite citizen-supporters into the campaign. The sorrow is that weblogging maintained a hierarchical relationship between citizens and the campaign and reinforced that citizen-supporters were not ultimately insiders.[32]

Every major presidential candidate posted a blog in the 2008 campaign. Some, like John Edwards and Mitt Romney, allowed people unaffiliated with the campaign to post comments. Most campaigns still avoid this because it can open a Pandora's box of unwanted attention.

Obstacles to Innovation

Given the multimedia competition for our attention—whether from the Internet, iPods, cell phones, music downloads, or television—capturing a person's interest has become a more difficult task. Furthermore, interest may ebb and flow over a long campaign, especially one as long as the 2008 presidential campaign. State and local campaigns have also gotten longer, and they generally attract less interest to begin with. The U.S. Senate race in Maine, between the incumbent Susan Collins (R), and challenger Rep. Tom Allen (D), began eighteen months before the election (as did the presidential campaign). Campaigns ask a great deal when they ask activists to get involved so early and stay involved so long. The social media we have been discussing requires an active, interested audience, willing to watch videos or forward messages to friends. Most Americans are not active and interested until close to election day, and many never become interested. U.S. voting rates tend to hover in the 50 percent to 60 percent range in presidential election years and around 40 percent or less in midterm election years. So although campaign videos on YouTube have been viewed hundreds of thousands of times, it is important to remember that only 15 percent of Internet users have *ever* seen a political video online.[33] The potential impact of new media in political campaigns must be considered in relation to low audience interest in politics and how that interest fluctuates over the course of the campaign.

As we have said, campaigns are conservative and risk averse: They generally lag behind consumer marketing in the use of new media. Promoters of rock concerts, soft drinks, and popular music are all more willing to innovate online. Innovation in political campaigns often borrows from marketing and advertising, and the innovators have often been insurgent or third-party campaigns. Candidates struggling for attention may be more willing to innovate with technology. For example, in April 2007 congressman and presidential candidate Ron Paul (R-Texas) visited a Georgetown University dorm room to be interviewed by a college student for a YouTube video.[34] As the field narrows, candidates will not take such risks.

Competition also fosters innovation online. In 1996 and 1998, when a challenger built a Web site the incumbent followed. Candidates in competitive congressional races were more likely to use Web sites, and candidates in wide open primary campaigns seem more willing to take chances with new media. The innovative spirit at the beginning of a campaign, when more candidates are viable, may give way to more tried-and-true methods of campaigning when the field is winnowed. As a campaign progresses, it also needs to broaden its reach from its core of active supporters to the entire potential electorate.

On the other hand, although large audiences capture the imaginations of political campaign organizers (and those of entrepreneurs and academics), large audiences may not mean much. Large audiences can rapidly coalesce around a new Web site, but that does not mean the site will make money from those visitors, communicate its messages, or mobilize the viewers in some way. That is why the focus of new media in politics has moved from the mass audience to the elite. When politics first went online, the focus was educating and motivating the broad, popular audience in the United States. During the 2000 campaign cyber-utopians envisioned a nation informed and mobilized to action by information available online, and a host of nonpartisan political Web sites were founded with just that goal in mind. The entrepreneurs and nonprofit foundations that funded them were deeply disappointed when most sites closed after the election. The philosophy behind their efforts suggests the most interesting academic questions about new media in politics: Have they changed our interest in civic life? Are we more engaged than before? The answer seems to be that the Internet is good at reaching supporters, but it has proved much less effective at influencing people who are not interested. Seeing this, political organizers have turned to focusing on those who already have some interest and devising Internet tools to empower that smaller group of activists.

How Will Innovation Occur?

We should look for change where change is being attempted. Innovation is more likely to occur where it is being fostered. At this writing, the 2008 campaigns were working hard to find people with an interest in politics, predisposed toward their candidates, and to use new media to empower them. The key is giving activists a sense that their opinions are being heard and then giving them the means to act. Campaigns are experimenting with online social networks, mobile technology, video, and e-mail. It is among these efforts that we should look for real innovation.

Emerging Trends in Online Social Networks

In no place is innovation being fostered so intently as with social networks. In the future, social networks will be the arenas wherein activists will coalesce at all levels, from local to national politics. These networks will cross media into face-to-face interaction, and the networks will reside within and outside the campaigns. The Meetup.com discussion groups in the presidential campaigns of Howard Dean and Wesley Clark in 2004 were examples of the online/face-to-face connection, and they were both within and outside the campaigns. Groups of supporters organized online but met in person, and many groups continued to meet long after the campaigns ended.

These networks are more diverse than social networking brand names such as Facebook or MySpace. They will coalesce around blogs, mobile technology, Web sites, or a combination of media. Salem Communications, a radio network that specializes in conservative and Christian broadcasting, launched Townhall.com in 2006 as part of its effort to become a "multi-platform political movement." Townhall.com gives its audience a voice by enabling them to call in to talk radio or post messages to a series of interconnected Web sites; it has helped build a social network across platforms among a community of people connected by similar interests.[35] New media give these communities political power through the easy and rapid mobilization of their members.

Emerging Trends in Mobile Technology

The future of new media for the operation of campaigns is in mobile technology. The newest mobile technology used in campaigns consists of devices with greater database capabilities and constant Internet connections. As we are already seeing with Blackberrys, smart phones, and the iPhone, devices are adding more and more capability with easier Internet access. The iPhone, for example, can use a local wireless network, avoiding cell phone usage costs. The key is greater capabilities and greater access to enormous databases of demographic and consumer information. We are also seeing more use of ordinary cell phones to raise money or muster public support.

Cell phone parties are already popular. In a cell phone party, campaigns encourage local activists to sign up friends with cell phones (especially ones with unlimited calling plans). The group then gathers with a list of potential supporters from the campaign to be called for donations or get-out-the-vote efforts. This sort of directed local activism is easy to organize online and gives the campaign great flexibility while cutting costs. The phone banks of the past were much more expensive because of the costs of organization, installation, and long distance service. Text messaging has also been added to the mix. John Edwards's 2008 presidential campaign accepted cell phone text messages. Campaigns will also use text messaging for get-out-the-vote efforts, mobilizing people quickly, and raising money.

With most people now carrying a cell phone, a candidate can turn a public appearance into a fundraiser by asking audience members to call with their credit card number or, easier still, text message a donation. The text message service bills the user and shares that charge with the campaign. Rock concerts already have used this technology to raise money from concertgoers; for example, the group U2 has raised money during concerts for African poverty relief.[36] Federal Election Commission regulations require campaigns to collect information about donors and how much they have given, but such reporting could be coordinated through the service provider.

Mobile devices also facilitate mobilization in ways that, until now, have been used most effectively by protesters. Cell phones can organize collective action quickly and easily. During the 2004 Republican National Convention, in New York, protesters text-messaged Web sites to share news of police movements and to organize protests quickly in locations where they would have the most impact (and the least official interference). Cell phone cameras instantaneously transmitted photos of police to "protest news" Web sites, avoiding the mainstream media. All of it was done for only a few thousand dollars. This sort of instant mobilization has been seized upon more vigorously overseas. Activists in Spain turned to text messaging and e-mail groups to organize gatherings before elections, despite a moratorium on demonstrations. A text-messaging campaign against Philippine president Joseph Estrada resulted in his removal from office in January 2001. "Go 2 EDSA [an acronym for a Manila street]," read the text message, passed from person to person. "Wear Blck." [37]

Emerging Trends in Video

The next step is video transmission to mobile devices, and that again has already taken off overseas, especially in South Korea. Only about a third of cell phone users in the United States have text-messaging capability, and even fewer can access video, but those numbers will increase.[38] Sports highlights on mobile video, for example, are becoming increasingly popular. Sen. Norm Coleman (R-Minn.), among others, makes video available on his reelection Web site.[39] Several television news outlets post free video news on their Web sites, and both major parties post podcast video on their sites. Users download the podcast for viewing on an iPod or a phone with video capability.

Video will be ubiquitous at campaign stops. John McCain said in May 2007, "I assume that there's a camera there at all times. You really have to, and frankly it doesn't bother me." [40] McCain was taped singing "Bomb Iran" at a campaign stop at a VFW hall in South Carolina (sung to the tune of the Beach Boys' song "Barbara Ann"). For candidates in the future, the camera is always on.

Finally, candidates have turned the camera on themselves. In the 2008 presidential campaign, Democratic candidate Sen. Chris Dodd's (D-Conn.) staff started DTV (or DoddTV). The purpose was to show the campaign at work. At times the camera followed the campaign manager and other senior staff around the office. It also followed the candidate on the campaign trail. Senate candidate Tom Allen is doing the same thing with his TomTV.[41] In essence, the campaign has created its own version of reality TV for supporters. Furthermore, DTV and TomTV are available to online sites such as YouTube or more conventional media Web sites or networks. They are another creative way of attracting earned media. Looking into the next decade, online television is likely to become a staple of both congressional and presidential campaigns. At some point we should not be surprised to see a campaign interject drama into its daily deliberations or use humor to attract attention. These tactics might attract online viewership and appeal to younger voters raised on *The Daily Show.*

Emerging Trends in E-Mail

The use of e-mail to cast a wide net for potential activists and donors will increase in future campaigns. In 2004, the Republican firms Voter Contact Services and the Voter Emailing Company built a database of 24.8 million contacts.[42] This project was integral to the Republican get-out-the-vote effort. Enormous databases of contact information and consumer data have been acquired for 2008. E-mail can link someone to a candidate and keep them apprised of a campaign's activities, but for many people e-mail is a passive medium. Most political e-mail is not opened. Direct-mail experts believe that for many donors the inclination to donate needs to be piqued before the e-mail arrives. The e-mail does not convince someone to donate but provides an immediate reminder and easy opportunity to act on their impulse to give. E-mail will also be segmented to a much greater degree, using microtargeting to send smaller batches of specialized e-mail to particular audiences. In 2008, e-mail is also incorporating more interactive features to give recipients a chance to respond to the campaign, watch videos, or connect to the Web site. Especially early in the campaign, e-mail is the doorway through which activists connect with the campaign and join other, more engaging social networks.

Interactive Features in Political Campaigns

The Hillary Clinton campaign emphasized a "conversation," suggesting a role for everyone in the campaign. California representative George Miller (D) received questions from constituents via video, blog posts, and social networks in a project called "Ask George." The questions were aggregated, and Miller would post a video response. (Similar activities have been under way for years in Great Britain.) John Edwards held a "Demand and Be Heard" contest, in which supporters could "demand" that John Edwards visit their hometown. Columbus, Kentucky, won the visit from Edwards after 1,842 residents cast their votes. All of these efforts give people a greater sense that they are being heard and are a part of the political process. They attract media attention and seem to energize and mobilize support-ers.

But this sort of interactivity is a drain on the resources of a political campaign and on the time of a candidate. What's more, as we have already mentioned, there is a risk in this sort of uncontrolled communication. For example, in 2004 the lib-eral advocacy group MoveOn.org invited users to submit their own video adver-tisements about the presidential campaign. One user posted an ad comparing President Bush to Adolph Hitler. Although the ad was quickly removed from the Web site, MoveOn came under strong criticism that resonated among its political opponents and continued for months, as Republican operatives e-mailed the ad to millions of supporters. These things occurred despite the fact that MoveOn did not produce the ad but only provided a forum for a constituent to post it. Campaigns with open blogs or social networks run similar risks. In 2004, supporters of Howard Dean began their own campaign to win the endorsement of Sen. Tom Harkin (D-Iowa) without any prompting from campaign organizers. The campaign eventually had to ask supporters to stop phoning Harkin's office. The Dean campaign, the most successful in using the Internet to develop a community among its support-ers, also had to deal with supporters who considered themselves entitled to a voice and were upset when they felt they were not being heard.[43]

We should anticipate that this greater communication with supporters will diminish as the campaign progresses, especially when the nominees emerge. We have discussed some of the costs and risks of an open communication environment. The focus of a campaign's message can become warped or diffused. The risks grow as a candidate becomes the front-runner, then the nominee, and press coverage of him or her grows. Press attention to every misstep and every aspect of a campaign constrains candidates; they take fewer risks. Candidates for state and local offices, who have smaller constituencies and less press attention, may still see advantages to operating open, interactive campaigns.

Conclusion

The promise of new media in politics has always been their potential for substan-tive change to our political system. That hope for change influences our thinking when we try to predict what the future might hold. Many people hope that new media will encourage a more engaged electorate and a more responsive government, but we must not wear our hopes like blinders. We need to recognize the importance of the desires of the audience and the intentions of political campaigns. Despite the best intentions of Web site organizers in the 2000 presidential election, American voters did not flock online to the wealth of political information easily available for the first time in our history. Making political information available online is important, but it is not enough. In a similar way, new media will serve democratic ideals only if their use is consonant with the intentions of a political campaign. It is a boon for the electorate when candidates appear on YouTube, give interviews to bloggers, and engage college students on Facebook. But a political campaign is about winning, and if ever a campaign believes that these innovative uses of technology no longer serve the campaign, they will stop.

Many innovative uses of new technology are helping more people become engaged in the political process. Some of the forms of engagement are fleeting, such as receiving a political e-mail, but others offer a rich and meaningful way for citizens to take part in political life. Few of the new ways of engagement will touch the lives of all, but each has a niche of interested users. Some people will follow their candidate on Facebook or send text messages of support, whereas others will read the news magazines or watch *The Daily Show*. New media technology has introduced greater richness and diversity into our political lives, and that is a potentially promising change.

Notes

1. Joseph Graf et al., *Small Donors and Online Giving: A Study of Donors to the 2004 Presidential Campaigns* (Washington, D.C.: Institute for Politics, Democracy and the Internet, 2006), 18–19. Includes all data in the paragraph.

2. The greatest example of this was the Web site Freedom Channel. Its history is summarized in Joseph Graf, *Pioneers in Online Politics: Nonpartisan Political Web Sites in the 2000 Campaign* (Washington, D.C.: Institute for Politics, Democracy and the Internet, 2004). Freedom Channel attracted thousands of users, but never the Internet traffic that was hoped for.

3. Susannah Fox, *Digital Divisions: There Are Clear Differences among Those with Broadband Connections, Dial-up Connections, and No Connections at All to the Internet* (Washington, D.C.: Pew Internet and American Life Project, 2005).

4. John Burgess, "Clinton Goes On-Line with E-Mail; His Electronic Address Plugs Computer Users into White House," *Washington Post,* June 2, 1993; T. R. Reid, "Writing Letters to the White House, the High-Tech Way," *Washington Post,* August 16, 1993.

5. Dave D'Alessio, "Adoption of the World Wide Web by American Political Candidates, 1996–1998," *Journal of Broadcasting and Electronic Media* 44, no. 4 (2000); Karen MacPherson, "Need Another Political Fix? Try the Web," *Pittsburgh Post-Gazette,* October 3, 2000.

6. Mary Madden, *America's Online Pursuits: The Changing Picture of Who's Online and What They Do* (Washington, D.C.: Pew Internet and American Life Project, 2003).

7. Chris Casey, *The Hill on the Net: Congress Enters the Information Age* (Boston: AP Professional, 1996).

8. MacPherson, "Need Another Political Fix?"

9. Yuval Levin, "Politics after the Internet," *The Public Interest* 149 (2002): 80–94.

10. Described in Graf, *Pioneers in Online Politics.*

11. Gary Wolf, "How the Internet Invented Howard Dean," *Wired* magazine, January 2004.

12. Paula Dwyer et al., "The Amazing Money Machine: Defying Doomsayers, the Dems—by Some Measures—Are Outraising the Republicans," *Business Week* online, www.businessweek.com.

13. John Palfrey, "Internet Politics 2004: The Good, the Bad and the Unknown," www.personaldemocracy.com (accessed July 6, 2006).

14. D'Alessio, "Adoption of the World Wide Web by American Political Candidates," 567.

15. Tom Hockaday, as quoted in Steve Davis, Larry Elin, and Grant Reeher, *Click on Democracy: The Internet's Power to Change Political Apathy into Civic Action* (Boulder: Westview Press, 2002), 57.

16. Mark Singer, "Running on Instinct," *New Yorker,* January 12, 2004.

17. Alexandra Samuel, "Internet Plays Wild Card into U.S. Politics," *Toronto Star,* October 18, 2004.

18. The importance of personal communication through opinion leaders is discussed in Ed Keller and Jon Berry, *The Influentials* (New York: Free Press, 2003).

19. Dan Morain, "Internet Uncovers Ad Spoofer; An Anti-Clinton Video on YouTube Was Made by an Operative Tied to the Obama Campaign," *Los Angeles Times,* March 22, 2007.

20. All of these Web sites are defunct.

21. The history of these sites is reviewed in Graf, *Pioneers in Online Politics.*

22. Andy Sullivan, "Online 'Friends' Could Be Pivotal in 2008 U.S. Race," washingtonpost.com, August 23, 2007.

23. Kathleen Craig, "Making a Living in Second Life," www.wired.com.

24. E-mail from the 2004 election and data on e-mail from the George W. Bush reelection campaign acquired by the author. Campaign committees include the House, Senate, national, and campaign committees. Graf et al., *Small Donors and Online Giving: A Study of Donors to the 2004 Presidential Campaigns.*

25. Ibid.

26. Andrew Paul Williams, "Self-Referential and Opponent-Based Framing: Candidate E-Mail Strategies in Campaign 2004," in *The Internet Election: Perspectives on the Web in Campaign 2004,* ed. Andrew Paul Williams and John C. Tedesco (New York: Rowman and Littlefield, 2006).

27. Tim Craig and Michael D. Shear, "Allen Quip Provokes Outrage, Apology; Name Insults Webb Volunteer," *Washington Post,* August 15, 2006.

28. Joyce Howard Price, "Internet Technology Uprooting Campaign Stump," *Washington Times,* May 6, 2007.

29. Daniel W. Drezner and Henry Farrell, "The Power and Politics of Blogs," paper presented at APSA Annual Meeting, Chicago, August 2004; Joseph Graf, *The Audience for Political Blogs: New Research on Blog Readership* (Washington, D.C.: Institute for Politics, Democracy and the Internet, 2006).

30. Esther Scott, " 'Big Media' Meets the 'Bloggers': Coverage of Trent Lott's Remarks at Strom Thurmond's Birthday Party" (Boston: Joan Shorenstein Center on the Press, Politics and Public Policy, 2004).

31. Jennifer Stromer-Galley, "On-Line Interaction and Why Candidates Avoid It," *Journal of Communication* 50, no. 4 (2000).

32. Jennifer Stromer-Galley and Andrea B. Baker, "Joy and Sorrow of Interactivity on the Campaign Trail: Blogs in the Primary Campaign of Howard Dean," in *The Internet Election: Perspectives on the Web in Campaign 2004,* 129.

33. Mary Madden, *Online Video* (Washington, D.C.: Pew Internet and American Life Project, 2007).

34. Linda Feldmann, "Web 2.0 Meets Campaign 2008," *Christian Science Monitor,* May 16, 2007.

35. Chuck DeFeo, "Call in Now! How Townhall.Com Turned Talk Radio Fans into a Community of Bloggers," in *Person-to-Person-to-Person: Harnessing the Political Power of Online Social Networks and User-Generated Content,* ed. Julie Barko Germany (Washington, D.C.: Institute for Politics, Democracy and the Internet, 2006), 29.

36. Antony Bruno, "Acts, Audience Connect via Text Messaging," Billboard.com, December 10, 2005.

37. Maki Becker and Bob Port, "Protesters Click with New Media to Mobilize," *Daily News,* September 3, 2004; Cathy Hong, "New Political Tool: Text Messaging," *Christian Science Monitor,* June 30, 2005.

38. Lee Rainie, *Pew Internet Project Data Memo: Cell Phone Use* (Washington, D.C.: Pew Internet and American Life Project, 2006).

39. See home page, colemanforthesenate.com, where the senator does a welcoming interview with Minnesota farmers (accessed August 20, 2007).

40. Steve Grove, "Senator John McCain: The Youtube Interview," www.youtube.com.

41. See chrisdodd.com and tomallen.org home pages for reference to links for live-action television (accessed August 20, 2007).

42. "24.8 Million Email Addresses Now Available for Political Communications from the Voter Emailing Company; Political Groups Can Target Voters through Email Just Like Direct Mail," *Business Wire,* August 6, 2004, www.businesswire.com (accessed August 29, 2004).

43. Stromer-Galley and Baker, "Joy and Sorrow of Interactivity on the Campaign Trail."

CHAPTER 5

Polling—Trends in the Early Twenty-First Century

Candice J. Nelson

IN THE INFANCY OF MODERN SURVEY RESEARCH, survey interviews were conducted in person. But beginning in the mid-1970s, when the telephone spread to over 90 percent of households, telephones became the mechanism of choice for the vast majority of surveys.[1] The key to the success of telephone surveys was their ability to select respondents in a particular population at random—be it a national, state, or district population—using random digit dialing (RDD). RDD uses the area codes for the geographic population being surveyed. Computers generate random numbers that allow survey administrators to call random respondents within the survey population. Among the many advantages of RDD is that it enables pollsters to reach potential respondents with unlisted phone numbers. The advent of computer-assisted telephone interviews (CATI) allowed computers to place the calls, rather than individuals, reducing the time needed to make calls and thus complete surveys.

Random digit dialing and computer-assisted telephone interviews were the standard methods for reaching survey respondents in the later part of the twentieth century. But with the increased use first of answering machines, then caller ID, and finally cell phones, RDD became a less-reliable method of reaching potential respondents. At the same time, with the growth of the Internet, online polling, a new option, appeared on the horizon. Technological advances at the start of the twenty-first century have called the future of RDD into question, presenting survey researchers with their biggest challenge for the future—how best to reach prospective voters. The debate in the survey research community today, and likely in the years to come, is about using phones versus using the Internet for surveys. As this chapter will show, both techniques have pros and cons. Moreover, the best method for a particular survey may depend on the survey's purpose.

In this chapter I will briefly review where survey research is today, the issues pollsters face, and the changes that have already occurred as a result. I will examine the options for pollsters going forward and where polling is likely to be in the next five years—from now through the 2012 elections. Similar trends appear across the board in the survey research industry, from commercial to campaign polling.

Phone Surveys: Practices and Problems

Phone surveys' major advantage is their ability to randomize the survey respondents, which enables pollsters to generalize from the survey sample to an entire population. Pollsters can survey as few as 400 respondents and generalize to an entire congressional district or state. National surveys typically have approximately 1,000 respondents, largely to allow some comparisons among demographic groups (men compared to women, Democrats compared to Republicans, and age, income, and educational level comparisons, for example). But pollsters have begun to find it difficult to get people to answer phone surveys. With answering machines and caller ID, potential survey respondents are able to screen their calls and simply not answer when the caller seems to be a polling organization. It once took four calls to obtain a completed survey, but it now takes ten calls. John Zogby, president of Zogby Interactive, a political polling firm, states, "When I started in 1984, average response rates were 65 percent nationally. Today, we're at about 28 or 29 percent. If you get into select metropolitan areas like New York City and Southern California, it's 8 to 9 percent. People mostly don't want to be bothered." [2] That obviously increases both the cost of surveys and the time they take.

A second, and growing, problem for phone surveys is the increased use of cell phones, particularly the growing number of individuals who only have cell phones. A National Health Interview Survey in December 2004 found that 5.4 percent of Americans had given up their landline phone and lived in households with only a cell phone.[3] Two years later the number of American households with only a cell phone had more than doubled, to 11.8 percent.[4] The cell phone–only phenomenon is most problematic for surveys of young people. For example, the Pew Research Center found that between 2000 and 2006 the percentage of respondents in the eighteen-to-thirty-four age group in their unweighted surveys declined from 31 percent to 20 percent.[5] A survey of eighteen-to-twenty-four-year-olds in March 2007, by the Institute of Politics at Harvard University, concluded that because just 48 percent of that age group had landline phones, RDD polling was unreliable, and so the Institute used an online survey for its 12th Biannual Youth Survey on Politics and Public Service.[6]

Landline versus Cell Phone–Only Users

The decline in landline phone use in favor of cell phones only, poses potentially serious problems for phone survey research for a number of reasons. First, as we have said, the main advantage of surveys using RDD of landline phones is the ability to generalize from the sample to the entire population. But the population that uses the cell phone only and the one that uses the landline phone are different, so generalizing from landline phone users to the entire population mischaracterizes the cell phone–only population. Today, the cell phone–only population is between 10 percent and 15 percent, but as that group grows, the differences will become more important.

In March 2006, the Pew Research Center for People and the Press conducted a survey to compare landline and cell phone users.[7] Cell phone–only users are younger; 48 percent of those in the Pew survey were under thirty. Cell phone–only users are also less affluent, less likely to be married, and less likely to own their own homes, all characteristics no doubt related to their age.[8]

Clearly, young people pose the most risk to RDD surveys' ability to generalize from landline phone users to the general public. At the moment the problem is not serious for two reasons: First, although the cell-only population differs from the general population, their political views are not very different from those of their landline counterparts in their age group. The same Pew study found that "young cell-only users and landline users do not differ widely in their political attitudes and partisan affiliation. . . . Most of these differences do not achieve statistical significance. The modest nature of these differences suggests that young people—whether cell-only or not—are more similar than different politically." [9] Mark Mellman, president of the Mellman Group, a Democratic polling firm, reaches the same conclusion. Mellman's research has shown that

> so far, while cell-only voters are different from the electorate as a whole, they are quite similar to other voters their age. Overall, voters under 30 gave Kerry a 14-point margin [in the 2004 presidential election], close to his 17-point margin among cell-only, under 30s. Terrorism was most important to 16 percent of those under 30 and to 17 percent of those who were wireless-only in the same age cohort. As a result, ensuring a poll has the correct percentage of younger people now yields accurate results, overall.[10]

A second factor mitigating the young-cell-phone-users problem is that campaign pollsters are most interested in the views of potential voters. The youngest age cohort, those eighteen to twenty-nine years old, are least likely to vote and thus of least interest to pollsters working for candidates for office. If young people become more interested and involved in politics, as some research suggests they are doing, the difficulty of reaching them by landline phones will become a bigger concern.

The Future of Phone Surveys

As response rates to traditional RDD phone calls decline, pollsters have sought alternative means to reach sample respondents. Pollsters doing surveys for political candidates have been turning to voter lists.

From Random Digit Dialing to Voter Files.   Most campaign pollsters now use voter lists provided by state election officials or by the political parties because, in the words of Dotty Lynch, former senior political editor at CBS News, "there are just too many lack of responses with RDD." Lynch adds, "With voter lists at least you are dealing with registered voters." [11] Bob Carpenter, senior vice president at American Viewpoint, a Republican polling firm, said in an interview for this project that for national surveys, he still uses random digit dialing, but for congressional or legislative races, and maybe even statewide races, he would use a list of registered voters or a voter file.[12] A voter list is a list of registered voters provided by the state election agency. A voter file is an "enhanced" voter list, which includes more information about registered voters. Voter files are put together by vendors such as Bob Blaemire.

Blaemire Communications is one of the most respected Democratic voter file companies in the United States and counts as its clients some of the major Democratic polling firms. In discussing the advantages of doing surveys from voter files, Bob Blaemire, the firm's president, and Bill Russell, its marketing director, pointed out that voter files contain party identification (in states where there is party registration) and voting history, including frequency of voting. Pollsters therefore have on the voter file information that they would have to obtain by using screening questions in an RDD sample. Blaemire and Russell argue that although drawing a sample from a voter file is more expensive than drawing an RDD sample, the advantages of having information on the voter file that would otherwise have to be asked for ultimately make sampling from a voter file less expensive.[13] Given that the costs of phone surveys are determined largely by the number of phone calls made and the length of the survey, Blaemire and Russell argue, voter file surveys are less expensive for two main reasons: First, fewer questions need to be asked. Second, because the phone numbers on the voter file are the residential numbers of registered voters, fewer calls have to be made to get the sample.[14] Blaemire and Russell confirm, however, what survey researchers have found: young people are harder to reach by phone. They find that it is harder to get phone matches for young people than other age groups.[15]

Complications with Cell Phones.   Although drawing phone samples from voter lists seem to solve some of the problems of RDD samples, surveying cell phone–only households is still difficult, even using voter files. Currently almost all, if not all, survey firms use some form of automated dialing device to make their calls.

However, federal law prohibits making CATI calls to cell phones, so all phone calls to cell phone users must be dialed manually. As a result, sampling cell phone users, even off a voter file, is considerably more expensive than sampling landline phone users. Mark Mellman estimates that interviews of cell phone users are five to fifteen times more expensive than interviews of landline phone users.[16] As part of the Pew Research Center study described above, researchers conducted a survey of cell phone users to "assess the feasibility of conducting a telephone survey in a cell phone sampling frame." The study concluded that "such surveys are feasible, but they are more difficult and expensive to conduct than landline surveys." [17]

The Pew survey found that cell phone users were easier to reach than landline phone users (76 percent of cell phone users answered, compared with 68 percent of landline phone users) but less likely to agree to be interviewed. Fifty percent of those reached on landline phones completed the interviews, compared with 28 percent of those reached on their cell phones.[18] Among those in both groups who agreed to be interviewed, the Pew study found little difference in either levels of cooperation or levels of distraction during the survey. The study estimated that the cost of the cell phone survey was two-and-a-half times that of the landline survey, less than Mellman's estimate but still considerably higher than traditional RDD landline surveys. Particularly for campaigns, which must weigh research costs against the costs of voter contact activities such as TV, radio, and direct mail, even twice as much for cell phone surveys may make them infeasible.

Finally there is the problem of acquiring cell phone numbers. The Pew study pulled its sample from a nationally representative cell phone number database,[19] but such databases are not widely available and reliable. For any survey in which the geographic location of the respondent is important—and that would include all campaign surveys—using cell phone numbers creates problems. Because cell phones are portable, they go with their owners when they move from one jurisdiction to another. A cell phone owner may move to another state but not change his or her cell phone number. Landline phone area codes represent real physical jurisdictions. Bob Carpenter, one of the pollsters surveyed for this research, noted that he used to live in Maryland, with a 301 area code, but now lives in Virginia, yet still has a Maryland area code on his cell phone.[20] This problem is greater, once again, with respect to young people, who often have cell phone numbers tied to their parents' home address, even when away in school or working in a different area or state.

Online Surveys

The question of where survey research will be in the future inevitably raises the question of online surveys, which a number of companies are now using. However, for any survey that wants to generalize from the sample to the entire population, the lack of randomness in most online surveys is a serious problem. That we can generalize from phone surveys is still their greatest strength. The lack of the ability to generalize from Internet surveys remains their biggest weakness.

Harris Interactive was one of the pioneers in online survey research and is still one of the largest online polling firms. The Harris Poll OnLine claims to have over six million participants.[21] All online polling firms use variations of a technique called "opt-in": The firms solicit respondents through a variety of means—Web sites, advertisements, and sweepstakes, for example. Respondents who agree to be part of these large surveys are periodically sent surveys online, and the respondents choose whether or not to participate in any particular survey. Many of these large online surveys are done for market research, but many also have some political content.

The opt-in component is what critics of online polling see as these polls' greatest weakness. Because respondents opt to participate, the sample is not random, and thus generalizations cannot be made. Moreover, individuals who are online are not representative of the entire population; the online community is younger, whiter, more affluent, and better educated than the population at large. According to a Pew Internet survey conducted in February and March 2007, 87 percent of eighteen-to-twenty-nine-year-olds use the Internet, compared with just 32 percent of those sixty-five and older. Seventy-eight percent of English-speaking Hispanics and 73 percent of white non-Hispanics use the Internet, compared with 62 percent of black non-Hispanics. Fifty-five percent of those with yearly incomes of less than $30,000 use the Internet, compared with 93 percent of those with incomes of $75,000 or more. Only 40 percent of people with less than a high school education use the Internet, but 91 percent of those with a college degree or more do.[22] For political polling, particularly predicting election outcomes, these data are particularly worrisome because seniors are the least likely demographic group to be online but the most likely to vote.

Accuracy of Online Surveys

Online surveys claim that they are able to correct for the lack of a probability sample in a variety of ways. One way is to use a mathematical procedure called "weighting" to correct for the underrepresentation of certain demographic groups.[23] Harris Interactive claims that its weighting scheme leads to accuracy in its online survey results. One way to measure accuracy, of course, is to look at success in predicting election results. In 2000, Harris Interactive polled 300,000 adults between October 30 and November 6. Berrens and his colleagues reported that

> overall, the Internet poll did better in predicting state-level presidential votes than did the final telephone polls of other firms conducted on or after October 27. For the 38 states in which HI polled by Internet, its polls were off an average of 1.8 percentage point for Gore and 2.5 percentage points for

Bush. The telephone polls were off an average of 3.9 percentage points for Gore and 4.4 percentage points for Bush.[24]

Zogby Interactive is another political polling firm with a large online presence. In the 2004 presidential election, Zogby claims, it called seventeen of twenty states correctly and predicted that George W. Bush would defeat John Kerry by a margin of 50 percent to 49 percent.[25] The actual election result was Bush 51 percent, Kerry 48 percent. Zogby's methodology, like Harris Interactive's, relies on large databases of respondents who opt into the polls. *Campaigns and Elections* magazine, in a study of online polling, described Zogby's methodology as follows:

> The firm has compiled a database of several hundred thousand voters. These people were solicited since 1998 on the company's Web site to participate in online polls. The database also includes participants of Zogby International's random telephone surveys who then were asked to submit their e-mail addresses. Zogby Interactive calls about 2 percent of the online respondents to validate their personal data, such as home state, age and political party. . . . Roughly 100,000 respondents are picked randomly for each online poll. Interactive polls are supplemented by telephone surveys to "ensure proper demographic representation, especially among hard-to-reach groups," the Zogby International Web site states. Those telephone follow-ups allow Zogby to weight his polls against the under-representation of blacks and Hispanics.[26]

Two other online polling organizations, Knowledge Networks and Polimetrix, have tried other innovative ways to make online surveys representative of the general population. Knowledge Networks, which counts CBS News as one of its clients, uses random digit dialing to recruit a panel of respondents to survey online. Knowledge Networks provides respondents who do not have Internet access with the technology to respond to surveys online.[27] In return for the equipment, panel members agree to participate in an agreed-upon number of surveys.[28] Polimetrix, on the other hand, uses lists of registered voters obtained from election officials to draw a random sample of the population. It then matches the random sample to its list of opt-in respondents based on a series of demographic variables.[29] Douglas Rivers, the founder of Polimetrix, claims that his samples "look exactly like the registered voter population in terms of things that we can measure."[30] To prove the accuracy of its sample-matching methodology, Polimetrix plans to try to predict the outcome of the 2008 presidential election in all fifty states, using a sample of 1,000 respondents in each state.[31]

The Advantages of Online Surveys

The previous discussion has illustrated the ways that online polling firms try to correct for the main disadvantages of online polling—the lack of randomness in the sample and the disproportionate reach of the Internet to some demographic populations. However, online polling also brings with it some very important advantages. The first and foremost is cost savings. Online polls are much less expensive to conduct than phone surveys. Once the survey is posted on a Web site or e-mailed to respondents, there is virtually no cost to the administration of the poll, unlike phone surveys, which require phones and interviewers. A second advantage of online surveys is they are often faster. Nancy Belden, a partner in the survey research firm Belden, Russonello and Stewart and past president of the American Association of Public Opinion Researchers, is one pollster who has serious reservations about online polling but still recognizes that "the allure of Internet polling has several parts to it. . . . It's much cheaper. It's a lot faster." [32] Joseph Graf, an assistant professor in the School of Communications at American University, was one of the researchers in a survey of small donors and online giving in the 2004 presidential elections. The survey was a mail survey, but the respondents were given the option of taking the survey online. Twenty seven percent of the respondents did so, and Graf reported that the online responses saved a lot of money in labor and postage costs. [33]

The Future of Survey Research: Phones versus the Internet

Most campaign pollsters still think that phone surveys are the most reliable for predicting voter behavior and campaign outcomes and dismiss online surveys. The following quotes give a sample of the views of political pollsters: Nancy Belden says, "There are grave sampling limitations trying to do a horse race survey with an online sample. . . . They're ignoring the people who are totally not online at all. Just because you get it right once or twice, or some of the time because you correct your sample through weighting doesn't mean you're not missing something that's out there." Jeff Pollack, president of Global Strategy Group, agrees with Belden. "Telephone polling is still going to be far more accurate. Not everybody is online. There are all sorts of problems with online sampling. If you call 10 campaigns and talk to 10 candidates, not a one will accept an online poll for their candidate because they believe it would be skewed." Mark Mellman joins the refrain: "There are a lot of things you can do online. Getting a pinpoint-accurate survey is not one of them at the moment. . . . Online polling has generated a lot of controversy and a lot of heat, but so far there is certainly no consensus that online polling is an efficacious method of getting accurate results." Republican pollsters are just as skeptical as their Democratic counterparts quoted above. Rob Autry, vice president of political polling for

Public Opinion Strategies, one of the largest Republican polling firms, says, "Of all the political campaigns we're doing, we'll not do a single one of the polls online. . . . What scares most political pollsters away from doing online surveys is the generational gap. No one uses them for political work, certainly not campaigns." [34]

Yet these same pollsters also recognize that the use of phones is going to be more problematic in the years to come, particularly because of the proliferation of cell phones. Pollack states, "Over time, the phones are going to be more problematic for us as researchers. We all know that." [35] Mellman agrees: "For now, wireless households should be giving pollsters pause, but in the near future, they could cause real heartburn." [36] Carpenter observes that although there are still enough people aged thirty-five and younger who have landline phones, reaching that demographic by phone "will definitely be a problem in the future." [37] So, what form is survey research likely to take in the coming years?

The Future of Phone Surveys

In the realm of phone surveys, it seems that random digit dialing has seen, or will soon see, its demise. For the 2008, 2010, and 2012 election cycles it seems quite certain that campaign pollsters will draw surveys from state-compiled voter registration lists or voter files put together by voter file vendors. Given the widespread skepticism that pollsters express about online surveys, in seems unlikely that Internet surveys will see widespread use in campaigns in the near future. Moreover, as the Help America Vote Act (HAVA) is implemented, voter lists should become increasingly accurate and reliable to use.[38]

Yet more accurate voter lists do not address the complications presented by cell phone–only users. It is not known at this point how the growth of cell phone–only use might affect the reliability of sampling from voter lists in the future. Even if cell phones numbers could be appended to voter registration lists, the portability of cell phone numbers, the fee structure for calls to cell phones, and the prohibition on using computer-assisted dialing to call cell phone numbers make cell phones an unlikely successor to landline phones for the purposes of survey research.

As we have already discussed, research has shown that cell phone–only users differ from landline users in their lifestyles: they are less likely to be married, to own a home, and to have children than landline users, primarily because they are younger. If, as these cell phone–only users marry, have children, and buy a home, they come to mirror the lifestyles of older cohorts and acquire landline phones, then the cell phone–only problem will continue to be primarily one of reaching the youngest cohort of voters. If they continue to be cell phone–only users, then using phones for survey research becomes yet more difficult.

The Future of Online Surveys

Although online surveys may not be part of the polling equation in the next five years, it seems inevitable that they will play more of a role in survey research in the future. One key to online polling is the availability of e-mail lists. For example, if e-mail addresses could be appended to voter files, it would be possible to pull random samples of e-mail addresses off a voter file and conduct random sampling online.[39] However, Bob Blaemire thinks that voter files cannot now be matched with e-mail addresses in a way that is useful to pollsters. Phone numbers can be matched to about 55 percent to 60 percent of voter files, but e-mail matches on a voter file are 10 percent to 15 percent.[40] Moreover, Blaemire thinks that favorable responses to an e-mail request to respond to a poll would be far less than to a phoned request, exacerbating current problems with survey response rates.

If e-mails are not widely available on voter lists, then for the foreseeable future it is unlikely that e-mails can be used for survey research in the way phones have been used during the past thirty years. Joseph Graf thinks that a national list of e-mail addresses "is not likely anytime soon—2012 or beyond at the earliest." [41] Although large lists of e-mail addresses are available, they are not representative of any population and thus are not helpful for survey research. In the words of prominent pollster Warren Mitofsky, "At best, we end up with a large sample representing nothing but itself." [42] Seniors, again, are the least likely to have e-mail addresses. However, as Bob Carpenter points out, "While eighty-year-olds don't have computers, more and more sixty- and even seventy-year-olds do, and this is the demographic that would be most likely to answer Internet surveys, for the same reason they are most likely to vote. They have the time." [43]

Another problem with using e-mail addresses for survey research is that many people have several of them. In Bill Russell's words, "One they give out, and others that they use when they actually want someone to contact them." [44] People are also more likely to change e-mail addresses than they are to change phone numbers, particularly landline phone numbers. People do not have to give an address to obtain some e-mail accounts, such as Gmail, Hotmail, and Yahoo, so there is no way to know where they live, making those e-mail accounts useless for survey research in political campaigns. As Blaemire points out, campaigns are unlikely to spend money to get e-mail addresses if they cannot be sure the person is registered to vote, and without an address, there is no way to verify registration.[45]

Between Now and the Future: Survey Research Possibilities

For the near term, it is likely that phone surveys of samples drawn from lists of registered voters will define survey research in political campaigns. In the long term, online surveys may be the norm. In the middle, as Carpenter suggests, "surveys may be a hybrid—phone surveys with an Internet component." Carpenter thinks that there is the potential for "wholesale changes" in how polling is done. He thinks there may come a time when pollsters use different technologies with different groups of people. "While now we would not combine a phone survey with an Internet survey, in the future, we may do so. For example, a phone survey for seniors, an Internet survey for young people. After all, there is not that much difference between asking where someone is on a one-to-seven scale on the phone and on the Internet." [46]

Understanding Voters and Candidates

In thinking about the future of survey research, it is important to keep in mind the purpose of a survey in a campaign. The primary reason campaigns use survey research is to understand voter attitudes about candidates and issues and then use those attitudes to predict candidate choices at the polls. Because online polling, with its lack of randomness, cannot accurately predict attitudes, opinions, and behaviors, it is not likely to supersede phone surveys for political campaigns in the next five years. However, there are many other uses for Internet surveys in campaigns, and most pollsters have yet to tap those possibilities. Graf thinks that "most online surveys don't take advantage of the possibilities that online surveys present. They are just paper surveys online." [47] Others interviewed for this chapter agreed.

Because of time and cost constraints, questions on phone surveys generally force the respondents to select one of a set of responses predetermined by the pollsters. There are few open-ended questions that ask, for example, why a respondent holds a particular attitude or opinion. A common survey question is, "Generally speaking, would you say things in this country are heading in the right direction, or are they off on the wrong track?" Rarely is there an open-ended follow-up question that asks the respondent why he or she believes the country is heading in the right direction or on the wrong track.

Today, research into the "why" behind attitudes and opinions is done in focus groups. Focus groups bring together ten to twelve people to enable survey researchers to probe why different demographic groups hold the opinions they do. Focus group participants typically share a demographic characteristic—gender, age, or race, for example. The small size of focus groups and the lack of randomness of the participants (focus group members are usually recruited by advertisements and paid a modest honorarium) prevent generalizing from their comments. However, they enable the moderator to probe the attitudes and opinions of a small group to try to understand why people hold the opinions expressed in larger surveys. For example, it was a focus group held in New Jersey in 1988 that led Republican operatives to discover the voter anger over a Massachusetts prison furlough program supported by then-governor Michael Dukakis that allowed convicted felons in Massachusetts prisons weekend furloughs. One prisoner, Willie Horton, furloughed as part of the program, did not return to prison at the end of the weekend. Ten months later he raped a Maryland woman and stabbed her fiancé.[48] The results of that focus group led to the infamous advertisement in the 1988 presidential election focusing on the Willie Horton case.

Online surveys also provide opportunities to explore the "why" questions because they do not have the same time and cost constraints as phone surveys. Online surveys allow more open-ended questions. In fact, Carpenter suggests that it is possible that online surveys could become entirely open-ended, "to allow the respondent to free-think rather than force them into a predetermined set of responses." [49] If the research of Rivers and others proves fruitful, and online surveys are able to achieve some level of randomness, they could combine the current capabilities of phone surveys and focus groups, at much less cost to campaigns.

The Internet, in the short term, also presents opportunities for online focus groups. Without the time and expense of flying to a city or cities to do focus groups, pollsters could recruit and conduct focus groups online, saving the campaign valuable dollars. Recruiting participants may also be easier, as people could participate from their homes rather than having to travel to a focus group session. The demographics of the online citizenry, however, discussed earlier in the chapter, will again make online focus groups more feasible among some demographic groups than others for the immediate future.

While randomness is important for generalizing the attitudes and opinions of a survey population, it is less important in testing campaign messages. Both Carpenter and Lynch say that online surveys have the potential to allow pollsters to do some of the things that in the early years of survey research were done with in-person surveys but cannot be done over the phone. One obvious example is to show visuals. The Internet could be an effective medium to test ad or direct-mail messages with various subgroups in a population. Ad testing is now done in focus groups, but it would be much less costly to do online.

Polling and Microtargeting

A part of campaigning that has received substantial attention in recent elections, particularly in 2002 and 2004, is microtargeting, which is described in more detail in the voter mobilization chapter of this volume (chapter 6). Microtargeting can complement survey research but not replace it. Indeed, the success of microtargeting is based in polling. During the 2004 election, the Bush campaign polled 5,000 people from a consumer database on their political attitudes and behavior. An important attribute the Bush campaign was looking for was "anger points"—issues that would motivate survey respondents to turn out to vote.[50] The campaign then used those anger points to target messages to potential Bush voters to motivate them to turn out on election day. Sosnick, Dowd, and Fournier, the authors of

Applebee's America, a study that describes how the Bush campaign used microtargeting in 2004, acknowledge the importance of polling to microtargeting in their critique of the Kerry campaign, commenting that "Kerry's team failed to do the polling and analysis required to segment the electorate into like-minded groups and determine what issues angered or excited them." [51]

Although the Bush campaign's microtargeting and subsequent turnout operation are credited with the campaign's success in 2004, some think that Karl Rove and the Bush White House placed too much reliance on microtargeting in the 2006 elections, ignoring the findings of traditional survey research. In an article in *Newsweek* shortly after the 2006 elections, Richard Wolfe described Rove's views of phone surveys: "Rove thought the polls were obsolete because they relied on home telephones in an age of do-not-call lists and cell phones. . . . Rove placed so much faith in his figures that, after the election, he planned to convene a panel of Republican political scientists—to study just how wrong the polls were." [52]

Given the costs of phone surveys and the limited number of questions that can be asked, it is unlikely that lifestyle questions, like those used in microtargeting will find their way into phone surveys. For every lifestyle question asked, one attitude or opinion question would have to be dropped. However, if and when Internet surveys become more commonplace, lifestyle questions could become part of the question bank. Because they lack the time and cost constraints of phone surveys, it may become more cost-effective for campaigns to ask lifestyle questions in online surveys rather than acquire costly consumer databases.

Conclusion

Online surveys are not likely to replace phone surveys in the next five years. Although random digit dialing, which defined survey research for the past thirty years, is no longer the methodology of choice, phones will still be the primary means to survey voters in political campaigns. Random digit dialing has been replaced by samples from voter lists, assuring campaigns at least that survey respondents are registered voters. However, online surveys, in at least some forms, are the wave of the future. Pollsters at Knowledge Networks, Polimetrix, and other Internet survey organizations will continue to experiment with techniques to draw probability samples from online populations. In the interim, online surveys likely will be used to supplement phone surveys.

As this chapter has shown, phone surveys off of voter lists have replaced random digit dialing, but phone surveys still face the problem of the growth in cell phone use, particularly among the youngest age cohort. As researchers at Internet survey organizations test ways to make Internet surveys representative, with the growth of wireless technology there may come a time in the not-too-distant future when the phone and computer are one device. Five years from now, the question may not be online versus phone; there may be one common communication device that combines both. Research cited earlier in the chapter found that cell phone users were roughly half as likely as landline users to complete interviews. Will survey researchers be able to reach voters on their iPhone or T-Mobile phone? At this point, a great deal more is known about the problems that survey research faces in the coming years than is known about their solutions.

Notes

1. Robert P. Berrens, Alok K. Bohara, Hank Jenkins-Smith, Carol Silva, and David Weimer, "The Advent of Internet Surveys for Political Research: A Comparison of Telephone and Internet Samples," *Political Analysis* 11, no. 1 (2003): 1–23.
2. J. Todd Foster, "Is Online Polling: a. Representative b. Accurate c. Efficient d. Don't Know Yet," *Campaigns and Elections,* September 2006, 33.
3. Mark S. Mellman, "Pollsters' Cellphonobia Setting In," *The Hill,* May 23, 2007, 14.
4. Ibid., 16.
5. Pew Research Center for People and the Press, "National Polls Not Undermined by Growing Cell-Only Population: The Cell Phone Challenge to Survey Research," news release, May 15, 2006, 2.
6. Institute of Politics, Harvard University, "The 12th Biannual Youth Survey on Politics and Public Service," April 17, 2007, 2.
7. The Pew Center sampled 1,503 U.S. adults. Seven hundred and fifty two were sampled on their landline phones; 751 were interviewed on their cell phones. Pew Research Center for People and the Press, "National Polls Not Undermined," 2.
8. Ibid., 4.
9. Ibid.
10. Mellman, "Pollsters' Cellphonobia," 16.
11. Dotty Lynch, executive in residence, School of Communication, American University, and former senior political editor at CBS News, personal interview, April 10, 2007.
12. Bob Carpenter, senior vice president, American Viewpoint, Alexandria, Virginia, personal interview, May 31, 2007.
13. Bob Blaemire, president, and Bill Russell, marketing director, Blaemire Communications, Reston, Virginia, personal interview, June 14, 2007.
14. Ibid.
15. Ibid.
16. Mellman, "Pollsters' Cellphonobia," 16.
17. Pew Research Center for People and the Press, "National Polls Not Undermined," 9.
18. Ibid.
19. Ibid., 2.
20. Carpenter, interview.
21. See www.harrisinteractive.com/partner/hpolpanel.asp (accessed June 27, 2006).

22. Pew Internet and American Life Project, "Demographics of Internet Users," February 15–March 7, 2007 Tracking Survey, www.pewinternet.org/trends/User_Demo_6.15.07 .htm (accessed June 27, 2007).

23. Berrens et al. describe the Harris Interactive weighting scheme as follows: "HI has developed a method of applying propensity weights . . . to make the sample representative in terms of selected covariates. The method involves adding attitudinal and behavioral questions to RDD and Internet surveys being conducted contemporaneously, though typically for different purposes. The telephone and Internet data are merged and the attitudinal questions and standard demographic variables are used to predict the probability of being in one sample rather than the other. These probabilities, or propensities, then serve as the basis for weighting the Internet sample so that its pattern of covariates, including the attitudinal and behavioral questions, match[es] those in the telephone sample." Berrens et al., "The Advent of Internet Surveys," 13–14.

24. Ibid., 13.

25. Foster, "Is Online Polling," 32.

26. Ibid.

27. Lynch, interview.

28. Berrens et al., "The Advent of Internet Surveys," 14.

29. See www.pollster.com/blogs/internet_polls (accessed June 7, 2007).

30. Foster, "Is Online Polling," 34.

31. Thomas Crampton, "About Online Surveys, Traditional Pollsters Are: (C) Somewhat Disappointed," *New York Times,* May 31, 2007, www.nytimes.com/2007/05/31/business/ media/31adco.html?ei (accessed June 7, 2007).

32. Foster, "Is Online Polling," 31.

33. Joseph Graf, assistant professor, School of Communications, American University, personal interview, June 6, 2007; also Institute for Politics, Democracy and the Internet, *Small Donors and Online Giving: A Study of Donors to the 2004 Presidential Campaigns* (Washington, D.C.: Graduate School of Political Management, The George Washington University, 2006), appendix A.

34. Foster, "Is Online Polling," 34.

35. Ibid., 32.

36. Mellman, "Pollsters' Cellphonobia," 16.

37. Carpenter, interview.

38. The Help America Vote Act was passed in 2002 to help states improve their election procedures. The act was passed as a result of the ballot problems in the 2000 presidential election. The provisions of HAVA were to be implemented by the 2006 elections, but some states are still working to bring their election procedures into compliance.

39. Lynch, interview.

40. Blaemire and Russell, interview.

41. Graf, interview.

42. Warren Mitofsky, "Pollsters.com," *Public Perspective,* June/July 1999, 24–26, as quoted in Berrens et al., "The Advent of Internet Surveys," 13.

43. Carpenter, interview.

44. Blaemire and Russell, interview.

45. Bob Blaemire, e-mail to author, July 18, 2007.

46. Carpenter, interview.

47. Graf, interview.

48. See www.insidepolitics.org/ps111/independentads.html (accessed August 6, 2007); http://en.wikipedia/wiki/Willie_Horton (accessed August 6, 2007).

49. Bob Carpenter, e-mail to author, July 18, 2007.

50. Douglas B. Sosnick, Matthew J. Dowd, and Ron Fournier, *Applebee's America* (New York: Simon and Schuster, 2006), 36.

51. Ibid., 43.

52. Richard Wolffe, "The Architect's Faulty Specs," *Newsweek,* November 20, 2006, 57.

CHAPTER 6

Voter Mobilization — Into the Future

Richard J. Semiatin

THE SHORENSTEIN RULE NO LONGER EXISTS. It was the paradigm of how votes were delivered to the polls for nearly a century. Hymie Shorenstein was the Democratic Party political boss in the Brownsville section of Brooklyn. He once delivered a twenty-to-one majority in favor of his party's presidential candidate, Franklin D. Roosevelt.

Once a nervous office seeker came to see Shorenstein. The boss turned to the candidate. "Ah, you're worried? Listen. Did you ever go down to the wharf to see the Staten Island Ferry come in? . . . You ever watch it, the chewing-gum wrappers, and the banana peels, and the garbage? When the ferryboat comes into the wharf, automatically it pulls all the garbage in too. The name of your ferryboat is Franklin D. Roosevelt—stop worrying!" [1]

The Shorenstein rule implied that party was the single, dominating political force delivering votes to candidates. Hymie Shorenstein, if alive today, would be stunned at the complexity and precision with which candidates and parties now mobilize to turn out the vote.

The task of getting voters out to the polls has changed dramatically over the past half-century. Political parties used to be the engines that delivered votes for candidates from the presidency all the way down to the local level, as Shorenstein did. Today, campaigns are much more on their own—campaign staff use Blackberrys and PDAs to call up voter information on streets. Campaigns are now developing greater precision to target a voter down to that voter's household. They will know what someone eats, where they shop, and what they watch on television. Given all the personal information out in public and cyberspace, presidential, senatorial, congressional, and gubernatorial campaigns will become more individualized. The process of voting will become less of a civic ritual, less communal, and more personalized. The future of campaigns may find that presidential candidate organizations, not parties, will be the vehicle to identify and target citizens and get them out to vote. We begin here with a look at the background of get-out-the-vote (GOTV) operations, then proceed to the current state of traditional and new methods of voter mobilization, and finally to where such efforts are headed in the future.

The Tradition of Parties' Delivering Votes

The political science literature and history books about presidential campaigns have focused on the historically central role of political parties that candidates could rely on to bring out their voters on election day. Political scientists of the 1950s and 1960s discussed the symbiotic bond between candidates and parties—that candidates owed their allegiance to parties and supported the party platform accordingly and that parties would provide the organizational muscle to bring enough of their voters to the polls to win elections.[2] The long-standing model of party-driven politics was ended by the era of television, as candidates, beginning with John F. Kennedy, became their own electoral entrepreneurs. With television, candidates no longer needed parties as ambassadors to introduce them to voters in presidential elections and later in elections for the Senate and House.

Candidate-driven politics emerged, but parties still played a role in delivering votes on election day. It was a hybrid system in which parties provided a basic organization and delivery system for each campaign. Campaigns supplemented that effort with their own campaign workers, who would target key precincts and neighborhoods, identifying likely and marginal voters for their candidate. Under the Federal Election Campaign Act (FECA) Amendments of 1974 parties could provide "coordinated expenditures" to help candidates for Congress, Senate, and president get out the vote. These expenditures, based on population, were for general election purposes and could be for advice, tactical planning, and organizational help to identify key groups essential for victory, contact them, and get them out to vote.[3]

The Traditional Model of Targeting Voters

For the last several decades campaigns have used voting data, voter registration lists, turnout mail, radio, and ID calls as the basis for their voter identification and GOTV operations. Parties and their candidates, Democrats and Republicans, seek out their voters in precincts throughout a congressional district. They then prioritize the precincts in the district depending on their partisanship and voter turnout rates.

Voting Data

Nothing is more important to start with than the basic tool for GOTV operations—voting data. The voting data from the past several elections are distilled by the campaign to identify precincts (or districts) on a zero-to-ten point scale. Ten is a maximum-performing district for the candidate, and zero is a district where there is no hope. Thus, for a Republican a ten-point district would be the strongest Republican district and a zero the weakest; Democrats classify their districts in a similar way. The precincts that are rated in the middle—four, five, and six—are dominated by neither party and are called "swing" precincts.[4] If the election has a high number of undecided voters (as in the 1992 presidential election among George H. W. Bush, Bill Clinton, and Ross Perot), then swing precincts are the focus of both parties, as they seek to persuade undecided voters or weakly identified voters of their own party. However, in base-driven elections, such as the 2004 campaign for president between incumbent George W. Bush and Sen. John Kerry, where there are few undecided voters, the emphasis for Democrats and Republicans is more firmly on squeezing every vote out of their high-performing precincts.

Federal party organizations coordinate their efforts with the campaigns to identify voters, often assisting them (as an in-kind service) with advice on how to develop a voter contact list. Moreover, parties have often served as the source to find individuals who can run field operations for important campaigns. The Bush campaign of 2004 drew on the services of Terry Nelson, who had served as deputy chief of staff at the Republican National Committee in 2002 and 2003. Nelson moved over to the Bush/Cheney reelection campaign as political director in charge of the campaign's massive field operation.

All targeting operations begin with the average vote of the party. In statewide federal races, that would be the average performance of the party in senatorial and presidential races over three to five election cycles. For example, if we were to average statewide federal races in Missouri from 2002 to 2006, the data would show Republicans getting approximately 51 percent and Democrats 47 percent of the vote.[5] On the other hand, congressional races differ from statewide races when computing average turnout. Congressional districts often traverse county lines, therefore computing the average performance data for congressional districts is more difficult and technical.

Voter Registration Lists

Supplementing voting data are voter registration lists. The voter registration lists are matched up with voting data for precincts to see where candidates have performed as well as expected, underperformed, or overperformed. For example, a precinct of 500 voters might show that Republican candidates in federal races were winning, on average, 60 percent of the vote, compared with 40 percent for Democrats. However, if the voter registration figures show that the precinct has 50 percent registered Democrats, then that district is underperforming for Democrats, meaning that the Democratic candidates are averaging ten percentage points less than they should.

Underperforming precincts are of highest concern to a candidate because they are potentially the greatest source of votes. After identifying the problem, the party and candidate have to figure out why the district is underperforming. Is it because candidates are out of step with their own voters? Is it because of neglect by previous campaigns? Has the district started to change its behavior (voting for the opposing party's candidate), even though party registration is still in their favor? The campaign then has to decide what tactics it will employ to target that district (in statewide or federal races) or precinct (in congressional races).

Will Robinson, a political consultant, believes that in low-performance areas it is best to have a precinct captain who is a resident. The reason is that their residence can be the "precinct house," which the campaign can use as a base to enhance its voter turnout on election day.[6]

Voter Registration

Increasing party registration is key for any voter mobilization effort. Parties, partisan interest groups, and 527 organizations (independent political organizations) work at increasing their voter bases. In particular, the Democratic Party has conducted extensive voter registration drives in the past focusing on the African American and Latino communities in urban areas, which tend to have lower voter registration rates and thus lower voter turnout rates. Republicans sometimes counter with voter registration efforts in rural areas to offset increased registration of Democrats in urban areas. The U.S. Census Bureau reported that in 2004, 142 million adults, or 72.1 percent of the adult population, were registered to vote. Of those registered voters, 88.5 percent voted on election day.[7] Thus, voter registration is highly predictive of who actually turns out.

Turnout Mail

As election day approaches, turnout mail is critical to GOTV plans of both candidates and parties because it does two things: it advertises candidates to citizens, and it reminds those citizens to vote. Sometimes mail comes in the form of a literature drop at your doorstep by the candidate.

Most critical is the message that a direct-mail piece conveys about the importance of voting on election day. Turnout mail messages frequently state that the upcoming election is "critical to the future of the country" and that your "active participation" in voting is essential to winning on election day. Turnout mail messages from parties say, "Vote Democratic" or "Vote Republican." However, in an era of candidate-centered politics, you will rarely find a direct-mail piece that identifies a congressman, senator, or gubernatorial or presidential candidate as a Democrat or a Republican. Candidates are their own electoral entrepreneurs.[8]

Suppressing voter turnout can also be the object of direct mail, even the less-overt kind that is not about race or character. In 2005, Tim Kaine's (D) winning campaign for governor of Virginia used an issue approach to convert GOP voters or deter them from casting their ballots for Republican nominee Jerry Kilgore. The left-hand side of Kaine's brochure said, "An important message for Republicans!" and featured a picture of the Republican elephant. The mail piece claimed that Kilgore was a closet tax raiser. Therefore, Republicans should call the Kilgore campaign to find out if he could be trusted on taxes.[9] The mailer could have an inverse effect on voter turnout if sent to nonpartisan voters in Virginia; the message being to get out and vote for Kaine, for otherwise Kilgore will raise your taxes.

Radio

Radio has been a classic method for GOTV operations, especially for niche populations, which are hard to influence by turnout mail or phone banks. Lower-middle-class or poor voters and African American and Latino communities are often targeted by radio ads. Promos run on hip-hop, rap, R&B, soul, and gospel stations with messages urging people to vote. Other promotions have included hip-hop conventions urging people to vote. In fact, in 2004 rapper P-Diddy was promoting his own T-shirts that said, "Vote or die." [10] The P-Diddy message addressed the fact that young male African Americans have had very low rates of voter participation.

ID Calls

ID or identification calls help to locate supporters, ascertain their voting plans, and ensure that they get out to vote. ID calls are the surest and most direct method to reach voters personally, and voter registration lists plus other available voter lists are used to help ensure that the population they reach can vote. The calls help to identify the candidate a citizen might vote for and assess the likelihood of their voting. The purpose of ID calls is to build a relationship between the voter and the caller (whether the latter is from a candidate or party organization). Wally Clinton, a consultant who specializes in phones and communications for Democrats, has said that building a relationship with a potential voter is "about listening, not yelling". [11] Clinton says this is particularly important since the terrorist attacks on September 11, 2001, as nurturing voters has become even more important, given the sensitivities of the time.

ID calls normally begin several weeks before the election to determine the level of support, where it is located, and where the candidate has to go to increase support. As the election approaches, the campaign ascertains the likelihood that individuals on the list will vote. If a citizen is infirm or aged or lacks transportation, the campaign identifies that person, sets a time, and provides transportation to take them to the polling place.

Given that landline phone charge rates have decreased in real terms, phone banking has become even more cost-effective. Moreover, phone banks are key to turning out voters. Extensive voter contact research and effective messaging can help energize and mobilize individuals to vote. In the 1998 runoff election for lieutenant governor of Georgia, Democrat Mark Taylor's campaign used a very focused, targeted message—"He'll make sure small Georgia is not ignored." In the counties the Taylor campaign targeted, the turnout was 10 percent, and Taylor won 75 percent of the vote. Turnout in counties not targeted by the Democrat's campaign was only 6 percent, and there Taylor won 47 percent of the vote. The phone bank ID calling made the difference in turning out the vote for a Taylor victory.[12]

Phone banks are more important in researching senior than young voters. Young voters often use cell phones exclusively. Seniors are less mobile and more reachable, particularly in the evening. According to political scientist Susan McManus, phone banks are twice as likely to reach "persons 50 and older versus persons 18 to 29." [13] Moreover, McManus shows that election eve reminders to seniors to vote are critical, since they are more likely to vote in the morning.[14]

ID calls are among the most effective techniques to boost GOTV efforts. According to research by Green and Gerber, phone bank contacts by volunteers will add about one vote for every thirty-five calls made. Yet that rate, which runs at a relatively cheap $35 per hour, is hardly a ringing endorsement.[15]

Door to Door

Despite being labor intensive, the most effective form of traditional voter contact is door-to-door canvassing. That voters meet face to face with representatives of local parties and candidates can make a difference. According to Green and Gerber, this method yields one vote for every fourteen contacts, which is substantial.[16]

The sophistication of door-to-door canvassing reached new heights in 2002, when the campaign committee for House Republicans, the National Republican Congressional Committee (NRCC), instituted the Strategic Task Force to Organize and Mobilize People, or STOMP, to get out the vote in congressional races. "Republicans from safe districts contributed staff and volunteers to work in competitive congressional races across the country." [17] This was the Republican "72-Hour" GOTV program, in which dozens of experienced staff and campaign workers were shifted to key races to help incumbent Republican senators and House members in tight election campaigns. The STOMP campaign was coordinated with a nonstop barnstorming blitz across the nation by President George W. Bush over the final week of the campaign. Republicans gained four Senate and six House seats in 2002, marking the first time since Franklin Roosevelt (1934), that a president's party gained seats in both houses of Congress during his first term in office.[18] The coordination of political targeting and personal contact, combined with extensive media coverage of the president jetting across fifteen states in five days, was unprecedented. It reached voters locally (individual contact) and nationally (viewer contact through television).

Each of the aforementioned tactics demonstrates the importance of candidate organization and field operations. In fact, the field division is the largest in any campaign because it involves dozens, or hundreds, or thousands of volunteers communicating candidate or party messages urging people to get out and vote. In the end, the old Tip O'Neill adage that "all politics is local" is manifest even in presidential campaigns because national organizations have to translate potential support into votes, turning macro-level strategies into micro-level performance. The parties have continued to refine and adapt their strategies in the modern campaign era, as campaigns move away from television and voters become more diverse consumers of new technologies.

Voter Mobilization in the Twenty-First Century

Campaigns are moving into a new era of customer-driven campaigning. Voters have increasing control of media content, which enables them to manipulate or alter information. For example, voters can decide what content appears on their Yahoo home page. Furthermore, as television viewing decreases and people are spending more time online, campaigns have to develop new techniques to entice voters to their Web sites. In terms of voter mobilization, this means creating a virtual community in which voters participate in the online campaign through blogs, e-mail, and Web campaign events, where they are part of an interactive audience even though they are at home. Thus campaigns have to develop more personalized and stylized messages to interest voters who are barraged with visual cues at the click of a mouse. As statistical methods of predicting turnout have become more precise, the new age of voter mobilization strategy is vested in merging consumer or lifestyle information with traditional targeting models. Major campaigns and political parties are now able to target individual homes based on profile information available through public files or obtained through purchasing lists; this is known as "microtargeting." New technology helps expedite the process of locating, contacting, and getting out voters. So much personal information is becoming available to private industry, and thus to campaigns and parties, that it has raised privacy concerns: What are the parameters that determine what personal information should or should not be available to political campaigns?

Traditional-model GOTV operations have incorporated voting behavior histories and issue polling to mobilize interested citizens to vote. However, new elements have been added to the targeting process to make voter mobilization more precise and effective. They look at voters as customers and consumers to understand their lifestyle. Understanding a voter's lifestyle enables a campaign to engage that voter and get them out to vote on election day, as long as they are persuadable.

Thus, today's GOTV effort incorporates voting history, and issue salience, plus consumer or lifestyle behavior.

According to TargetPoint, a Republican firm specializing in GOTV, "The control has switched from seller to buyer. Voters and consumers now have multiple sources for information and entertainment." [19] Direct mail and personal contact alone will no longer suffice. The consumer—that is, the voter—must be reached by multiple sources of information, multiple times for a campaign to get out their vote.

Lifestyle or Microtargeting and the 2004 Campaign

The new modus operandi of campaigns is lifestyle or microtargeting. According to an article in *Winning Campaigns* magazine, "Survey research that focuses on crosstabs such as income, gender, race . . . only provide[s] a fraction of the story. . . . By using hundreds of data points, comprised of voter information, life cycle information, life style information, financial data, consumer behavior, geographic data, and political attitudes and preferences," voters can be placed into clusters or "segments" that provide precision methods of reaching them.[20] The George W. Bush reelection campaign used this approach successfully to get out its base vote in 2004.

The Bush campaign realized early on that Democrats had a natural base advantage heading into the 2004 election. They reasoned that the Gore vote plus Ralph Nader's gave Democrats a 51 percent majority. Moreover, the Bush campaign knew that the president's popularity was sliding downward toward the critical 50 percent approval range, largely because of the increasingly unpopular war in Iraq. Matthew Dowd, who was the campaign's pollster and strategist, believed that Republicans "had to find and motivate new GOP voters" and that meant new strategies. "Dowd had one in mind: targeting people based on their lifestyles rather than just their voting histories and policy views." [21]

The Bush campaign assembled profiles of nearly 5,000 voters and "grouped [them] into thirty-four segments." [22] For example, Michigan segments included "Archie in the Bunker," "Religious Independents," and "Wageable Weak Democrats." Each potential GOP segment was valued in terms of its size and commitment to George W. Bush. The Bush team was able to predict with 80 percent to 90 percent accuracy how likely the segment was to vote for President Bush.[23]

The Bush campaign was able to locate Republican voter segments that might be in strong or weak Democratic precincts and get out their votes. For example, if a precinct's voting history was 70 percent Democrat and 30 percent Republican, that district would not be targeted by a Republican campaign. But lifestyle/microtargeting enabled the Bush reelection campaign to locate that Republican 30 percent, target them with messages to mobilize them to vote, and get them out to vote on election day. No campaign had done this on such a large scale in the past. In fact, 2004 voter turnout jumped to 60.8 percent, from 49.3 percent in 2000, or 17 million more votes. Voter participation went up in Democratic areas, too, but lifestyle targeting made a dramatic difference for Republicans.

According to the Bush campaign political director, Terry Nelson, in Florida the Bush campaign contacted 33 percent of its voters in 2000. In 2004, that number jumped to 84 percent.[24] As the election approached, the Bush campaign reported contacting 400,000 people a day in the critical swing state of Ohio.[25]

Another major break from the past was that the Republican GOTV effort was effectively being run by the Bush campaign, not the Republican National Committee. The *Washington Post* reported that the Bush campaign was spending approximately $125 million on its GOTV efforts, whereas the Democratic National Committee was spending about $60 million on GOTV efforts on behalf of Kerry.[26] (Kerry GOTV efforts were aided by 527 groups such as America Coming Together and labor unions.)

The implications are critically important because the presidential campaign is now assuming functions that have traditionally belonged to the national parties. Presidential campaigns are subsuming the major organizational functions of parties. We will discuss later on what this portends for the future.

Technology and GOTV

Modern technology has put critical information into the hands of campaign field organizations. Voting history, issue preferences, and lifestyle/consumer information are now available in PDAs and Blackberrys for precinct workers. A precinct worker in the 2008 New Hampshire primary, for Hillary Clinton, Rudolph Guiliani, Barack Obama, Mitt Romney, can be in a neighborhood in Manchester's fourth ward and find out which voters need to be mobilized for support on election day. No one wants to be caught napping. In 1976, one of the leading Democratic candidates for president, Sen. Birch Bayh (D-Ind.), asked his campaign for their GOTV plan on the weekend before the New Hampshire primary. No plan existed.[27]

Technology must be tested well in advance of election day. The Bush reelection campaign planned its GOTV operation well in advance—and the president was not burdened by having a primary opponent. The Bush campaign tested its GOTV effort in a simulation in July 2004,[28] enabling the campaign to determine what was working well and what needed fine-tuning. The Kerry campaign did not have such a luxury, given the early and contentious primary season, which shortened planning time for its GOTV effort. It put much of the planning in the hands of the party and pro-Democratic interest organizations (unions and 527 groups). Because the election had so few undecided voters (perhaps 6 percent), both campaigns treated the election as base driven rather than focusing on undecided voters.

The Bush campaign also had an e-mail list of six million voters by November 2003; that was ten times the number of any Democratic campaign.[29] The Bush team used the list to maintain contact with potential voters. E-mail could drive voters to the campaign's Web site to enhance their interest. Finally, e-mail could also enable the campaign to recruit workers for its GOTV efforts; the Bush campaign eventually had a field organization of one million volunteers.

Heading into 2008 and beyond, Web sites are playing an increasingly critical role for field organizations. Sen. Barack Obama's (D-Ill.) presidential campaign advertised "Camp Obama," on its Web site, which it used to recruit volunteers, the focus clearly on youth. The campaign offered two- to four-day training dates in Chicago during June 2007, for potential for interns and volunteers. Its idea was to build campaign communities for Obama across the country. The program demonstrates the Web site as a tool to build an effective campaign organization for voter contact (for example, through phone banks and door-to-door canvassing), melding the traditional approach with modern technology.[30]

Congressman Tom Allen, challenging incumbent Susan Collins for a Maine Senate seat in 2008, has used a two-pronged voter recruitment and mobilization effort that was advertised on his Web site. Twice on Allen's home page the icons "Volunteer" and "Build Our Base" appear. The first term is self-explanatory, and the second, "Build Our Base," asks potential supporters to "tell family and friends about Tom." [31] When visitors click on the second icon they see an e-mail form to send, with an optional message to support Tom Allen. It enables the supporter to edit or change the message to personalize it. The campaign thus uses the Web site as a conduit to transmit information without its active intervention. It empowers individuals, who act as part of the team to contact people and mobilize support. Technology enables virtual voter contact by volunteers, complementing traditional voter contact methods. The result is that the campaign covers a potentially larger base of supporters than it could have a decade ago.

"Meetups" enable "virtual" volunteers to share information and thoughts about a campaign through blogs and comments. Well-designed meetups enable campaigns to generate volunteers who are willing to do the footwork of voter contact and mobilization. Meetups were pioneered by MoveOn.org, a liberal, online, grassroots organization that recruited more than three million members in less than two years.[32] The Howard Dean campaign for the Democratic presidential nomination in 2004 employed meetups not only to increase interest in the campaign but to raise money and recruit an army of 177,000 volunteers (more than three times what any other candidate had at the time).[33]

Instant messaging (IM) may have a dramatic effect on voter turnout in the 2008 U.S. elections. IM enables campaign organizations to keep instant tabs on turnout, from multiple sources simultaneously. The advantage IMs have over telephone calls is rather simple—campaigns can receive multiple messages rather than wait for messages to be verbally transmitted one at a time. Text messaging worked quite successfully for GOTV efforts in the Spanish election of 2004, according to Sandra Suarez of Temple University, and American campaigns have taken note. American presidential campaigns actively used and refined this technology for 2008 as first evidenced in the Iowa caucuses as Obama targeted young voters, propelling their turnout.[34]

Voter Mobilization of Mail and Absentee Voters

National political campaigns in the twenty-first century have to address larger numbers of voters who are casting their ballots by mail, early, or absentee. For example, Oregon allows voting by mail, and Florida allows early ("in-person absentee") voting. Thirty-five states allow voters to request an absentee ballot without supplying any excuse or in-person absentee voting.[35]

These provisions create havoc with traditional GOTV operations, which focus on election day. States such as Washington (89.4 percent), Nevada (51.6 percent), and Tennessee (47.4 percent) had a tremendous percentage of votes cast by mail. The implications are that campaigns and parties have to organize their GOTV operations, establish phone banks, send out targeted voter mail, and canvass earlier than ever before. "Election weeks of voting" mean that campaigns have to mobilize sooner than in the past. Election weeks enable voters to cast a vote during a time period prior to election day at a place designated by the local election board. Separate plans have to be developed for GOTV efforts on election day and those prior to election day. According to Curtis Gans, for the Committee for the Study of the American Electorate, "No-excuse absentee-ballot voters are middle-class, upper middle-class and upper-class voters who are lazy. They want their convenience." [36] If such voters are lazy, Gans implies, some may not vote. Thus, not only are campaign GOTV contact and mobilization efforts becoming more costly, but in the future they may be less cost-effective.

The Cutting Edge of Change: Into the Future with Voter Mobilization

If candidates—not party organizations—are going to provide the GOTV effort, it will affect the electoral process. What will be the implications for GOTV efforts with new immigrants/citizens? Can technology boost turnout? What about the effect on voters' privacy of using information lists for microtargeting? All of these questions have profound implications for the future of the electoral process.

Presidential Campaigns as Party Organizations

The Democratic and Republican nominees of 2008 will likely raise between $500 million and $1 billion *each*. By 2012 that amount could easily increase by 50 percent or more. Given that presidential candidates are eschewing the voluntary federal campaign funding system because they can raise much more on their own, presidential candidates are soaking up more of the available political capital that might otherwise be contributed to congressional and gubernatorial races.

The Bush campaign established its own GOTV effort, partly in concert with, and partly independent of, the Republican National Committee because, unlike the Democrats, the GOP does not have traditional interest groups or organizations doing its voter mobilization. Because neither party's nominee will take federal funding for the 2008 general election, even less money may flow to the national party organizations. As a result, presidential campaigns are becoming full-service organizations, not only for their own campaigns but for other party candidates on the ballot during White House election years. The substantial costs in manpower and money will tie presidential and congressional candidates closer together, suggesting that the winning presidential candidate will be in a more powerful position to demand support from senators and House members of their party. For the loser, defeat is a self-explanatory consequence.

Greater Citizen Diversity Makes GOTV More Complex

Over the next fifty years, a majority of the U.S. population will become nonwhite and Latino, according to demographer Leon Bouvier. That means that candidates will have to communicate not only bilingually but multilingually to get out the vote. The 2000 campaign was the first in which both presidential candidates—Gore and Bush—recorded campaign messages in Spanish.[37] As Latino, eastern European, and southeast and central Asian populations increase, campaigns will need more field organizers who are bilingual or multilingual to canvass potential voters whose second language is English. During the last great immigration wave, after World War I, ethnic neighborhoods in large cities made it easier to find campaign workers who were fluent in English and their native tongue. Migration and mobility within the country make such efforts less centralized today. Not only must campaigns communicate with diverse cultures, but they need multilingual staff to help build trust among those voters. It is easier to get someone to the polls when you speak their native language, because a natural bond is first established.

Will New Media and Technology Boost Turnout?

The cutting edge of campaigns would seem to reside in technology. After all, e-mail contacts, text messages on cell phones, and Web site communities would seem to attract voting consumers. PDAs, Blackberrys, and cell phones should enable campaigns to target potential voters with greater accuracy. But surprisingly, the preliminary evidence has not been so promising.

Green and Gerber have demonstrated that most GOTV methods, traditional and new, are not very cost-effective. The early results show that new approaches such as e-mail contacts and robo calls have no detectable effect on voter turnout.[38] Research is not yet available on the effectiveness of Web sites in contacting voters. As stated earlier, in the Spanish general election of 2004 text messages seemed to have a discernible, positive effect on turnout. Perhaps the reason is that young voters are more apt to communicate via cell phones and text messaging.

Although technology has changed and, some would say, has made the world more impersonal, it is the personal touches that make the difference. Gerber and Green found that personal contact through door-to-door canvassing is the only GOTV method that is highly effective (winning one voter for every 14 contacts). The next-most-effective methods are professional telephone canvassers reading scripts (one voter per 30 contacts) or volunteers reading scripts (one vote per 35 contacts).[39] Again, as stated earlier, campaigns are becoming more consumer oriented, and that means personal contact is as important as ever.

That makes the quality of information available to field organizers even more important. The more information available to the campaign about individual voters, the better the message can be targeted to the individual. Companies such as Acxiom keep massive files on consumers, which grow in complexity as more personal information is available to retailers through purchases and online services. The most recent estimate on Acxiom's database comes from *Wired* magazine, which reported that the company had a database of 176 million Americans in 2003.[40] That number has surely grown half a decade later.

Information Supply versus Privacy Concerns

The implications of the changes we have been discussing are daunting in terms of where to draw the line between the right of individuals to privacy and the desire of campaigns to win their votes. The amount of individual identity information available through public databases is substantial. According to the Electronic Frontier Foundation (EFF), an organization established to protect privacy rights, the United States is moving toward a national ID system:

> On March 1, the Department of Homeland Security (DHS) released draft regulations for implementing REAL ID, which makes states standardize drivers' licenses and create a vast national database linking all of the ID records together. Once in place, uses of the IDs and database will inevitably expand to facilitate a wide range of tracking and surveillance activities. . . . [T]he Social Security number started innocuously enough, but it has become a prerequisite for a host of government services and been co-opted by private companies to create massive databases of personal information.[41]

How might such information help campaigns? The United States is a highly mobile nation; the most recent data show that 14 percent of the population moves every year. Having standardized information to track driving registration would enable campaigns and parties to track potential voters with greater ease.[42] Paradoxically, whereas Democrats are more likely to oppose such strictures, the data availability may be of greater benefit to them than Republicans because younger voters (who are less settled and more mobile) seem to be trending Democratic, based on data from 2004 and 2006 exit polls. Ultimately the courts will decide how much information is available to the government and private companies, but such decisions tend to be narrow and piecemeal because the intersection of new technologies and privacy involves numerous technical issues.

Cost

As national advertising becomes less appealing to presidential candidates, and as television and the Internet converge, driving down costs, campaigns may allocate more of their resources to voter mobilization. Currently, about 50 percent to 70 percent of a campaign's budget goes for paid advertising. For example, a typical Senate campaign in 2010 may cost $12 million. A 5 percent change in allocation of resources from paid advertising to voter mobilization would increase the GOTV budget by $600,000, yielding approximately 120,000 new voters at $5 per vote.

Parties and independent organizations, not campaigns, carry out voter registration activities. In the future, presidential campaigns may subsume the GOTV effort by the parties during White House election years, as previously noted. However, parties still raise money for voter education activities under the auspices of the Federal Election Campaign Act Amendments of 1979 (what are called "nonfederal" funds). Moreover, special campaign committees that can raise unlimited individual contributions (527 groups) will continue to register voters in targeted areas.

Republicans will continue to put more of their resources into mobilizing their existing base through lifestyle targeting. For Democrats, however, the future may be different. Given that minorities have lower voting rates and thus lower voter registration rates, will the Democrats spend more on harder-to-reach populations, to bring more African American, Latino, and young voters into the voting population? Or will they shift their focus away from voter registration and focus more on turnout, as Republicans do? That is a dilemma that Democrats will have to face. The choice for Republicans, whose cohort groups have higher voter registration rates, is less problematic.

The Technological Future of Voter Mobilization

The future of voter mobilization will be in more direct interface between candidate and voter, without the filter of television. The key is for campaigns to obtain access to more databases of information to enable them to communicate by cell phone, PDA, and e-mail. Getting such lists will make it easier to reach each voter through several media.

Traditionally campaigns have used mass media and direct mail to reach voters—they know that oft-repeated messages (usually ten times) tend to have a cumulative effect on a voter. In the future, not only can the number of messages be increased, for GOTV operations as well as for voter persuasion, but there can be multiple points of contact, including paid advertising, direct mail, and the much cheaper newer technologies such as e-mail, cell phone text messages, and perhaps recordings for download on an iPod or iPhone.

E-mail and its interaction with mobile technology will become more common. In essence, e-mail can be tailored for each voter. The first stage is contact and introduction; the second stage is persuasion; and the third stage is mobilization to vote. For example, one possibility is that candidates will be able to e-mail videos to potential supporters (targeted by the methods we have been discussing). That can be followed up by virtual zip code captains, who can e-mail their neighbors using a handheld device such as an iPhone. (Of course, this depends on campaigns' obtaining actual addresses or zip codes that match e-mail addresses.) Virtual zip code captains can engage in dialogue, perhaps through text messaging, with potential voters for persuasion and mobilization and perhaps to volunteer. The campaign coordinates the activities among the virtual captains and the actual precinct captains in that zip code to ensure that there is no overlap or overcommunication with any potential voter.

Cell phone numbers are not made public; however, campaigns can build phone trees through their field organizers. If campaign organizers can obtain lists of cell phone numbers, they can contact individuals both actively (ID calls) and passively (text messages) about the importance of voting.

Finally, campaigns may be more active in recruiting rock stars and celebrities to record a message for iPod or post-iPod download. That message could be attached to a song recorded especially for the candidate. These are ways to reach voters under thirty-five, whose consumer patterns have changed the music industry from being CD driven to being single-song-download driven.

These examples illustrate how campaigns might harness technology to transform campaign mobilization. All may not be successful. Many of them, however, are relatively cheap or almost free (e-mail, for example) compared to turnout mail and paid advertising. Campaigns will use an increasing number of such tactics to reach voters through different media, and the number of GOTV contacts per person is thus likely to increase. Campaigns will have to learn by trial and error how not to burden voters with too much pressure or information, which could backfire and deter voter turnout.

Long-Term Planning: Redistricting and Voter Turnout

Democrats and Republicans are planning for the long term, as the next U.S. Census approaches. The Republicans have long been successful in using business models to implement long-term planning for the Census, as they did following the 2000 election. In 2006, two Democratic-affiliated organizations, the National Committee for an Effective Congress (NCEC) and the Democratic Legislative Campaign Committee (DLCC), formed a 527 organization called Foundation for the Future. "The Foundation will use computer data to analyze existing districts, voting patterns, demographic trends and potential district lines. It will then develop a political strategy to influence important redistricting decisions." [43] The data will help Democrats maximize their effort to apportion congressional districts for the next decennial Census after 2010. Long-term planning enables Democrats not only to influence future redistricting but also to ascertain where votes are to be maximized in future GOTV efforts.

Conclusion

The future of voter mobilization is much more complex than it was for Hymie Shorenstein and his precinct captains of seventy years ago. While personal, door-to-door contact is still the preferred method of inducing persuadable voters to vote, how those potential votes are identified and contacted is far more complex than in the past. Campaigns will play an increasing role in identifying and getting out voters—particularly in presidential elections—because nominees will be soaking up a disproportionate amount of the available money, and that may diminish the role of political parties. The new voter mobilization may mean that the emphasis of party-driven GOTV operations may be the midterm congressional elections. As new technologies are developed, and methods to identify, track, and predict the likelihood of voting for individuals become more specialized, the sophistication of congressional campaigns will eclipse that of today's presidential campaigns. Understanding how to mobilize voters in the future means understanding what each potential voter wants.

Notes

1. Theodore H. White, *The Making of the President 1960* (New York: Pocket Books, 1961), 49.

2. See Samuel Eldersveld, *Political Parties in American Society* (New York: Basic Books, 1982); Austin Ranney, *Political Parties: Democracy and the American Party System* (New York: Harcourt, Brace, 1956); and V. O. Key, *Southern Politics in State and Nation* (Knoxville: University of Tennesee Press, 1984).

3. Anthony Corrado, "Where Are We Now? The Current State of Campaign Finance Law," in *Campaign Finance Reform: A Sourcebook,* edited by Trevor Potter (Washington, D.C.: Brookings Institution Press, 1997), 8–9.

4. Information confirmed by Tim Crawford, New Models Consulting, personal interview, August 8, 2007.

5. That includes the special Senate election of 2002 to fill the remaining term of Mel Carnahan (Jim Talent, Republican, winner), the 2004 senatorial (Kit Bond, Republican, reelected) and presidential (Bush winner) races, and the 2006 Senate race (Claire McCaskill, a Democrat, defeating Talent).

6. Will Robinson, "Organizing the Field," in *Campaigns and Elections American Style,* (Washington, D.C.: Brookings Institution Press, 1995), 146.

7. Kelly Holder, "Voting and Registration in the Election of 2004," report P20-556, U.S. Census Bureau, Washington, D.C., March 2006, 2.

8. See Martin Wattenberg, *The Rise of Candidate-Centered Politics: Presidential Elections of the 1980s* (Cambridge: Harvard University Press, 1991); and David E. Price, *The Congressional Experience: The View from the Hill* (Boulder: Westview Press, 1992) for a discussion of entrepreneurship.

9. MSHCdirect.com (accessed June 1, 2007). MSHC is a major direct-mail marketing firm that works for Democratic candidates. It has offices in Washington, D.C., and San Francisco.

10. Scott Mervis, "Hip-Hop Convention Seeks to Rap Out the Vote," *Pittsburgh Post-Gazette,* October 1, 2004 (accessed from postgazette.com on August 25, 2007).

11. Walter D. Clinton, "Building Relationships with Voters," in *Winning Elections,* edited by Ronald Faucheaux (New York: M. Evans, 2003), 567.

12. John Jameson, Chris Glaze, and Gary Teal, "Phone Contact Programs and Good Data," in *Winning Elections,* ed. Faucheaux, 573.

13. Susan A. McManus, *Targeting Senior Voters* (Lanham, Md.: Rowman and Littlefield, 2000), 84.

14. Ibid., 85.

15. Donald Phillip Green and Alan G. Gerber, *Get Out the Vote!* (Washington, D.C.: Brookings Institution Press, 2004), 94.

16. Ibid., 94.

17. Richard J. Semiatin, *Campaigns in the 21st Century: The Changing Mosaic of American Politics* (Boston: McGraw-Hill, 2005), 219.

18. Richard J. Semiatin, *The 2002 Midterm Elections* (Boston: McGraw-Hill, 2003), 1.

19. See Target Point Consulting Web site, at targetpointconsulting.com/MicroTargeting (accessed June 12, 2007).

20. Alex Lundry, "Microtargeting: Knowing the Voter Intimately," *Winning Campaigns,* vol. 4, no.1, date unknown. Also much background information on how microtargeting is used, as described in this chapter, was confirmed by Alex Lundry and Mike Myers, of Target Point Consulting, in an interview on July 9, 2007.

21. Douglas B. Sosnik, Matthew J. Dowd, and Ron Fournier, *Applebee's America* (New York: Simon and Schuster, 2006), 33.

22. Ibid., 36.

23. Ibid., 37.

24. Ibid., 43.

25. Dan Balz and Thomas B. Edsall, "Unprecedented Efforts to Mobilize Voters Begin," *Washington Post,* November 1, 2004, A1 (accessed from washingtonpost.com, June 12, 2007).

26. Ibid.

27. Martin Schram, *Running for President: A Journal of the Carter Campaign* (New York: Pocket Books, 1977), 23.

28. Terry Nelson, Powerpoint presentation on the Bush 2004 campaign, American University, Washington, D.C., February 15, 2006.

29. Dan Balz and Mike Allen, "Election Is Now for Bush Campaign," *Washington Post,* November 23, 2003, A1 (accessed June 12, 2007, from washingtonpost.com).

30. From my.barackobama.com/page/s/campobama (accessed June 12, 2007).

31. See tomallen.org (accessed June 12, 2007).

32. MoveOn.org reports on its Web site (moveon.org) that the organization has 3.3 million members (accessed August 26, 2007).

33. Declan McCullagh, "Newsmaker: The Cyberbrains behind Dean," CNETnews, January 16, 2004, new.com.com (accessed August 26, 2007).

34. Michael Alvarez, blog, "New Technologies for Voter Mobilization—Instant Messaging?" electionupdates.caltech.edu/2005 (accessed June 12, 2007).

35. Eva Galanes Rosenbaum, presentation, and Paul Gronke, director, "Early Voting and Technology," Early Voting Information Center, Reed College, presented at Cal Tech, March 2007.

36. Carol Anne Clark Kelly, "Early Voting: Getting the Jump on Election Day," NPR, November 4, 2006 (accessed from npr.org June 12, 2007); includes voting data references.

37. Semiatin, *Campaigns in the 21st Century,* 230; includes reference to Bouvier.

38. Green and Gerber, *Get Out the Vote!* 94.

39. Ibid.

40. Ryan Singel, "Acxiom Opts Out of Opt-Out," *Wired,* November 17, 2003 (accessed from wired.com/politics on August 26, 2007).

41. From eff.org, "Repeal the Real ID Act," EFF Action Center (accessed June 13, 2007).

42. "Geographic Mobility: 2004–2005," table, U.S. Census Bureau, at census.gov (accessed August 26, 2007).

43. Gerald McEntee, "Rethinking Redistricting," The Huffington Post, August 18, 2006 (accessed from huffingonpost.com/gerald-mcentee August 26, 2007).

Part II:

The Evolving Campaign— Adaptation by Political Institutions and Implications for Democracy

CHAPTER 7

Political Parties—On the Path to Revitalization

Ronald G. Shaiko

THIRTY YEARS AGO POLITICAL SCIENTISTS WERE PREDICTING the demise of the party system. The esteemed journalist David Broder wrote that the "party" was over. He meant that the era of the political party system that had controlled individual campaigns was over and that the parties were becoming less relevant for election to national office.[1] Broder's obituary, however, which seemed prescient at the time, turned out to be premature. Political parties may not have the degree of control that they had fifty years ago, but they have had a resurgence over the past two decades, the seeds of which were sown as far back as the 1960s. The demise of the party system has not come to pass—today, parties are alive and well.

Political parties are at their best in political campaigning when they keep in mind that they have the sole responsibility for governance or for loyal opposition to the governing party. That is when they serve voters best. When parties become just another organized interest in the political campaign context, they lose their distinctiveness. Political parties have great responsibilities in the political system—far greater than corporate or union PACs, far greater than so-called 527s (independent political organizations), and far greater than even the individual citizens who fund campaigns and vote. Political parties and the candidates they field in elections are the only truly accountable actors in political campaigns. In this chapter I will discuss what political parties do in political campaigning. The bulk of the assessment here will focus on federal campaigns. The parties remain relevant as national party and campaign organizations and have a role to play in the future.

National Party Organizations

The Democratic National Committee (DNC) and the Republican National Committee (RNC) are the centers of national party activities and are the parent bodies of the fifty state party organizations and those of the federal territories, including the District of Columbia, Guam, and Puerto Rico. The Democratic Congressional Campaign Committee (DCCC) and the National Republican Congressional Committee (NRCC), for the House of Representatives, are also member organizations. Democratic House members and Republican House members are the respective primary constituencies of the DCCC and NRCC. Each organization has as its first priority the protection of incumbents, and its second is to pursue races for open seats (in which no incumbent is running) and seats whose incumbents of the opposing party can be defeated. The similar bodies in the Senate, the Democratic Senatorial Campaign Committee (DSCC) and the National Republican Senatorial Committee (NRSC), are structured the same way in terms of membership (senators) and priorities.

Each organization has divisions that include finance (fundraising), administration (office operations and payroll), legal (interpreting campaign finance laws), political (candidate recruitment, training, advisement, tactical advice, and voter mobilization efforts), and communications (earned media, paid media, and new media), as well as an office of the chairman or chairwoman.

National Committees as Campaign Organizations

During the past two decades, the DNC and RNC have gravitated toward providing services to candidates in what is known as the "service party" model of political campaigning.[2] This model is critical to understanding how the parties struggled and developed into the modern organizations we see today.

Development of the Service Party Model

The Republican Party was first to embrace the idea of party organization as service provider to candidates and campaigns. More than forty years ago Republican National Committee chairman Ray Bliss moved the national party apparatus into the service provision mode by engaging state and local party organizations in efforts to build and maintain party infrastructure. Following the Watergate electoral debacle in 1974 and his own defeat for reelection to the Senate from Tennessee in 1976, Bill Brock was tapped to lead the RNC in 1977. Under his leadership the GOP implemented the "southern strategy" envisioned by President Richard Nixon. This top-down strategy of winning southern states in the presidential race, followed by inroads into congressional races, transformed the Solid (meaning solidly Democratic) South of the 1950s and 1960s into a solidly Republican region of the country at both the presidential and congressional levels.

In 1975, before Republican implementation of the top-down strategy, Democrats held more than three-quarters of the House seats of the South and more than half of its Senate seats. By 2005, Republicans held almost two-thirds of the House seats and 85 percent of the Senate seats from the South.[3] Chairman Brock professionalized all fifty state party organizations by providing salaries for all state executive directors; he also provided technical expertise in fundraising, organizing, and campaign management to state and local parties across the nation.[4]

Unfortunately for the Democratic Party, a series of its leaders in the 1960s and 1970s were more concerned with internal procedural reforms and the descriptive representativeness of the Democratic National Committee and delegates to the national conventions than with building an enduring party infrastructure. Despite some strong DNC leadership in the 1980s and early 1990s by chairmen Charles Mannatt, Paul Kirk, and Ron Brown, the party lagged woefully behind the Republican Party in service provision.

By this time both parties were building their senatorial and congressional committee organizations. Whereas the national committee operations used to eclipse those of the senatorial and congressional campaigns, that became less true during the 1970s. Senators and members of the House of Representatives became increasingly independent in running their own reelection campaigns, relying less on the DNC and RNC for candidate recruitment, fundraising, and technical assistance. Congressman Guy Vander Jagt (R-Mich.) "began overseeing the recruitment and election efforts of House Republicans as chairman of the National Republican Congressional Committee, crisscrossing the country to raise money for candidates and trying to build the party through sophisticated forms of direct mail." [5] Democrats lagged behind. They lost in a landslide to Ronald Reagan, creating a new urgency. Democrats also lost control of the Senate and lost thirty-four seats in the House. Tony Coehlo (D-Calif.), who was chair of the DCCC from 1981 to 1986, aggressively recruited new candidates to run for open and competitive seats and worked to help them raise money. Democrats regained twenty-six House seats in 1982 and were never in danger of losing their majority for the rest of the decade.

The Republicans had equally strong leadership at the RNC in the 1980s, continuing into the 1990s. Frank Fahrenkopf (1983–1989) oversaw the establishment and growth of an unmatched voter file/direct mail operation. Haley Barbour (1993–1997) brought the RNC into the television age with state-of-the-art television production facilities. Jim Nicholson (1997–2000) brought the RNC into the computer age by establishing Internet communications. Again, the Democratic Party failed to match the growth and innovation of the RNC throughout the 1990s. Despite holding the White House, the Democratic leadership was wandering in the wilderness while the Republican Party continued to build on its organizational dominance.

The one bright spot for the Democrats was the Democratic Senatorial Campaign Committee, which successfully used soft money (unregulated spending in coordination with state parties) to help win narrow races. It was particularly successful in 1998, the year of the Monica Lewinsky/ Bill Clinton scandal. On the surface the scandal hurt Democrats. But "party contributions helped make a difference in Nevada, California, New York, North Carolina and Washington Senate races. . . . [T]he massive amounts spent in [these] Senate races were not by Republicans but by Democrats." [6] Democrats won all of them. Also that year, the NRCC spent $10 million in the last few days of the election campaign on anti-Clinton ads in districts where Democrats were deemed vulnerable. But the controversial ads backfired after they received national network news coverage. Republicans ended up losing five seats in the House; whereas predictions earlier that summer had been that they might win thirty seats.[7]

Democratic Party Organizations in the Twenty-First Century

The DNC was the source of many of the technical and strategic organizational changes for Democrats. When Terry McAuliffe took over as DNC chairman in 2001, following Al Gore's defeat by George W. Bush, the national party organization was in disarray; it was basically a money pit. The party had just lost the presidential election (or had it stolen from them, as McAuliffe continues to claim) and the DNC was roughly $17 million in debt. As a service provider, the party was an abject failure. McAuliffe has recounted the dismal state of affairs that he inherited at the DNC: "Our direct mail efforts summed up the problem perfectly. The DNC had raised $1.6 million in 1979 through direct mail. That doesn't sound bad until you hear that it cost $850,000 to bring in that money—53 cents on the dollar. Not much had improved by 1999 when we raised $17 million at a cost of $8 million—47 cents on the dollar." Given the comparatively high cost of direct mail, McAuliffe sought to adopt a more diversified strategy to raise money but was met with significant roadblocks: "I was stunned when my tech people told me we had only 70,000 e-mail addresses in our DNC files. That was one e-mail address for every 729 Al Gore voters out there. . . . I was also eager to tap our voter files, which were records of individuals' party affiliation, name and address, history of giving, and other useful bits of information. Despite nearly 51 million Democratic voters out there, we did not have a single voter file at the DNC," said McAuliffe.[8]

His first plan of attack was a $40 million capital campaign that would engage the wealthiest supporters of the Democratic Party, but would also reach out to donors via the Internet. The consummate fundraiser, McAuliffe wasted little time raising the money necessary to reach solvency and then build a party organization worthy of its competition. With the imminent threat and subsequent reality of a ban on soft money contributions to parties, the DNC launched an eleventh-hour quest for soft money to restore its solvency. After a single fundraising dinner, hosted by former president and Mrs. Clinton at their new Washington, D.C., residence, and a coast-to-coast round of "asks," McAuliffe met half of his fundraising goal with just eight checks. Media mogul Haim Saban topped the list with a check for $7 million.[9] It is truly ironic that it took the threat of a soft money ban to force the Democratic Party to use soft money for its intended purpose—party building. Four years later, in 2005, when McAuliffe handed over the gavel to current DNC chair Howard Dean, the party had no debt and $4 million in the bank. According to McAuliffe, the party "brought in $70 million online, and built a new, state-of-the-art headquarters that doubled our workspace, gave us modernized database and Web platforms, built a satellite TV studio, updated IT backbone, and added training facilities and a conference center—and paid for it all in cash." [10]

Howard Dean continues the organizational transformation of the DNC in his own distinct manner. Clearly enamored of the Internet, Dean believes that the future of the DNC lies in connecting with voters in a different way. Although he was not the choice of the Democratic establishment in Washington, D.C., in 2005, his vision of party building has been successful in the short term and may pay even larger dividends in the long term. Dean has implemented a "fifty-state strategy" aimed at building Democratic support from the grassroots level. His strategy, however, has been controversial and has led to conflicts between Dean and DCCC chair Rep. Rahm Emanuel (D-Ill.).

Republican Party Organizations in the Twenty-First Century

While the past six years at the DNC has been a vibrant time of political catch-up, the Republican Party has had a series of RNC chairmen who have served more as organization caretakers than as transformational leaders. Jim Gilmore, Marc Racicot, and Ed Gillespie all served during the time McAuliffe chaired the DNC. Since then Ken Mehlman and current chair Mike Duncan have managed the national party.

Republicans have chosen political operatives as chair more often than Democrats, who rely more on current or past elected officials (such as Howard Dean, the former governor of Vermont). Gillespie and Mehlman were longtime political operatives associated with President George W. Bush. Gillespie was communications director for the Bush/Cheney campaign in 2000. Mehlman managed the Bush/Cheney reelection campaign in 2004. A decade earlier Haley Barbour, who was the last transformational leader of the Republican Party, rebuilt the RNC as an effective and cohesive campaign organization, helping to bring Republicans majorities to the U.S. House and Senate. McAuliffe was the only true political operative to chair the DNC full-time during the past fifteen years.

Republican staff tends to turn over less frequently, particularly at the NRCC. Long service is not unusual. For example, Carl Forti served as both deputy director and communications director for the NRCC from 1999 to 2006. New chairs at the NRCC have tended not to shake up the staff as long as they performed well. Democrats have had much greater turnover (usually every two to four years). Even after successful elections new chairs sweep out old staff and bring in their own people, including Rep. Patrick Kennedy (D-R.I.) and Rahm Emanuel. The substantial defeat that Republicans suffered in the 2006 midterm elections, however, in which they lost control of both the House and Senate, led to major staff shakeups at all three major party committees.

Following the 2006 elections, both parties began gearing up for the 2008 presidential election. As in other presidential election years, the DNC and RNC will be involved not only in fundraising and in contacting and mobilizing voters, but also in communicating with them through television advertisements. Those communications are independent of the candidates' organizations. In 2004 the DNC hired the media firm of Murphy, Putnam, and Schorr to produce ads independent of the Kerry campaign. In 2008 and beyond, the parties will be able to produce more ads because the Internet, in addition to television, will be available as a medium to reach base voters.

Surviving Campaign Finance Reform: National Parties Post-BCRA

When Congress passed and the president signed the Bipartisan Campaign Reform Act (BCRA) in 2002 (it took effect after the 2002 election), the parties were hard-hit. The BCRA barred national and state parties from raising "soft," or unregulated, money. Soft money, individual donations to parties for "voter education" purposes, formerly had no contribution limit. Thus, a Bill Gates or Warren Buffett could conceivably give hundreds of thousands of dollars to the parties to spend on voter education, or what has become better known as "issue advocacy." But as it turned out, data from 2000–2006 demonstrate that the parties were just as effective in raising money, even though contributions for issue advocacy are now limited.

As Table 7.1 illustrates, the Democratic and Republican committees raised $1.62 billion in 2004, after BCRA, compared to $1.23 billion in 2000, before BCRA went into effect. What makes that all the more remarkable is that nearly $500 million of the parties' 2000 total had been soft money.[11] How did the parties manage to flourish financially despite BCRA?

The parties were effective in tapping new, as well as old sources of revenue—whether the Internet, direct mail, or telemarketing. They worked harder to attract more money. They expedited their efforts to apply precise methods of attracting new contributors through lifestyle or geotargeting techniques (see chapter 6, on voter mobilization). The new law forced the parties to seize on new strategies to make up for the revenue sources lost because of the new BCRA rules. Contrary to the conventional wisdom, not only have the parties adapted, but they are financially stronger than one might have anticipated following the law's enactment.

TABLE 7.1 Total Receipts: National Political Party Organizations, 2000–2006

Party organization	2000	2002	2004	2006
Democratic Party	$520,433,199	$463,312,470	$730,935,853	$599,412,184
DNC	260,560,928	162,062,084	311,524,471	130,821,232
DSCC	104,206,648	143,441,173	88,657,573	121,376,959
DCCC	105,096,499	102,889,031	92,945,101	139,891,645
Republican Party	$715,701,784	$691,646,873	$892,792,542	$707,486,826
RNC	379,006,604	284,028,091	392,413,393	243,007,131
NRSC	96,127,865	125,587,504	78,980,487	88,812,386
NRCC	144,610,249	210,766,756	185,719,489	179,549,131

Source: Center for Responsive Politics, www.opensecrets.org/parties/index.asp.
Note: Total receipts include donations to all party committees reporting to the Federal Election Commission. DNC = Democratic National Committee; DSCC = Democratic Senatorial Campaign Committee; DCCC = Democratic Congressional Campaign Committee; RNC = Republican National Committee; NRSC = National Republican Senatorial Committee; NRCC = National Republican Congressional Committee.

The Necessary Tools for Voter Engagement in the Future

Political party organizations apply the same techniques as campaign organizations do. The difference is that individual campaigns end. For political parties, the tools or techniques they use must transcend each election. And through both traditional fundraising tools, such as direct mail and telemarketing, and twenty-first-century tools, such as new media, party organizations have more avenues than ever to communicate with voters and raise money. Moreover, given the massive changes of the information era, parties seeking to reinvent themselves after an electoral defeat now have far less time to reflect on how they might want to change. They have to adapt quickly to the political environment.

Direct Mail

For at least the next decade or two, direct mail will continue to be a significant means for political party organizations to connect with voters. Microtargeting by the parties has improved and will continue to improve. It is difficult to wean an organization from direct mail once it has engaged in this method of fundraising, especially because of its reliability in the past. In general, a mass mailing breaks even with a response rate of 1 percent to 2 percent. That is, for every one hundred pieces of mail sent out, ninety-eight can end up in the trash, and as long as two citizens respond the organization will not lose money on the effort.

Both parties have made significant improvements in collecting and managing voter files for direct-mail purposes, especially the DNC. Both parties now have at their disposal quite elaborate voter file management systems—Voter Vault at the RNC and Datamart/Demzilla at the DNC. Both parties are using customer relationship management (CRM) techniques that are the new wave of communications and selling from Madison Avenue. CRM integrates databases that include demographic, voting, political, lifestyle, and consumer orientation information on voters. Today Republicans and Democrats do not target a city block, but rather specific houses on a street, so as to custom-tailor messages to voters and fundraising prospects.[12] The messages cater to micro-audiences.

Both parties' systems have direct applications to the Internet (to be discussed below). Their data gathering and management efforts will bear fruit in both direct mail and online mobilization and targeting.

Now that the Democratic Party is approaching parity with the Republican Party in providing services to party leaders at the national, state, and local levels, as well as to candidates for office, Republicans will have to rethink their strategy over the next decade to stay ahead.

Telemarketing

Although telemarketing is not terribly cost-effective in initial ("cold call") fundraising efforts, it is very effective for mobilizing voters (GOTV) and fundraising from existing members or contributors. Dollars for Democrats was the largest nonfederal fundraiser for the Democratic Party in 2006; all of its money was raised via telemarketing. A more recent form of telemarketing in the campaign context is "robocalling," which both parties engage in. Leading robocalling firms include Democratic Dialing for the Democrats and Conquest Communications for the Republicans. During the 2006 cycle, the NRCC, in an "independent expenditure" campaign on behalf of twenty Republican candidates, targeted twenty Democratic-held congressional districts with prerecorded messages against the Democratic candidate. Conquest Communications received more than $180,000 from the NRCC to target these phone calls to selected voters.[13] The robocalls were uniformly targeted against the Democratic incumbent, rather than in support of the Republican challenger. Similar efforts by Democrats in 2006 were equally negative.

Given the general hostility toward telemarketers (as evidenced by the federal "do not call" list for commercial solicitors), caller ID displays, and the growing percentage of the population without landline telephones, telemarketers will have to focus on an older demographic of contributors who, among other things, are less likely to rely on cell phones. People over sixty-five years old make up 13 percent of the entire U.S. population in 2008. The figure is expected to reach 15 percent by 2015.[14] In a May 2006 survey by the Pew Research Center, 90 percent of the sampled population over age sixty-five reported using landlines only. That contrasts with the 23 percent of the population between the ages of eighteen and twenty-nine who uses landlines only.[15] Thus, the future of telemarketing will probably skew even more to an older demographic.

Traditional Media — Television and Radio

Even though television and radio are losing their appeal as voters turn to other means of information gathering, the traditional media outlets will continue to play a significant role in political campaigns in America. Candidates and parties will continue to generate "earned media" coverage to spread their messages and will continue to pour hundreds of millions of dollars into traditional paid media campaigns. In the context of paid media (i.e., the purchase of thirty- or sixty-second advertisements on television, cable, or radio stations), the most pressing issue for the major political parties and their candidates is the crowding out of the legitimate contestants by unaccountable organized interests.

For example, 527 groups bought up air time in the 2004 presidential campaign, supplanting parties and candidates as the primary actors in the political dialogue. The prime example is Swift Boat Veterans for Truth, a 527 group that questioned Sen. John Kerry's (D-Mass.) service during the Vietnam War and the medals he received for valor in combat. After Kerry had won the 2004 Democratic presidential nomination, when the Kerry campaign was conserving its money for the fall general election campaign, the group's ads began appearing in August. The ads went unanswered for more than ten days, and the result was that the Kerry campaign and the DNC spent several weeks trying to defuse the charges—which contributed to the Massachusetts senator's defeat.

The Internet and the Blogosphere

For the past decade, parties and their candidates have scrambled to engage voters via the Internet. Today, we have reached virtually complete use of the Internet by parties and campaign organizations. In 2002, only 55 percent of major-party Senate candidates had Web sites. Today, nearly all Senate candidates have them.[16] All of the party organizations discussed in this chapter have Web sites. Some are more elaborate than others, but each entity makes an effort to engage voters in some way.

The Democrats have harnessed the Internet much more effectively than Republicans, thus far. In fact, as stated earlier, the DNC raised $70 million online in 2004—or 23 percent of the total sum raised that year.[17] Final data on party fundraising for the 2007–2008 election cycle were not available when this book went to print, but we know that Democratic candidates had outraised their Republican counterparts online three-to-one ($28 million to $9.4 million) through the first half of 2007.[18] Furthermore, given that raising money online is cheap (less than a penny per dollar raised) compared to traditional means (such as direct mail, which costs about fifty cents per dollar raised), the anecdotal evidence suggests that Democrats in general are benefiting from online fundraising more than Republicans.

DNC chairman Howard Dean, for one, is sold on the idea of the Internet as the next wave of civic engagement:

> The Internet is the most significant tool for building democracy since the invention of the printing press. . . . The implications for political parties are tremendous. Political power resides with the public; it has only been loaned to us politicians. It does not work its way from the top down. It grows from the grassroots up.[19]

Although Dean is correct in theory, in practice it is less clear that political parties can be the democratizing forces in political campaigns that he wishes them to be.

At their best, campaign and party Web sites serve three distinct purposes: (1) as an administrative tool, (2) as an active campaign tool, and (3) as a participatory and organizational tool.[20] In all three, the Internet is a means to an end, not an end unto itself. For the Web sites of the major parties to be the democratizing force that Dean suggests would require a way to expand the political discourse significantly among voters and candidates and their parties via the Internet. Thus far, party Web sites have imitated candidate Web sites in seeking to generate revenue. At the RNC Web site, one can click on "GOP Stuff," enter the virtual store, and buy an MP3 holder emblazoned with the symbolic Republican elephant. Democrats have initiated something different—rather than offering a store, they ask viewers to invest in the Democratic Party by buying "Democracy Bonds." Thus, a suggested contribution of $20 per month is regarded as a personal investment by the contributor in the Democratic Party.[21]

In addition to Web sites, each of the national party organizations and their campaign committees in the House and Senate supports a blog, with the exception of the National Republican Senatorial Committee. If one were seeking to uncover some degree of political discourse, one would expect to find it in the parties' blogs, whose purpose is to keep activists in touch with each other and the party. This is a very high-maintenance process, especially for Democrats. "Democratic bloggers are more demanding and require more care from the committees than their Republican counterparts. Democratic bloggers have sought recognition as strategists, particularly on resource allocation and candidate recruitment, rather than just fundraising." [22] Moreover, parties cannot control the content that bloggers post on the party's Web site. That creates a great risk that both parties seem willing to accept to mollify their base. By placating activists, the party gets return customers to its Web site, and that means more opportunities to organize and raise money.

Finally the Dean campaign of 2004 should suggest caution to those who view the Internet, and in particular the blogosphere, as the savior of modern party politics. Blogs can be a way to manipulate users:

> After a careful reading of the Dean blog posts and citizen comments, it seems that the campaign was interacting *at* citizens rather than interacting *with* citizens. Rather than genuine interaction between the staff and citizens, the weblog was used in a way to relay information to citizens, but was not used as a forum to dialogue with citizens.[23]

Blogs can be methods to feed information to users using "strategies that gave the impression that they were involved in the conversations taking place on the blog," as the Dean campaign did. The campaign's Internet staff rarely responded to more than one request per individual via the blog.[24]

Lisa Miller, director of communications at the RNC, clearly views the Internet as an important means of connecting with voters, but she acknowledges that the RNC's Internet audience is not looking for prolonged political discourse. The average length of time that an RNC visitor spends online at the Web site is eight minutes—hardly enough time to engage in a serious political dialogue.[25]

The DNC Web site includes an innovative tool developed by the Dean leadership team that other party organizations might want to replicate—"partybuilder." Clearly defined as a tool, rather than an end, this online model of voter mobilization uses the Internet to develop grassroots infrastructure for the Democratic Party. This is the kind of Internet use that will serve the longer-term goals of the parties, rather than seeking the goal of furthering the national political discourse. According to Dean, "PartyBuilder isn't the typical online tool set. Individual users control most of the activity—from blogging, to setting up and managing groups or activists, to organizing and managing real-world events, to fundraising. Democrats are entrusted to build the space and the Party." [26]

The New Voter Mobilization

Both political parties have extensive voter mobilization infrastructures in place. The Republican National Committee's mobilization efforts have largely remained under the radar of the traditional news media. RNC leaders tend not to flaunt their prowess in voter identification and mobilization, yet they are quite successful. The Democrats, conversely, tend to divulge their strategic planning to anyone who will listen.

STOMP and GOP Voter Mobilization

When Karl Rove arrived in Washington in 2001, he understood that the Republicans had to change the dynamic of voter mobilization. Since 1932, Democrats had competed effectively with Republicans, despite their shortfalls in fundraising, because their get-out-the-vote (GOTV) effort was better than that of the GOP. Democrats and their labor union allies provided organizational muscle to get the working class out to vote, enabling the Democrats to hold their New Deal and Great Society coalitions together from the 1930s through the 1960s. Despite the decline of union membership and power, Democrats were able to muster strong voter mobilization efforts that enabled them to maintain majorities in the House and Senate for most of the forty years from 1954 to 1994. Moreover, Democrats were more effective than Republicans in getting their base voters to vote in the 2000 election, giving Al Gore a slight popular vote margin (0.4 percent) over George W. Bush, who triumphed in the Electoral College.

Afterward Rove and his team analyzed the 2000 election. If one added populist Ralph Nader's vote to Gore's, Democrats had a natural 51 percent voting base. Rove, a student of voting history, sought to build a Republican Party majority that would last for a generation.

The first step in this endeavor was creating a party-managed GOTV program for the 2002 midterm election called STOMP (Strategic Task Force to Organize and Mobilize People). STOMP is also known as "the seventy-two-hour program." "Republican members [of Congress] enlist their district supporters to aid GOP candidates in neighboring, more competitive House races." [27] Operatives often include congressional staff from other offices, many of whom have campaign experience; they take leave, and on their own time spend the last seventy-two hours of the election campaign in a district where an incumbent is vulnerable. The STOMP plan was highly successful in enabling Republicans to gain seats in the House during Bush's first midterm in office—a rare occurrence. The last time a first-term president's party had made such gains was during Franklin Roosevelt's administration in 1934.

GOP efforts were broadened in 2004, as the party and the Bush campaign worked in tandem to increase voter turnout (as discussed in chapter 6). Republicans won 50 percent of the aggregate House vote, compared to 47 percent for Democrats.[28] But the Republicans' majority-building plans fell apart in 2006, when the Democrats won control of both the House and Senate, largely because of the unpopularity of the Iraq war and ethics lapses by congressional Republicans. Republican losses would have been far greater without the coordinated GOTV plans the party had developed that extended from the national party to the state parties. The strategic and tactical changes that the RNC and the Bush campaign made will continue to benefit Republican candidates beyond the 2008 election. However, even a one or two point drop in turnout could result in the loss of more

Republican House and Senate seats. In a close election, turnout becomes critical for organizational control of Congress and the difference between winning and losing the White House.

The Fifty-State Strategy and Democrats: Mobilization, Change, and Conflict

When Howard Dean took over as chairman of the Democratic National Committee, he sought to build the party from its grass roots. He wanted to make the Democratic Party more competitive across the country, focusing on building support in regions such as the Mountain states, Midwest swing states, and even parts of the upper South (especially Virginia). We learned a great deal about Dean's "fifty-state strategy," as well as the sometimes conflicting plans that the DCCC and the DSCC laid out for 2006.

There was conflict between Dean and Democratic Congressional Campaign Committee chairman Rahm Emanuel throughout the 2006 campaign. Dean felt strongly that the fifty-state strategy of engaging voters in all regions of the country, along with targeted efforts in congressional districts that the DNC identified, was the most effective plan. Emanuel wanted far more DNC resources handed over to the DCCC to fund its strategy. In the end, both sides were able to claim credit for the electoral success. Yet Dean insisted that the crucial factor was the value added by his plan: "Of the thirty-five initial races targeted by the DCCC, they only won nine of those races. An additional seventeen seats were picked up in unexpected places that many largely credit to the fifty-state strategy, which enabled grassroots candidates to get their campaigns off the ground." [29]

An assessment of the fifty-state strategy by former White House official Elaine Kamarck supports Dean's conclusion. In contested congressional races in 2006 ($N = 390$), Democrats, on average, received 4.7 percent more votes than in similar races in 2002, the last midterm election. In the districts with DNC-paid organizers in 2006 ($N = 35$), Democratic candidates received 9.8 percent more votes than in 2002. The DNC was active in four additional districts where no Democrat ran in 2002.

> This is a powerful testament to the value of a long-term party building approach. Gains in the Democratic vote occurred where the Democrat won and [where] the Democrat lost. The Democratic candidate won in 20 of the 39 districts where the DNC had organizers[,] but this should not detract from the accomplishment of dramatically increasing the vote in those districts.[30]

DCCC financial support in those districts also had an impact on voter turnout. In twelve districts where DCCC contributions to the Democratic candidate ranged from $10,000 to $100,000, Democratic vote totals increased by 8.4 percent over

2002; in the fourteen districts with DCCC support from $100,000 to $200,000, Democratic votes increased by 13 percent over 2002. "It is not surprising to find out that organizing matters and so does money." [31]

It is key that political parties not ask voters for their votes in a political vacuum. In politics, context matters. The 2006 elections represented a distinct political context that will not be manifest in 2008. According to pundit Charlie Cook, "Midterm elections are about punishing. They're driven by anger—anger and/or fear. And if Democrats see this as a mandate, I think they're crazy; if they see this as an opportunity, then I think they are smart. Because nobody voted for Democrats [in 2006], they voted against Republicans." [32]

Thus far it is not clear whether the new Democratic leadership is over-reading the party's electoral success in 2006, but there are hints that they are. The 2006 election was largely about the Iraq war and to a lesser degree about congressional ethics; little else elicited remotely comparable interest among voters.

Further, the strategies that Emanuel and Dean employed to win back the House for the Democrats have left the Party with a more diverse majority:

> Democrats won in 2006 in part by invading Republican turf and running more moderate or even conservative candidates in Republican-leaning districts. Pelosi will need to balance the interests of their newly enlarged Blue Dog faction with that of the old bull committee chairs, many of whom are from the liberal wing of the party, and the Congressional Black Caucus, another bastion of largely liberal-leaning voters.[33]

An additional problem facing the Democrats in their quest to maintain their majority status is that many of their newly elected members were swept in on the singular salience of their antiwar positions. In the political climate of November 2006, a pulse, "Democrat" after their name, and an antiwar stance were sufficient conditions for several candidates to win election to the House. Rahm Emanuel acknowledged as much in a May 2007 press conference: "We cannot be a one-trick pony [party]." [34]

The difficulty for the Democrats in retaining the House, in particular, according to Ken Spain of the NRCC, lies in the fact that "Democrats now hold sixty-one House seats in districts won by Bush; conversely Republicans now hold only seven seats in districts won by Kerry." [35] One can expect that the year leading up to the November 2008 elections will be quite volatile. With no real anchor for either party at the top of the ticket, voters and party leaders alike will be mulling over the candidates and party positions with added care. Furthermore, with redistricting coming up following the 2010 elections, both parties will be putting great emphasis on state legislative races, seeking to control the legislative bodies responsible for redistricting.

The political party role in voter mobilization has been reinvigorated. In a sense, both parties are returning to the roots that propelled parties half a century ago. Today, parties use modern technologies to organize and control GOTV efforts. But it will be hard to sustain the massive turnout level (60.6 percent) of 2004 in upcoming elections. September 11 and the Iraq war together energized voters who in other years might have stayed home to come to the polls for the primaries and general election.

Finally, states have been moving their primaries so far forward that the nomination process began nearly a year before the presidential election. Although the DNC took preliminary action against one state, Florida, stripping it of delegates to the Democratic National Convention, no one can be sure what the long-term implications are for the state and national parties. It might take an additional election cycle (2012) to sort out the primary schedule.

Conclusion

As we venture toward the second decade of the twenty-first century, both major political parties are poised to expand their roles in the political campaign process. The Democratic Party is quickly catching up to the Republican Party in fundraising and voter mobilization. Yet both remain minority parties in the electorate, as their bases become more and more distinct. To expand their bases, both parties need to make concerted efforts to engage voters currently not aligned with either party. That, however, requires that the parties clearly articulate reasons for voters to engage with them in governance, field credible candidates, and select credible party leaders to guide them. In recent years, both political parties have failed on all counts. Their messages and messengers are muddled. Even so, there is reason to be somewhat optimistic for the future of political parties in campaigns. A more pragmatic assessment of the electorate may serve both parties equally well:

> America's two parties have less in common in their composition, values, and objectives than was the case after World War II. Because they are minority parties in the electorate, neither Democrats nor Republicans can secure national majorities simply by appealing to their most committed supporters. . . . Republicans manifestly need more support from minorities and non-Christian whites, and Democrats need to improve their performance among white Christians.[36]

Furthermore, the parties need to put increasing emphasis on strategy. The demographics of the country are changing (it is becoming less white and more minority), and so is the population distribution. Today, the Northeast has the smallest population of any region of the country, and the South has the largest. Historically, the Democratic Party has pursued a demographic approach to political campaigning, particularly at the presidential level, and the Republican Party has pursued a more geopolitical approach. Democrats have sought to win various groups of voters within their diverse coalition; Republicans have sought to win states.

At the presidential level, the geopolitical approach has been, and will continue to be, the more effective avenue to electoral success. At the congressional level, as well as at the presidential level, the battle lines have shifted:

> The battle in coming cycles will focus on the more competitive Midwest and Interior West states. These 20 states were home to all but three of the eleven states decided by five points or fewer in the 2004 presidential race; the ideas that these states and regions will become the central battlegrounds for the future control of Congress makes perfect sense—especially in the wake of the 2006 midterms, which aligned national legislative control more closely with presidential performance.[37]

Both parties need to respond strategically to these new electoral facts while at the same time pursuing the longer-term goals of party building. To that end, there needs to be a meeting of the minds among Democratic Party leaders that allows room for both a fifty-state strategy and a cyclical approach to campaigning. For the Republicans, the task is even more difficult. The message that served them well in 1994—"We are the party of Main Street, not Wall Street"—no longer captures the imagination of prospective voters. During the decade of the 1990s, it is fair to say, the Republican Party won the war of ideas; its governing philosophy won the day more often than not, regardless of who occupied the White House (the passage of welfare reform during the Clinton administration is an example). Today, the Republican Party lacks both a coherent message that will appeal to voters beyond those it currently attracts and the key leaders who can guide voters into the next decade. Democrats are riding the tide of opposition to an unpopular war. What will happen once that chapter closes?

"The new regionalism encourages continuous battles between ideologically driven partisans—conservative Republicans and liberal Democrats—who represent minorities of the entire electorate. Under such conditions, governing the United States will remain an extraordinarily difficult challenge."[38] Recent elections have been base driven, with few undecided voters. Parties will need to prepare and reach out to voters in the next decade, when elections may become less base driven and more like they were two decades ago. That long-term strategic planning is key for beyond 2010 if the political parties are to remain viable and relevant.

Notes

1. David Broder, *The Party's Over: The Failure of Politics in America* (New York: Harper and Row, 1972).

2. See John C. Green, ed., *Politics, Professionalism, and Power: Modern Party Organization and the Legacy of Ray C. Bliss* (Lanham, Md.: University Press of America, 1994); Paul S. Herrnson, *Congressional Elections: Campaigning at Home and in Washington*, 4th ed. (Washington, D.C.: CQ Press, 2004); and Marjorie Randon Hershey, *Political Parties in America*, 12th ed. (New York: Pearson Longman, 2007).

3. Hershey, *Political Parties in America*, 310.

4. Green, *Politics, Professionalism, and Power.*

5. Jeff Zeleny, "Guy Vander Jagt, 75, Long a Leader in G.O.P., Dies," *New York Times*, June 23, 2007 (accessed from nrcc.org on August 31, 2007).

6. Richard J. Semiatin, *1998 Mid-Term Elections Update* (Boston: McGraw-Hill, 1998), 16.

7. Ibid., 22–23.

8. Terry McAuliffe, *What a Party! My Life among Democrats: Presidents, Candidates, Donors, Activists, Alligators, and other Wild Animals* (New York: Thomas Dunne Books, 2007), 279–280.

9. Ibid., 283–289.

10. Ibid., 305.

11. See opensecrets.org/softmoney/softglance.asp (accessed September 1, 2007).

12. Such techniques were utilized by the Bush campaign after being tested in the 2002 election by the RNC. See Douglas B. Sosnik, Matthew J. Dowd, and Ron Fournier, *Applebee's America* (New York: Simon and Schuster, 2006), chap. 1, about integrating lifestyle targeting with traditional political/demographic models.

13. Paul Kiel, "NRCC Robo Calls Hitting 20 Districts," November 2006, posted on www.tpmmuckraker.com (accessed July 2, 2007).

14. U. S. Census Bureau, Population Division, Tables NP-T3-C and NP-T3-D, Internet release, January 13, 2000, on population projections. Table T3-C covers projections from 2006 to 2010. Table T3-D covers projections from 2010 to 2015 (accessed September 1, 2007, from www.census.gov).

15. "The Cell Phone Challenge to Survey Research: Summary of Findings," Pew Research Center for the People and the Press, May 15, 2006 (accessed September 1, 2007, from www.people-press.org).

16. The Bivings Group, "The Internet's Role in Political Campaigns: Utilization by 2006 United States Senatorial Candidates" (Washington, D.C.: Bivings Group, 2006).

17. See Center for Responsive Politics, www.opensecrets.org/parties/index.asp, on party fundraising by year since 2000.

18. Marie Horrigan, "FEC Stats Highlight Democratic Party Committee's Fundraising Prowess," CQPolitics.com, August 15, 2007 (accessed September 1, 2007, from www.cqpolitics.com).

19. Howard Dean, "How the Web Is Restoring Democracy to Politics," *Fortune*, May 7, 2007, 94.

20. Stephen Ward, Rachel Gibson, and Paul Nixon, "Parties and the Internet," in *Political Parties and the Internet: Net Gain?* edited by Rachel Gibson, Paul Nixon, and Stephen Ward (New York: Routledge, 2003), 12–13.

21. See www.rnc.org and www.dnc.org (accessed September 1, 2007).

22. Nathan L. Gonzales, "The Webs They Weave," *Roll Call,* May 17, 2007, 14.

23. Jennifer Stromer-Galley and Andrea B. Baker, "Joy and Sorrow of Interactivity on the Campaign Trail: Blogs in the Primary Campaign of Howard Dean," in *The Internet Election: Perspectives on the Web in Campaign 2004,* edited by Andrew Paul Williams and John C. Tedesco (Lanham, Md.: Rowman and Littlefield, 2006), 129.

24. Ibid.

25. Lisa Miller, personal interview with RNC director of communications, Republican National Committee Headquarters, Washington, D.C., June 13, 2007.

26. See dnc.org (accessed September 1, 2007).

27. Mark Wegner, "CongressDaily: Reynolds Turns to RNC to Manage Get-out-the-Vote Effort," *The Hotline,* July 19, 2006 (accessed from hotlineblog.nationaljournal.com, September 1, 2007).

28. See Rhodes Cook, "Counting the 2004 Vote," from rhodescook.com (accessed September 1, 2007). Republicans received 56.1 million House votes, compared to 53.1 million for Democrats and 2.6 million for other candidates.

29. Howard Dean, personal interview with DNC chairman, Democratic National Committee Headquarters, Washington, D.C., May 17, 2007.

30. Elaine C. Kamarck, "Assessing Howard Dean's Fifty State Strategy and the 2006 Midterm Elections," *The Forum* (2006 Midterms: Post-Election Appraisal), Article 5, 2006, 6–7.

31. Ibid., 8.

32. Source quoted in William F. Connelly, "Wall vs. Wave?" *The Forum* (2006 Midterms: Post-Election Appraisal), Article 3, 2006, 9.

33. Ibid., 10.

34. Jonathan Weisman and Lyndsey Layton, "Democrats' Momentum Is Stalling amid Iraq Debate, Priorities on Domestic Agenda Languish," *Washington Post,* May 5, 2007, A1.

35. Ken Spain, personal interview with NRCC director of communications, National Republican Congressional Committee Headquarters, Washington, D.C., May 17, 2007.

36. Earl Black and Merle Black, *Divided America: The Ferocious Power Struggle in American Politics* (New York: Simon and Schuster, 2007), 259–260.

37. Philip A. Klinkner and Thomas F. Schaller, "A Regional Analysis of the 2006 Midterms," *The Forum* (2006 Midterms: Post-Election Appraisal), Article 9, 8.

38. Black and Black, *Divided America,* 260.

CHAPTER 8

Interest Groups and the Future of Campaigns

Nina Therese Kasniunas and Mark J. Rozell

CANDIDATES FOR PUBLIC OFFICE IN THE UNITED STATES may differ in their rhetoric on many issues, but they all seem to agree on this point: interest groups are entirely too powerful. In truth, candidates need interest groups more than ever—not only as easy targets of attack to win public approval, but also to facilitate campaigns. Interest groups have become the potent intervening force in political campaigns by influencing the choices of voters. In recent years, interest groups have often resembled political parties in their ability to inform, influence, and mobilize hundreds of thousands or even millions of voters to get to the polls.[1]

Americans are long accustomed to complaining about the influence of "special interests" on U.S. politics. Nonetheless, most would agree that even if they are too influential, interest groups have a right and even a duty to try to promote their views in a democratic republic. Groups spend a lot of their time and financial resources on lobbying government—either through contacting public officials directly or by activating their supporters to put pressure on leaders. But groups also realize that if they can influence exactly who reaches elected office, the task of lobbying those officials becomes much easier. Thus, interest groups are heavily involved in electoral politics and see such activity as an essential means to achieve their preferred policy outcomes.

Groups become involved in electoral politics in a variety of ways. For example, groups try to identify voters who are sympathetic to certain issue positions and then provide resources to ensure that those people vote. Many groups purchase campaign broadcast ads in areas of the country where there are competitive elections. Some groups train activists in the techniques of campaigns. And some groups actively recruit and train candidates for public office. These are among the many ways in which interest groups try to affect the outcomes of U.S. elections at all levels.

Groups' efforts to influence elections have become increasingly sophisticated. Groups with substantial resources make use of the latest technologies to communicate with large numbers of activists, supporters, and other potential voters. New technologies have made it possible for groups with fewer resources also to communicate with large numbers of people in campaigns.

In this essay, we examine the various ways in which interest groups are using traditional and new technologies to influence electoral campaigns. Our emphasis will largely be on the modern techniques of interest group mobilization and communication. Groups today employ a variety of techniques to pursue their electoral and policy goals. Some place a strong emphasis on building a community of supporters that they can activate when necessary, and others mostly raise money to contribute to candidates. When it comes to the technologies that interest groups employ, some groups are at the forefront, implementing the newest devices and techniques, while others lag far behind.

Campaign Activities of Interest Groups

Although new technologies are rapidly transforming the ways in which groups become involved in campaigns, most still rely on tried and tested techniques. If anything, technology is enabling more efficient use of those methods. Recently there has been a lot of media buzz about the important roles that Web sites such as Myspace and YouTube are playing in the latest election cycles. In the 2006 elections, for example, a brief video posted on YouTube, in which Sen. George Allen (R-Va.) made what many considered a racially charged comment at a campaign rally, completely altered the dynamics of his reelection race. Observers attributed Allen's stunning loss to a political novice to that single video snippet, which provided an unflattering look at the senator.

Cutting-Edge Fundraising

A fundamental but extremely important strategy of interest groups in campaigns is raising and contributing money. Since the Federal Election Campaign Act (FECA) was enacted in the early 1970s, interest groups that want to contribute to a candidate or party have had to do so through a political action committee (PAC). PACs are simply organizations that exist to raise and contribute money in federal elections. Although some PACs are unconnected—they are not affiliated with another organization—most are the fundraising entity of a parent organization. For example, BANKPAC is the PAC of the American Bankers Association. BLUEPAC is affiliated with the Blue Cross and Blue Shield Association. An example of an unconnected PAC is the Prostate Cancer Research PAC, which was formed as an organization in its own right, without ties to any other.

Interest groups have various reasons for wanting to make campaign contributions. Some contribute to try to affect the membership of Congress. They want to elect members of Congress who support the ideas, ideologies, and policy positions of their organization. This is the case with labor unions, which are among the most prolific fundraisers. Because labor unions follow this strategy, they almost always support Democratic candidates; few Republican candidates have platforms that are compatible with unionism. Other interest groups make campaign contributions to the candidates they believe are most likely to win, so as to be in favor with them once they become elected officials. For that reason many PACs tend to favor the incumbents in a race, regardless of their party affiliations or ideologies.

Even if an interest group chooses not to engage in elections by making campaign contributions, it has an interest in raising money. No organization can maintain itself without financial resources; rents, salaries, and other bills need to be paid. Interest groups that are businesses, corporations, or other for-profit entities use a portion of their profits to cover the costs of their lobbying efforts. Some support themselves financially through foundation or government grants or through the generosity of patrons. But other groups, especially membership groups, solicit contributions from individuals. Such solicitation has traditionally been done through massive direct mailings. The mailings typically make emotional appeals in the hope of influencing the recipient to make a financial contribution. Purchasing the mailing lists for these appeals can be costly, as is creating a professional, attractive brochure or packet.

Most interest groups now maintain their own Web sites, which characterize their personality. Some, such as the National Rifle Association (NRA), have a lot of live-action video and movement, highlighting action and independence. Others, such as the Communication Workers of America's Committee on Political Education (CWA-COPE), display a blog-style menu that invites group participation. Technology now makes it possible for a group to collect contributions securely through its Web site. An interest group site may feature a page that enables the visitor to contribute using a credit card or check. At the very least, the Web page can provide the user with a downloadable contribution form, which can be printed and sent to the organization. In some sectors of membership groups, such as civil rights and human rights, environmental, and single-issue groups, almost every Web site allows the user to donate money.

Few, if any, businesses have this donation option on their Web sites, even when they feature a "governmental affairs" page. Business Web sites are geared toward consumers and investors rather than political activists or employees, so that an option for making political contributions would not be appropriate. Labor unions similarly do not make this option available, at least not through the public Web sites. It is likely that once the user enters the "members only site" the option is available. Even without enabling contributions to be made over the Internet, these same businesses and unions are notable contributors to campaigns. For example, Goldman Sachs contributed $3,398,866 in the 2006 midterm elections, and AT&T

contributed $2,905,747. Representing labor, the National Education Association contributed $2,371,427, and the American Federation of State, County and Municipal Employees contributed $2,390,338.[2] Not giving Web site visitors the opportunity to contribute hasn't hampered their ability to raise significant amounts of money.

Some groups are using their Web sites for more aggressive fundraising. Both Handgun Control Inc. and Planned Parenthood have had pop-up windows soliciting donations that confront the visitor as soon as he or she enters the Web site. These pop-ups are more assertive in that the user does not have to look for and click on the fundraising section to see the appeal being made; the pop-up immediately appears, and the user has to click on it to close it.

Curiously, a visit to both these Web sites almost a month after the initial visit revealed that the pop-ups no longer existed—the pop-ups were being used strategically. Two events just prior to the initial Web site visit likely prompted unusually high traffic to both of the sites. First, was the tragedy at Virginia Tech University in which a student gunned down thirty-two of his classmates. Second, was the Supreme Court ruling in *Gonzales v. Carhart* (No.05-380, 05-1382 [2007]) that upheld the federal late-term abortion ban passed by Congress. That legislation disallowed exceptions to the third trimester abortion ban for women whose lives are at risk. These highly publicized events likely prompted some individuals to visit the two Web sites because they either wanted more information or they wanted to do something about the issues at stake. Playing on the possible emotional state of those visitors, the pop-up immediately was in the face of the user, asking for money. In this way, the pop-ups are akin to direct mail sent to individual households, soliciting money by making an emotional appeal. Although direct mail is used on an ongoing basis by some groups, some appeals are timed to follow events that might raise concern about the issue the group represents, a strategy we also see being used with the pop-ups.

Another feature of many of the interest group Web sites is an option to sign up for e-mail alerts. The National Organization of Women (NOW) Web site, for example, features this option under the "Take Action" section and once clicked reveals the message, "Sign Up to Stay Informed about Feminist Issues!" The National Rifle Association simply has a prompt for "E-mail Signup" on its Institute for Legislative Action Web page. On the home page of the World Wildlife Fund's site is the prompt, "Sign up to get conservation news and WWF's free e-newsletter." Most of these prompts are positioned to suggest that subscribers will receive informational updates about the issues of concern. However, as these are among the groups that frequently use direct mail to solicit contributions, it should be no surprise that some would then use the e-mail lists also to solicit contributions.

We collected e-mail updates from a number of these interest groups over several months. Analyzing their content reveals how most groups use this feature. The

League of United Latin American Citizens sends its e-mail network policy updates a couple of times a week. Although the e-mails are primarily informational, a prompt that is part of the template says, "Donate." Defenders of Wildlife uses its network similarly to the way that the NRA and NOW use theirs. All of these groups have similar templates and thus afford the same opportunity to their users. Greenpeace sends out an e-mail alert that breaks the pattern. Prominently featured on the right side of its e-mail, in an eye-catching green color, is the list "3 Ways to Help." The first is, "Donate."

A few groups use e-mail for the sole purpose of fundraising. Common Cause had a campaign to raise $50,000 to support a bill making its way through Congress to require voting machines to create a paper record. The e-mail alert urged the reader to make a contribution to help reach the $50,000 mark. The Wilderness Society distributed an e-mail urging contributions on behalf of saving the Tongass National Forest. Defenders of Wildlife has also employed this technique. At the same time, a number of groups send e-mail alerts that do not include the option of giving, not even in the background template. Among these groups are Environmental Action, the Natural Resources Defense Council, Friends of the Earth, Environmental Defense, Amnesty International, the National Center for Employee Ownership, and the National Taxpayers Union.

Although it seems as if an e-mail network would frequently be used to solicit contributions, most e-mail only includes a passive prompt in the background giving the option of making a donation online. Very few groups use the network solely to raise money, and even the ones that do more frequently send e-mails requesting some other type of political action. E-mails asking for money are used sparingly. During roughly the same period that we were monitoring these e-mails (both action alerts and the ones asking for money), a steady stream of direct mail was sent out explicitly seeking money. The Sierra Club, the American Civil Liberties Union (ACLU), Defenders of Wildlife, National Wildlife Federation, People for the American Way, Greenpeace, and Beyond Pesticides are just a handful of senders of the almost-daily direct mailings we received. Not only have groups not yet abandoned the age-old practice of using direct mail, but they are fattening their lists with addresses that are provided when individuals subscribe to e-mail alerts.[3]

Issue Advocacy and Independent Expenditures

The law limits how much money PACs can contribute to campaigns. The current campaign finance law stipulates that no more than $2,300 per election may be contributed to any candidate, and no more than $28,500 per year may be contributed to any national party committee (in the 2008 election cycle). For those PACs and interest groups that raise tens of millions of dollars each election cycle, these are severe constraints. Interest groups have found ways to circumvent them, however, raising and spending money in ways that are influential in elections yet still legal.

The first way is by engaging in issue advocacy. "Issue advocacy" is the term used to identify any money that is spent advocating some specific issue or policy position. For example, the League of Conservation Voters may seek to advance its anti–oil drilling position. During elections, its advocacy is constructed to highlight not only the issue but also a candidate's stance on that issue. During the 2004 election, for example, the League ran an ad highlighting President George W. Bush's support of drilling for oil off the coast of Pensacola, Florida. Although the ad makes clear that the group does not support the reelection of Bush, it never explicitly says so. Because they contain no explicit call for the election or defeat of a candidate, these types of ads technically are about issues, not the elections, and therefore are protected by the group's free speech rights. There is therefore no limit on the amount of money an interest group may spend on issue advocacy.

Issue advocacy often takes the form of "voters' guides." Ratings, scorecards, and voters' guides enable interest groups to provide helpful cues to members and the public. Ratings and scorecards evaluate incumbent legislators' support for an interest group's agenda, usually by listing votes on important bills and amendments and summarizing that information as a numerical score that ranges from zero to 100 percent support. Ratings, which generally provide longer and more complex evaluations of incumbents' votes, are aimed primarily at activists, lobbyists, and journalists. Scorecards, usually shorter and simpler, are aimed primarily at interest group members. Voters' guides present incumbent and nonincumbent candidates' positions on issues of concern to interest groups and their members.

For example, the National Federation of Independent Businesses rates legislators according to their roll call votes on bills affecting small business. The Human Rights Campaign issues a scorecard rating the voting records of legislators on issues of concern to gays and lesbians. As with endorsements, scorecards and voters' guides can have varied impacts on elections. A rural legislator might consider a 100 percent rating from the NRA a proud achievement, whereas an urban legislator might find a favorable ranking from the NRA a political liability. Once again, although they implicitly endorse some candidates over others, because they do not do so explicitly these voters' guides are considered issue advocacy and are subject to no spending limits.

When an advertisement explicitly calls for the election or defeat of a candidate, and it is made and paid for independently of the candidate's campaign, it is considered an "independent expenditure." Independent expenditures are any expenses incurred advocating for or against a candidate without any coordination with the candidates' campaigns. These expenditures are also protected by a group's free speech rights and are therefore not subject to spending limits. Although much independent-expenditure and issue advocacy activity by interest groups focuses on television commercials, they also purchase ads in newspapers, send out literature to voters, and buy radio commercials.

Independent expenditures and issue advocacy are strategies that have been tried and tested by interest groups and therefore remain extremely popular. Internet technology has brought these strategies to a whole new level. Most important in this regard are interest group Web sites and Web sites such as YouTube. Buying air time for commercials is extremely costly. Once a commercial is created, however, it can find a home either on the interest group's Web site or on YouTube, where it can be played over and over for free, living in perpetuity. Because such advertising over the Internet is free, it has also allowed interest groups to move beyond the thirty-second spot to make longer commercials, which can communicate more information to viewers. These longer commercials are being made exclusively for viewing over the Internet.

Since the 2004 elections a new type of interest group has emerged that engages exclusively in issue advocacy. The 527 committee is named after Section 527 of the Internal Revenue Code, which covers political organizations and traditionally has been used only by candidate or party committees. Engaging solely in issue advocacy, 527 committees or groups do not have to register with the Federal Election Commission. These groups have been raising and spending unprecedented amounts of money. For example, in the 2004 election the top five 527 committees spent a combined $168.6 million. The top five 527 committees spent a combined $53.4 million in the 2006 midterm elections. These groups have gained notoriety in a short time partly because of the controversial issue advocacy they engage in.

Sometimes an interest group, or a 527 committee, has created a controversial commercial with the intent of generating so much buzz that it gains free media, that is, mainstream news coverage. This type of media buy is often referred to as a "vanity" buy. The strategy was purportedly used by the Swift Boat Veterans for Truth, a 527 committee that spent $22.6 million in 2004 to help reelect President Bush. During August 2004, the group ran a television commercial that accused Democratic presidential candidate John Kerry of lying about his war record. The controversy lay in that the "swift boat veterans" featured in the ad claimed that they had all served with Kerry. Although that was true, only one of the men was actually a crewmate. The others had served on different swift boats. Analysts are convinced that this ad was a "vanity" buy because, although the group purchased air time for it in three swing states, the markets were small and the air time purchased was limited.[4]

In sum, interest groups that are able to raise large amounts of money do not allow the contribution limits of the current campaign finance laws to hamper their spending. To get around the restrictions, they engage in issue advocacy and funnel their money toward independent expenditures. Whether they buy air time for their commercials, buy advertising space in major newspapers, or compile voters' guides, they are finding ways to reach voters during elections.

Informing via Webcasts and Podcasts

Another way in which groups attempt to shape the issue agenda of elections is by providing information directly to like-minded individuals. That way the groups can frame the issue so as to emphasize their own policy positions. Technology has transformed this technique by enabling rapid transmission of news, campaign updates, and policy updates via webcasts and podcasts.

A webcast is a live video feed or broadcast over the Internet. Webcasts are scheduled for live airing much as television shows are. A group's leadership can schedule a webcast, advertise it to its membership and other interested individuals, and then be able to enter the homes of the many supporters watching. An added benefit of webcasts is that usually they are then stored as a video file, accessible on the Web site for multiple viewings after the initial broadcast. Podcasts are audio files that are fed over the Internet in a format that can be downloaded and listened to on an MP3 player. Podcasting enables a radio type of broadcast that is freely available to any subscriber. The advantage of podcasting is that the organization can feature news that is of interest to its members. The organization gets to pick the subject of the podcast and frame issues that serve its own interests.

Although only a small percentage of interest groups feature this technology on their Web sites, certain groups are more likely to use it than others. Webcasts are more frequently found on trade association and business Web sites, particularly those involved in the banking, finance, insurance, and real estate sectors and in the industrial, construction, and transportation sectors. This type of technology suits their needs, as these groups traditionally have used face-to-face meetings to communicate within their hierarchically structured organizations. Webcasts provide a cost-efficient alternative to meetings. They open a direct line of communication between the leadership and the workers or members. Podcasts, on the other hand, are particularly favored by membership groups in the civil rights and human rights sector. Rarely do the members of these groups meet with interest group staff or representatives. While webcasts might not serve their needs, podcasting is a viable method of feeding information to subscribers. Podcasting is likely to grow in popularity as more and more Americans choose to outfit themselves with MP3 players.

Recruiting and Training Candidates

By reaching out to potential candidates and offering encouragement and support, interest groups can also influence who decides to run for office. By offering training, groups can potentially influence who wins elections. Many groups find that the most reliable and loyal candidates are drawn from the ranks of their own organizations. The AFL-CIO, for example, decided that it can best promote its policy goals by recruiting its own members, rather than by recruiting and training candidates from outside the labor movement, who may agree with some—but not all—

of the labor agenda. In 2000, 2,141 union members either held or ran for public office in the United States. The AFL-CIO has announced an initiative called "Target 5,000," to raise the number of union members in public service to that figure.[5]

Although interest groups sometimes look within their own ranks to recruit candidates, many recruit nonmembers as well. Recruitment is very important for groups that traditionally have been underrepresented in U.S. politics, many of whom would lack the resources or the knowledge to compete effectively without the support of organized groups.

The National Women's Political Caucus (NWPC), for example, has mounted a large-scale effort to recruit women to run for public office. The caucus holds training events to teach state and local activists how to identify potentially strong candidates and campaign managers. The national organization provides a training manual to local recruiters to help them identify women who might fit the profile of a good candidate in a legislative district. The manual also offers advice to potential candidates to overcome various concerns they might have about the task of running for office. Thousands of women have participated in NWPC candidate training seminars, including Rep. Linda Sanchez (D-Calif.), who says that she got her start in politics by attending one of these events.[6] Many other groups hold training seminars for potential candidates and provide various other resources such as training manuals, video and audio tapes, and access to pollsters and campaign consultants.

The decision to recruit and train candidates is based on two considerations: first, whether the person agrees with the policy goals of the organization, and second, whether the person has a realistic chance of winning. Groups want to expend their resources strategically and may turn away from an ambitious person who supports key policy stands but is not likely to win an election for whatever reason.

Endorsements and Hit Lists

Many organizations issue formal endorsements to signal to their members which candidates best represent their viewpoint. Endorsements are primarily means to convince group members to vote for the candidates who will be most friendly to the group's interests once elected. Not all groups issue endorsements. Some do not so as to maintain tax-exempt status. Others make a strategic decision not to alienate candidates who might win and become unfavorably inclined toward those who had endorsed their opponent. Corporate and trade groups often avoid endorsements because they do not want to create controversy within their own organizations, or offend stockholders, or even give cause to consumer groups to initiate boycotts. Nonetheless, ideological and policy-oriented groups mostly favor issuing endorsements as a means to influence elections.

The endorsement is not only a signal to group members as to which candidates win the "seal of approval," but it is also a means to persuade a larger public. Thus, an endorsement from the Sierra Club or the League of Conservation Voters would be a strong signal to voters as to which candidate in a campaign is more environmentally friendly. A National Rifle Association endorsement tells many voters which candidate is likely to uphold the interests of gun owners. Groups have to issue endorsements carefully and strategically, however, because they can backfire. For example, a moderate GOP candidate running for Congress from an urban district could find his or her electoral chances hurt by an NRA endorsement, which would stand as a negative symbol to voters in that area. Similarly, a Democratic candidate running from a socially conservative district in the Deep South would probably not want the endorsement of the National Abortion Rights Action League Pro-Choice America.

In addition to issuing positive endorsements, interest groups may single out candidates for defeat via what is commonly known as a "hit list." Perhaps the best known hit list is the "Dirty Dozen" named by the League of Conservation Voters (LCV). It is a list of those the League considers the twelve most environmentally unfriendly members of Congress. By using a catchy and memorable name for the list, the LCV succeeds in attracting media and public attention to the races where it has targeted candidates for defeat. Some groups target candidates for defeat without calling the roll of names a hit list.

Hit lists are far less common than endorsements for a variety of reasons. First, a group may fear being perceived as excessively negative. Second, the lists antagonize incumbents, who will most likely go on to win reelection. Third, group members are more likely to quit a group because of a disagreement over targeting a candidate than because of an endorsement. As with endorsements, hit lists can backfire. The gay rights organization Human Rights Campaign targeted North Carolina senator Jesse Helms (R) for defeat in 1996, only to see the conservative senator hold up the attack on him as a badge of honor. It is likely that advertising Helms as the anti–gay rights candidate in a conservative southern state actually helped him to win the support of many voters.

Although groups use a variety of techniques to try to influence campaigns, technology is changing at a rapid pace and redefining how races are conducted. Groups that can offer resources to candidates, in an environment that is demanding more and more knowledge of how to exploit emerging trends, thus become more influential.

The Future of Groups in Campaigns: From Candidate-Centered to Group-Centered Politics

For years scholars have written about the evolution of the American electoral process from a party-centered to a candidate-centered system. According to the conventional analysis, political party organizations were once the focal points of campaigns. The parties controlled the process of candidate selection, and they had real influence on platforms and policies. Then beginning in the 1960s and 1970s, with a series of reforms, the parties started to lose their grip on nominations, platforms, and policies. Instead, candidates themselves began to seek nominations through popular primaries and often ignored the party apparatus. Party platforms became merely symbolic, and elected officials came to feel that they owed nothing to their party on policy. Campaigns thus became focused on candidates, and parties were, according to some, relegated to mere labels.

Although parties have always been stronger than the candidate-centered-politics thesis suggests, there is no doubt that campaigns have evolved to allow for more independence from the parties on the part of political candidates. That trend is being fostered in part by the ever-increasing role of interest groups. Candidates today do not need to rely so heavily on party organizations as in the past because they can benefit from the electoral activities of supportive groups to advertise a message and mobilize voters. After the Supreme Court decision in *Federal Election Commission v. Wisconsin Right to Life* (09-969 [2007]), which overturned the ban on issue advocacy, interest groups are likely to play a stronger independent role in the future. Although interest groups may not supplant parties, it is likely that as we approach the 2010 and 2012 elections the power of such groups will rival the power of political parties.

It is possible that the U.S. electoral system is undergoing yet another evolution, from candidate-centered to increasingly group-centered politics. Groups are more involved than ever before in electoral politics, and often their activities do more to influence campaign discourse than do the parties and the candidates themselves. This development raises an important question to ponder: How is democratic accountability affected when the voices of those whose names appear on the ballot are overwhelmed by the steady and ever-louder stream of noise from organized groups? In the past, interest groups fostered strong links to candidates and political parties and thus had a positive role in enhancing accountability to citizens. Interest groups have actually strengthened political parties in the past and helped define the issue agendas of candidates more clearly for the public. For example, labor interest groups such as the AFL-CIO have traditionally been known for their links to the Democratic Party, while the U.S. Chamber of Commerce has been known for its relationship with the Republican Party.

Today, not only is the symbiosis between interest groups and parties weakening, but so are the links between interest groups and candidates. Interest groups are becoming more independent as electoral entrepreneurs, advancing their own agendas and asserting themselves in election contests even when the candidates do not welcome their activities. Groups such as the NRA on the right and MoveOn.org on the left are not likely to be dissuaded by parties or candidates from involvement in individual races.

New Technologies Enhance the Power of Interest Groups in Campaigns

What then is the future of interest groups in campaigns? It is likely that groups will be increasingly active and influential as they exploit new technologies and means of communication. As one group leader put it, "The speed, scale, and precision with which issue groups can target candidates for communications from their membership and supporter base" will continue to advance. Viral communications techniques can "geometrically multiply the power of the membership base." [7] Whereas in the past groups focused on communication to mobilize a finite membership base to political action, in the future they will look not only to mobilize their base but to use it to create much broader and more diffuse political pressure in campaigns. The emphasis will be on pushing issue agendas out into the public, rather than on forming bonds with candidates and party organizations as in the past.

Groups are also experimenting with ways to connect to potential voters through popular social networking sites on the Internet. As the Sierra Club's Greg Haegle put it, the potential payoff for groups could be substantial, if they can find ways to tap into social networks without undermining the very thing that attracts people to the sites in the first place—social bonds. Influencing potential voters, especially young people, to think of political activism and group politics as part of a social bond is a special challenge but one with strong potential for groups to exploit. Young voters used to adopt the party affiliation of their parents and hold onto those political bonds for a lifetime. As voters have become increasingly independent of the parties, they have also sought out alternative sources of political identification and networking. Groups will need to look for ways to attract the attention of these potential voters and convince them that certain issues are more paramount than others.

Internet fundraising and organizing have been increasingly successful in recent election cycles, as particular issues or even candidates have attracted voter enthusiasm. For groups this means that it will be more difficult in the future to rely on traditional means of building a steady core of dues-paying members; they will have to exert more effort to attract the attention of issues-conscious citizens. Haegle, for example, may find convincing many environmentally conscious people to join the Sierra Club and write a check every year a greater challenge than did his predecessors. But he has available to him many more technologies to promote environmental issues before the public and to influence voters and candidates to place those issues at the forefront of campaigns.

Interest groups use their Web sites as receptacles for their members in the virtual world. They produce information, establish blogs for feedback, and enable their members to feel involved. The cyclical dynamic enables the interest group organization and its individual members to contribute and consume information. Alan Locke, publisher of *Winning Campaigns* magazine, argues that Web sites attract the interested and the "faithful." [8] Interest groups can use Web sites as effectively if not better than parties or candidates because they have an ideological constituency that will normally traffic to their site. In the next decade, interest groups will likely become more adept at mobilizing their existing base to participate in the elections process. Moreover, if interest groups can harness that advance to substantially increase their fundraising, then their potency and reach will increase as well.

Conclusion

Despite all of the work that groups do to advertise issues and promote the fortunes of sympathetic candidates, campaigns will continue to lambaste "the politics of special interests." Whether they are Democrats, Republicans, or independents, candidates find that attacking interest groups has populist appeal. But interest groups are healthier than ever today because sophisticated techniques to reach constituents—such as e-mail, blogs, podcasting, and online videos, as well as traditional snail mail—enable them to remain in continual contact with their members. This is critical not only for fundraising but for mobilization to get out the vote. Although interest groups may never be a popular feature of the electoral environment, they will continue to be at the forefront of campaigns in U.S. politics.

Notes

1. Mark J. Rozell, Clyde Wilcox, and David Madland, *Interest Groups in American Campaigns: The New Face of Electioneering,* 2nd ed. (Washington, D.C.: CQ Press, 2006); Richard J. Semiatin and Mark J. Rozell, "Interest Groups in Congressional Elections," in *The Interest Group Connection,* 2nd ed., edited by Paul S. Herrnson, Ronald G. Shaiko, and Clyde Wilcox (Washington, D.C.: CQ Press, 2005), 75–88.
2. Campaign contribution data come from the Web site maintained by the Center for Responsive Politics, www.opensecrets.org. They compile in a user-friendly format data that are publicly available through the Federal Election Commission.
3. Although the individual is signing up for an e-mail alert, the interest group typically asks for a name and home address in addition to the e-mail address. This technique helps them add to their own mailing lists, and the lists are also sold to other groups for profit.

4. This information was obtained from Source Watch, a Web site maintained by the Center for Media and Democracy, www.sourcewatch.org.

5. Mark J. Rozell, Clyde Wilcox, and David Madland, *Interest Groups in American Campaigns: The New Face of Electioneering,* 2nd ed. (Washington, D.C.: CQ Press, 2006), 37.

6. National Women's Political Caucus, "National Women's Political Caucus Training Program," www.nwpc.org/ht/d/sp/i/47229/pid/47229 (accessed July 16, 2007).

7. Greg Haegle, Sierra Club, personal interview by e-mail, July 5, 2007.

8. Alan Locke, editor, *Winning Campaigns,* personal interview, July 12, 2007.

CHAPTER 9

Campaign Press Coverage — At the Speed of Light

Jeremy D. Mayer

AMERICAN CAMPAIGNS ARE GETTING FASTER and, paradoxically, longer at the same time. Sound bites that played on the news for sixty seconds in 1968 have now been reduced to seven seconds. The rhythm of media coverage determines the pace of the modern campaign at all levels of politics. The speed of coverage makes for more volatile campaigns, where the dynamic of a race can be altered by a single posting on YouTube. Political attacks, which used to take weeks or at least days to hit the airwaves and make an impact on the voters, now reach citizens at the click of a computer button. Speed is the most obvious change but far from the only one that the Internet is making in the way campaigns appear to the American public—and the Internet is now an indispensable part of news coverage. Given the declining ratings for national news networks and the even more rapid decline in newspaper circulation, campaign news has begun to go online all the time. That is why the emergence of online media is the focus our attention in this chapter.

It is only natural to expect that the Internet will radically alter the way the news media cover campaigns. After all, the rise of television to media dominance fundamentally changed election coverage. Television reduced the importance of issues and raised the profile of personalities and private scandals, from the rise of John Kennedy to the depths of the Bill Clinton/Monica Lewinsky scandal. The Internet will have even greater decentralizing effects both on campaigns and on media power. This process has already begun, as campaigns put more emphasis on online media of both the free and paid varieties. The age of the Internet also raises fundamental questions about the distinctions among citizens, reporters, and political actors. The clear lines that separated those groups are fraying. The evolution of our media also opens new opportunities for "narrowcasting," in which discrete messages are targeted at specific groups, bypassing the traditional news media, and for rapid responses to emerging media themes.

However, the dangers that the new media present to campaigns are obvious. The Internet is taking away customers from the print and broadcast news. Yet the Internet is not producing reporters of the quality of those in the print media, at least. Beyond that, constant surveillance of candidates greatly exacerbates the brutal nature of modern politics. The most qualified candidates may simply decide not to take part in the new politics, in which there are almost no limits to what is covered. There are hordes of hostile Web sites waiting to seize on the smallest mistake that can be magnified and endlessly repeated on the Drudge Report or the Daily Kos. Web sites do not even abide by the few remaining rules of propriety that limit our mainstream media, and they fact-check much less.

This essay traces the role of the press in covering campaigns, then discusses the plight of the traditional media and its implications. Finally, I discuss trends in the way the Internet is shaping press coverage, as the net lacks traditional journalistic standards of review and any filter to confirm news stories. We call this "filterlessness." It is irrevocably changing press coverage because separating facts from rumors becomes muddled when campaigns must respond immediately. New media have increased the reactiveness of politics, as we shall see.

Origins and Development of American Press Coverage

The major venue of political discourse for most of U.S. history was newspapers. When America was deciding how to govern itself after the revolution, men such as James Madison and Alexander Hamilton wrote newspaper articles advocating the new Constitution (today we know those articles as *The Federalist Papers*). The national campaigns for and against ratifying the Constitution were fought in the pages of the nation's newspapers.

The First Century: Strong Links between Parties and Newspapers

During the nation's first century, newspapers had a relationship to campaigns that would surprise most of today's readers. Back then, most papers openly supported one party or the other. A survey of 359 newspapers published in 1810 could find only thirty-three that had no party affiliation.[1] The modern idea of separating the news section from the opinion page was also unknown. It was easy to tell by simply looking at the headlines of the day which party a newspaper supported. Indeed, many newspapers put the name of the party into their titles. For this reason, larger cities during the nineteenth century would have a minimum of two newspapers, one for each party. So tight was the relationship between parties and newspapers that often the local party would meet at the offices of the local newspaper, since parties lacked infrastructure at that time. Reporters were expected to follow the party line announced by the editor and the publisher in their coverage. The presses of supportive newspapers also were used to print party pamphlets, and even presidents picked one newspaper, called a "house organ," to publish their views and also to benefit from government contracts.[2] Mob violence against newspaper offices happened several times during America's early history, when supporters of one party would attack the newspaper controlled by the other party.[3] This "partisan press" era persisted well into the twentieth century in many American cities, where the newspaper was key to political machines run by local parties.

Links Weaken between Parties and Newspapers

At the national level, the strong linkage between parties and newspapers in campaigns began to weaken in the late nineteenth century with the rise of the mass media. Newspaper empires such as the ones created by William Randolph Hearst and Joseph Pulitzer were designed to appeal to readers across party lines; they could not be so directly tied to the interests of a single party. At the same time, standards of professional journalistic ethics began to emerge. More and more, journalists were expected to at least attempt to be objective as they covered political campaigns and to avoid conflicts of interest. During political campaigns, newspapers became more like referees in a boxing match, rather than the cheering supporters they had been in the partisan press era. There were notable exceptions, and certainly journalists, editors, and publishers were not perfect in their adherence to objectivity, to say the least. But now the norm was at least to appear to be fair, which was a significant change from the nineteenth century. Journalism also became a true profession during the early twentieth century, as the first schools of journalism were founded. In the past, those covering American campaigns were often working-class writers without college degrees or family wealth. Journalism, previously not a prestigious occupation, was becoming desirable and even occasionally well paid.

Emerging Mass Media

During the early years of the twentieth century, radio networks emerged across America and the world. Yet radio never became the dominant medium for campaign coverage or advertising. During the era of radio's greatest popularity, the major newspapers were still more important in setting the nation's agenda. However, radio's rapid rise signaled that newspapers were vulnerable to electronic media. Television emerged after World War II and eventually replaced the papers as the dominant means of political communication. The moment when television came to dominate U.S. presidential campaigns is commonly identified as the Kennedy-Nixon debates of 1960. Those listening on the radio believed the debate to have been a tie. Those watching on television believed that the far more charismatic Kennedy had won.[4] American political campaigns would never be the same. It had of course been an advantage in politics to be reasonably attractive. Yet prior to television we had elected men who were widely acknowledged to be homely, such as Abraham Lincoln, or morbidly obese, such as William Howard Taft. Television has forced American politicians at all levels to pay more attention to their looks than ever before. In 2007, presidential candidates Mitt Romney (R-Mass.) and John Edwards (D-N.C.) were both criticized for spending thousands of dollars of campaign money on makeup artists or hairstylists. But looking as good as possible on television has been a vital part of every American campaign since Kennedy and Nixon.

The Power of Television

The impact of television on campaigns has been vast and goes beyond makeup and hairstylists. It focused more attention on image and sound and less on logic and thought. Television contributed directly to the decline of issues in U.S. elections and the rise of personality and individual character as decisive factors.[5] And television may be more powerful in its campaign coverage than the medium of print ever was because it can have a dramatic effect on voter choice in presidential primaries.[6] It does so not only through directly making a candidate look competent or incompetent, corrupt or honest, charismatic or dull. The media also run the expectations game, which can make winners of losers and losers of winners. A candidate expected to win a primary overwhelmingly, such as Sen. Edmund Muskie (D-Maine) in the New Hampshire primary of 1972, is declared the loser for failing to win by a sufficient amount. A candidate could be anointed by the media (and himself) as the "comeback kid" even though he finished second, as Governor Bill Clinton did in New Hampshire in 1992. The point in some primaries has been not to win or to avoid losing, but simply to surpass expectations set by the media.

Fundamentally television put the media at the heart of political power in America by supplanting means of communication that favored political institutions, such as parties, and by separating those institutions from their own elected officials.

If American campaigns today are the worst examples of television's pervasive and perverting effect on politics, then it would be expected that the presidents elected during the television era would have been worse than those produced by the print era. However, that may not actually have occurred. Although some of the least successful presidents have been elected during the television era (Richard Nixon, Jimmy Carter, and possibly George W. Bush), some that have been widely acknowledged by historians as capable or even great leaders have also won the White House (Kennedy, Reagan). Certainly many mediocre and incompetent presidents, such as Warren Harding, managed to be elected long before television ads appeared.

An Era of Transformation: The Decline of Mainstream Media

The emergence of powerful broadcast media has often been correlated with the decline of the newspaper industry. According to the Project for Excellence in Journalism, the number of daily papers in the United States declined from over 1,900 in 1940 to slightly over 1,400 by 2000. Interestingly, the total circulation of newspapers did not begin to decline until 1990. Furthermore, the rise of national newspapers, such as *USAToday*, helped compensate for the loss of papers in rural, suburban, and urban markets.[7] It implies that national and local campaign coverage was being consolidated in fewer newspapers. For example, the *Houston Post* went out of business in 1995, leaving the *Houston Chronicle* as the only major daily in Houston. Large corporations such as Hearst (which bought the *Chronicle* in 1994) and News Corporation (which bought the *Wall Street Journal* in 2007) have been accused of homogenizing news coverage. According to FCC commissioner Jonathan Adelstein, "It raises a real question as to whether or not there is independence between ownership and the journalists." [8]

Consolidation occurred not only among newspapers but in broadcast television as well. News broadcasts have become more similar and more focused on ratings. Corporations hire consultants to improve the image of local and national news programs. *ABC News* anchor Charles Gibson points out the problem: "Well, news directors who rely on consultants wind up producing newscasts that look like every other newscast around . . . and program merely what they think people want to watch. . . . [T]hey're not directing anything, they're being directed." [9] The focus becomes less on reporting the news than on image, increasing the personality-driven aspect of campaigns.

The rise of cable television drove the network news ratings of ABC, CBS, and NBC down 20 percent from 1980 to 1992. Competition from new media (such as the Internet) has also reduced the audience for evening network newscasts. Nielsen Media Research has shown that the audience watching all network news (including cable) dropped from approximately 42 million in 1992 to 26 million in 2006—a decline of 38 percent.[10] More citizens are turning away from television news, while online audiences increase dramatically.

Cutting-Edge Cost Effects on Political Campaign Coverage

The Costs of the Digital Divide: Mass Media and End Users

The Internet changes the financial equation, creating a "digital divide" separating people who can fully consume information and news on the Internet and those with limited or no access. The divide used to be primarily between those who did or did not own a computer. Now, given how important Internet video has become, it is sometimes characterized as a divide between those who can afford broadband access and those who are still dialing up. Even though Nielsen/Netratings found that 80 percent of the Internet market now uses broadband, and the percentage of those using a dial-up connection is declining rapidly, in key regions of the country it remains a problem.[11] Broadband access means more opportunities to obtain information about politics, including campaigns. For example, news organizations now use broadband to broadcast political events such as debates live to voters. This is just the beginning.

In 2007, when YouTube and CNN jointly sponsored Republican and Democratic debates in which presidential candidates faced homemade video questions prepared by viewers, there was jubilation in the online media about the way the format would empower ordinary citizens to participate. However, during the Democratic debate in Charleston, South Carolina, the *Washington Post* pointed out, an estimated 40 percent to 45 percent of Charleston residents had no Internet access, and even more lacked the broadband access that would allow them to watch the debate, let alone submit video questions.[12] Although the digital divide limits democratic participation in some cases, it is less profound than the cost effects on the production side.

The Advantage of Online News Production: Costs Driven Down

It is on the production side that the Internet is having the greater impact, particularly for the new wave of media, bloggers. A blogger such as Andrew Sullivan or a "journalist" such as Matt Drudge has remarkably low overhead. The smaller Internet presences have even smaller budgetary outlays. For example, newspapers are limited because every inch of space has a fixed cost. On the Internet, however, there is limitless space. As a result Sullivan and Drudge, and lesser-known Internet journalists and bloggers, have had a tremendous impact on American politics, for better or worse. While still a relatively unknown Internet journalist, Drudge first reported the Monica Lewinsky scandal on his site. The story spread rapidly and became widely reported in the mass media. Reporters face competition from anyone with a laptop and Internet access, and that can matter in a campaign.

Part I. On the Edge of Change: Politics at the Speed of Light

Perhaps the greatest change the Internet has introduced into American campaign coverage is the pace at which politics is conducted. The twenty-four-hour news cycle was much discussed when cable television first rose to prominence, since it suggested that campaigns and government institutions would no longer have a full day in which to plan their reaction to a development and make decisions. The

Internet has sped this up even further. For example, on September 17, 2000, the Bush and Gore campaigns for president strafed the reporters on their press e-mail lists (consisting of 2,000 and 1,200 names, respectively) with fifty-six e-mails. Most of these concerned a sixteen-page "Blueprint for the Middle Class" issued by the Republican nominee. The Democrat's "pre-buttal" was twenty-four pages long. The fifty-six e-mails spun and re-spun around the topic of which candidate had the better economic plan for America.[13]

Lessons from the 2000 and 2004 Campaigns

If a reporter gets something that occurs at a public event wrong, an average citizen can challenge the media account directly to the reporter's Web site or on their own blog. Some of the most famous mistakes in campaign coverage might have been caught earlier if they had happened in the age of Internet dominance. For example, in 2000, two national reporters badly misquoted Vice President Al Gore as claiming he had been the first to bring the Love Canal chemical disaster to the nation's attention. What Gore actually said was factually correct, but the reporters' inaccurate account fit into the Republican portrayal of Gore as a serial liar and exaggerator. Although the Internet existed in 2000, it had not yet achieved the penetration that it has today. The false story about Gore was used to batter his reputation for weeks.[14]

Only four years later, a larger error was more quickly corrected. In 2004, *CBS News* ran a major story on documents that allegedly showed that President George W. Bush had refused a direct order to appear for duty during his service in the Texas Air National Guard during the Vietnam era. While the public had long known that Bush used family connections to get into the Guard during a time when it was a popular way for wealthy men to avoid the war, the documents revitalized the issue of Bush's wartime conduct and his later failure to fulfill the terms of his enlistment. Very quickly, thanks to conservative bloggers, questions emerged about the documents' authenticity. Experts and amateurs pointed out numerous factual and stylistic problems with the documents. In a massive humiliation for *CBS News* and the main reporter on the story, Dan Rather, the network was forced to admit that the documents were probably forgeries. Rather, long accused by conservatives of having a liberal bias, faced difficult questions about how he had so quickly accepted as legitimate anti-Bush documents that had been rejected by other mainstream media outlets as highly questionable. Without the Internet's amazing ability to link people rapidly, citizens would have lacked the ability to quickly challenge the *CBS News* story.

Both stories demonstrate the synergistic power between traditional media and the Internet today. Stories are reported rapidly, often without fact-checking, as more media compete in the marketplace. Not only does this have implications for what the press does, but it puts campaigns in a position where they have to be reactive. Damage control is now a 24/7 operation for major national political campaigns, as they have to respond rapidly to news events. Failure to do so can have serious consequences, as John Kerry (D-Mass.) found out in the summer of 2004 when he failed to respond to charges of the "Swift Boat Veterans for Truth," which questioned whether he truly was a Vietnam War hero. The Swift Boat Veterans advertisement was widely reported as news on the Internet, in major newspapers, and by national broadcasters. That Kerry was slow to respond gave greater credibility to the charges. Eventually an *ABC News Nightline* investigation in Vietnam, with eyewitnesses, gave a more accurate story, but it was already October and the damage had been done.[15]

Part II. On the Edge of Change: Citizen Groups as Campaign Reporters

Citizen groups have emerged as the new press in the twenty-first century. However citizen groups do not have the reporting standards that mainstream news organizations such as the *New York Times* or *ABC News* have in covering stories. Their agenda is to promote and persuade rather than report facts. As a result, they often fail to filter their stories and check them for veracity, as we expect the mainstream media to do. These unfiltered groups are a third force in national politics and campaigns today, and likely tomorrow.

Citizen Groups: An Unfiltered Challenge to Mainstream Media Covering Campaigns

In addition to speeding up campaigns and media coverage, the Internet makes it easy for a citizen activist to start up a Web page or blog or to comment on an existing one. This poses serious problems for mainstream media outlets, which now have competition for news and information. The grassroots fervor and involvement that voters experience on Web sites like Daily Kos and Free Republic confound the major media companies in their attempts to compete with these groups for "viewers."

At the Daily Kos, the largest left-wing political Web site in number of unique daily visitors, anonymous posters can become famous quickly if they write well, post frequently, and battle the right with panache. Similarly, the slightly less interactive and more filtered Free Republic is the leading spot on the Web where right wingers can (once they register and become trusted) interact with one another. Both Kos and Free Republic have been involved in rallying voters for mass demonstrations and fundraising.

Over the Edge: When Online Groups Become Campaign News

MoveOn.org, the nation's largest grassroots Internet political organization, decided in 2004 to hold a national contest called "Bush in 30 Seconds." MoveOn's Voter Fund invited submissions of thirty-second anti-Bush ads. The concept was brilliant—harness the wild and diffuse creativity of Americans, and somewhere ten or twenty unknown writers and directors will come up with a few ads that are better than the ones the professional political consultants come up with. The judging process, in which MoveOn members would watch videos and vote for their favorites, boosted the visibility of the site. Ultimately, MoveOn hoped that it would come up with unusual and vivid ads and simultaneously raise the money to run them. The contest was a huge success in terms of number of submissions, number of page views, the amount of money raised, and the stunning quality of the top thirty or so ads.

But two ads, out of 1,500 published on the site, had images of Bush speaking juxtaposed with images of Adolph Hitler ranting. Although MoveOn.org eventually identified and removed the offensive ads, the comparison attracted national mainstream media attention. The clips were prominently displayed on right-wing Web sites as examples of "MoveOn" ads. The fact that MoveOn merely provided a forum for the ads, and did not create, or sponsor, or in any way fund them, was irrelevant.[16]

The MoveOn Incident's Impact: Unfiltered Reporting Gets a Black Eye

The MoveOn incident suggests one reason why media outlets such as CNN and *The New York Times* cannot easily take advantage of filterlessness, or "wiki" (fast) technologies. If you go to most mainstream media Web sites, there are fewer blogs and very little opportunity for visitors to shape the content in a "wiki" fashion. "Wikis" are public sites that allow registered members of a community to alter the content of a blog or Web page. If CNN instituted an "Upload your own video of the 2008 campaign" feature, it would be inundated with hundreds if not thousands of videos from the hard-core partisans of both sides, as well as radical videos from the fringes of American politics. The major media companies realize they cannot afford to be associated with something offensive, and they cannot afford the staff that it would take to monitor such comments.

Thus, fervent partisans looking for a way to express their own views must go to Web sites like MoveOn, Daily Kos, or the Free Republic. In this way, the filterlessness of the Web weakens the mainstream media, siphoning off attention and money to new media sites. It should also be noted that most of the links to information at Kos and Free Republic are to mainstream media coverage because almost no actual reporting takes place at either site.

Part III. On the Edge of Change: Campaigns as Reporters—Opponent Surveillance Expands in the Twenty-First Century

In the nineteenth century, many men ran for president while seldom leaving their homes. These "front porch" campaigns were possible in an era of print discourse. Media scrutiny of the daily lives of the candidates was minimal. In the twenty-first century, candidates even at the congressional level are finding themselves trailed by opposition partisans who tape every moment of their campaigns and even their daily lives, hoping to find a gaffe, an unflattering or ridiculous image, or best of all, some hint of scandal.

The rise of the Internet combined with miniaturization of video technology has changed what is considered fair game for campaign coverage. Thirty years ago, when Larry Sabato wrote *Feeding Frenzy*, about how the media had taken over the presidential campaign, he wrote of the media's endless appetite for scandal and for negative information and images.[17] But the Internet has made the surveillance of candidates even more constant and damaging.

The contrast between today and 1968 is illustrative. On the campaign trail in 1968, film was shot of various candidates at most rallies, usually by the networks. Film cameras were heavy, bulky, and quite expensive. Typically, to get quality images required not only access to the equipment but training as well. And a news organization would have to rush the actual film to a studio for developing, and then processing, and later that day or the next day, broadcasting. Today, an amateur with a $400 digital video camera can capture images as good or better than the professional images of 1968. They do not need processing and can be up on YouTube or another free video distribution service within minutes. What's changed is not just the Internet; it is also the miniaturization revolution in electronics, making video cameras and editing equipment smaller and affordable for a citizen.

How Campaigns Monitor Opponents

Many campaigns in America now send campaign staffers to all public events held by their opponent; they are armed with a video camera in the hope of capturing a gaffe, a misstatement, or simply an embarrassing image. They are known as "trackers." The best-known tracker is S. R. Sidrath, who captured Sen. George Allen's (R-Va.) "macaca" slur against him during Allen's 2006 Senate reelection campaign. The slur aimed at Sidrath's ethnicity backfired and helped lead to Allen's defeat. Technology is cheaper and more advanced these days. It enables campaigns to do their own reporting cheaply, and obviously campaigns take advantage of it to get an edge over their opponent through surveilling and monitoring them. A campaign can post something on YouTube, and if it gets enough hits, it may not even require the mainstream media to give it attention.

Campaigns have always sought ways to make their opponents look bad, going back to the dawn of democracy. The 1960 campaign of John F. Kennedy used myriad ways to mock and get under the skin of Richard Nixon, the Republican opponent. Dick Tuck, the mischievous genius of the low blow in that race, came up with a tactic to make Nixon look like a loser in the presidential debate, regardless of how it turned out. The morning after Nixon's first presidential campaign debate with John F. Kennedy, Tuck asked an elderly woman to wear a Nixon button, hug the candidate, and say loudly, "Don't worry, son. He beat you last night, but you'll win next time." [18] The picture was captured nationally. What changes with the Internet is obviously not a lowering of ethics on the part of campaigns. What changes is the speed and impact of such dirty tricks. The Tuck trick was a minor moment in a long campaign. Today, a clip on YouTube can mean the end of a Senate career. Even simple audio, unaccompanied by video footage, can shoot around the world without mainstream media cooperation. In summer 2007 Sen. Larry Craig (R-Idaho) was caught in a scandal involving his arrest at an airport restroom where he was allegedly soliciting a man for sex. Craig's political position became untenable in part because of an audio clip posted on the Internet of the interview between him and the arresting officer, in which the cop accused the senator several times of lying about his bathroom conduct. Most analysts are certain Craig will not be reelected in Idaho. Today, cell phones, electronics, and recording devices make everything public.

Surveillance and Future National Campaigns

Constant surveillance of candidates will increase the emphasis on personality, appearance, and character and further lessen the importance of parties, platforms, and issues. In the print media era, the nation elected leaders who were poor speakers (Jefferson), remarkably awkward in personal interactions (Nixon), extremely tight-lipped (Coolidge), close to dying (Roosevelt in 1944), prone to drunkenness (Grant), and recklessly promiscuous (Kennedy). Most of those men could not be elected in the television era (Kennedy was at the turning point between the two eras of print and television). Could any be elected in the Internet age? The more access we have to the personalities and personal conduct of our leaders, the greater the likelihood that we might vote on such ephemera as appearance and personality. This is the picture in the 2008 election cycle, and there is nothing to suggest we should expect anything different beyond this election.

Part IV. On the Edge—What Is a Journalist?

When the distinction is blurred between who is a journalist and who is an advocate (for a candidate), the veracity of news coverage suffers. This has become more apparent as the Internet expands. The Internet has begun to alter political journalism in fundamental ways, most importantly by changing the definition of who is a journalist. In the past a journalist was someone who worked for the established print or electronic media. Credentials to cover the White House or other major political institutions were granted on the basis of employment by a respected media outlet. Is someone who sets up a Web site that talks about politics a "journalist"? What if the Web site is basically a subsidiary of one of the political parties and only covers news that favors that party?

When Journalism Is a Cover for Political Advocacy

During President George W. Bush's first term, an obscure news "service," Talon News, which shared a Web site with a Republican political group (GOPUSA), hired a "journalist" by the name of Jeff Gannon, who had no qualifications or training. He was known for asking "softball" questions that echoed Republican talking points. When Gannon asked a loaded question that was factually incorrect at a press conference in January 2005, "liberal bloggers uncovered his real name (James Dale Guckert) and raised questions about his background." [19] His salacious past (which included establishing sexually explicit Web sites and working as a male prostitute) came out as reporters wanted to know how an unqualified partisan with an extremely shady past had managed to get daily passes into the White House, one of the most secure sites on earth. But beyond the scandal a deeper question remains: Who exactly is a journalist? This has profound implications for campaigns. Ascertaining the legitimacy of a journalist becomes more difficult in the online world, where there is no journalistic entity of repute that can adequately police cyberspace. Who is making a claim or spreading a rumor about a candidate, particularly when exaggerated claims are made online during the heat of a campaign? Most such material is discounted, but some is not. Cynthia Webb of the *Washington Post* described the rumor mill of Web sites (such as ustogether.org) that maintain that Kerry won the 2004 presidential election, including the popular vote.[20] Some online Democratic activists have never accepted the Bush victory in 2004 to this day.

Bloggers and the Federal Election Commission

The definition of a "journalist" most directly affects campaign finance regulation. If a citizen is hired by a congressional campaign to write and distribute political leaflets, every dime spent must be reported to the Federal Election Commission (FEC). The author of the leaflets is not a journalist, and no one reading them would think so. If a campaign hired a newspaper columnist to write for it, on the other hand, both the campaign and the journalist would be seen as violating the sanctity of elections and of the free press.

In July 2005, the FEC held hearings on whether or not bloggers should be given the same general exemption from campaign finance regulation that journalists receive. Either option poses risks for our democracy. If anyone can become a journalist just by paying a few dollars a month to have a Web site, then the privileges of the press, such as immunity from campaign finance laws and the confidential-source shield laws in forty-nine states, will become cheapened by their universality. On the other hand, prominent political bloggers, such as Michael Krempasky of RedState.org, fear that government regulation of the Internet will kill its vitality and vibrant freedom.[21]

Ultimately the FEC decided not to regulate the Internet in campaigns, except by requiring that all expenditures by a campaign on the Internet be reported, as with any other expense. One possible alternative has been offered by ElectionMall Technologies. ElectionMall suggests that the FEC create a " 'Blogger Identity Seal' program that would allow bloggers to voluntarily disclose whether or not they receive funding relating to federal elections. The information would appear as a seal on the blogger's site." [22] At present, however, the FEC seems reluctant to extend its regulatory jurisdiction.

Part V. On the Edge: Choosing Your Campaign News?

The Internet is an interactive medium, and unlike television, which is a passive medium, it requires that the user be involved. Thus the Internet may also weaken the media's control over what citizens learn about politics. If they wish to be, citizens can become more independent of the power of media than at any time in human history. Compare a daily newspaper to a thirty-minute evening news broadcast to a CNN Web site. The 40,000 words of text available in the newspaper represent the editors' views of what an educated citizen should know about current events that day. A reader has some degree of independence; a committed Republican could choose not to read any upbeat reports about Sen. Hillary Clinton (D-N.Y.) soaring in the 2008 pre-primary polls, while a committed Democrat might choose not to read any positive stories about Republican presidential aspirant and former Tennessee senator Fred Thompson. This "selective perception" by the viewer is reinforced by the Internet because the person manipulates the medium to his or her own satisfaction, which is the opposite of what happens with mainstream mass media. When the Internet and television are merged (likely within the next decade), even that distinction may become blurred. The technology is here, but it is not yet cost-effective.

Limitless Information Online

The Internet fosters independence by providing more points of access to political information for both consumers and producers. The network is practically limitless in its capacity to send, store, and grant access to information. Online search engines such as Google can rapidly search billions of Web pages for information. In August 2007, approximately 117 million home and work Internet users browsed Google.[23] And Google underestimates the breadth of the Internet, since it does not index e-mail, a medium that has been widely used for political purposes by candidates and parties.

The information network is more open and accessible than ever. The question is how many people will solely trust the Internet as an information source. The virtual world makes the real world of symbolic politics and campaigning more remote. These users are often cocooning themselves in their own information world.

Anonymous Campaign Reports: Narrowcasting News without a Gatekeeper

Another possibility that the Internet raises is a new type of anonymous campaign messaging that masquerades as news. Narrowcasting enables the producer to send information to an end user who has logged on or registered at a Web site. In the past, the media could receive an anonymous or confidential tip on the campaign trail, as one side hoped to put a rumor or negative story into the coverage. In 1920, Franklin Roosevelt, running for vice president, hoped to get reporters to cover the allegations that Warren Harding, the Republican nominee for president, had black parentage.[24] Such machinations are as old as democracy. But typically, to distribute such messages widely required some element in the mainstream media to agree to cover it. Reverend Jerry Falwell produced a videotape called "The Clinton Chronicles" that he mailed to thousands of his supporters in the 1990s. "The Clinton Chronicles" falsely alleged that Bill Clinton was involved in a string of drug-related homicides in Arkansas. The mainstream media did not pick up the story because it was without factual basis, so it remained off the radar screen for most voters.[25]

Today a campaign can put wild, anonymous rumors into circulation with much greater ease and get attention. In 2007 an activist associated with the Mitt Romney campaign posted a Web site called PhoneyFred.org that said that Romney's Republican rival Fred Thompson was "Once a Pro-Choice Skirt Chaser, [and] Now Standard Bearer of the Religious Right?" This was presented as fact. The site also said that Thompson had once lobbied for Planned Parenthood.[26] The implication was that Thompson dated attractive women and was pro-choice on abortion and therefore was no friend of the religious right. The distinction between news and rumor becomes blurred even further because campaigns have to react immediately. The result is that narrowcast messages often end up being broadcast to large—not targeted—audiences as news, and that can throw a campaign off-message for days. Campaigns face a very difficult choice: Do they respond rapidly to a wild story or attack, and give it broader circulation, or ignore it, as John Kerry did with the Swift Boat Veterans for Truth ad?

Mobile News Technology and Campaigns

Laptops are bulky and cumbersome compared to new technology such as iPhones, which are handheld computers that provide text, superior video, and phone services. As mainstream media adapt to new technologies, mobile users will be able to access CNN, FoxNews, and MSNBC, for example, to get their news. That will put more pressure on news organizations to produce news headlines faster because handheld devices facilitate frequent access by users. Thus campaign coverage, as well as the rest of the news, may become more focused on headlines because the shorthand fits easily on the screen. Already on mainstream TV we see tickers at the bottom of the screen (on CNN and FoxNews, for example), to make all news accessible in shorthand to viewers. The danger is that news coverage will become even more superficial and the seven-second sound bite from candidates even more important.

Synergistic News: Combining the Mainstream with New Media

The recent News Corporation buyout of Dow Jones represents a major new media conglomeration. Owner Rupert Murdoch now owns a major network (Fox), a major newspaper (the *Wall Street Journal,* published by Dow Jones), and major Internet Web sites (Fox and MySpace). Such concentration boosts media power and influence in the news and financial worlds. News and video from mainstream media can now be channeled to the Internet and other new media. Unlike the largely unregulated Internet, the synergistic media trend is toward producing more homogenous news coverage. Thus, a Hillary Clinton campaign event may appear the same in print, broadcast, and online. The result is that campaign coverage may take two forms—one that is largely independent and unfiltered and another that is overfiltered and lacks any independence. On the other hand, unbiased news coverage can suffer whether the medium is in the hands of the conservative Murdoch or a liberal online publisher such as Ariana Huffington.

Conclusion: Media Coverage of Campaigns in the Twenty-First Century — Unfiltered, Uncontrolled, Unpredictable

The Internet will produce greater changes in campaign coverage than the rise of television did. In the Internet era, mainstream media elites will lose some power over political communication, although one does not expect the *New York Times* to disappear any time soon. Nevertheless, those empowered by the rise of the Internet are likely to be, not politicians and party leaders, but rather a mix of new media figures and citizen activists. Bloggers and leaders of nonparty organizations such as MoveOn.org and the Free Republic are the ones who will thrive in this new media environment.

There is value to having many independent media outlets, with reporters who strive for objectivity and do in-depth stories on important, unsexy issues such as Social Security and military preparedness. Ten thousand bloggers mostly repeating the talking points of their respective parties cannot adequately replace one top national print reporter investigating a vital national question in a rigorous and unbiased fashion. Yet the Internet makes traditional media outlets less profitable by stealing viewers and readers, thus forcing many newspapers to fire just the reporters we need.

The second challenge for media coverage is what Neil Postman called "infotainment." If we all get to select exactly how much campaign news we will receive, and the depth of that coverage, it may be that too many Americans will choose shallow, biased sources of news on the Internet.[27] As political commentator H. L. Mencken said in the early twentieth century, "For every complex problem, there is a solution that is simple, neat and wrong." [28] But the voices arguing for nuanced and difficult solutions to complex problems may be softer now than at any time in the past, thanks in part to the vitriolic and biased way in which Internet media often treat political campaigns and the popularity of such coverage among viewers selecting freely from a plethora of Web sites. The mainstream media are not disappearing, but the Internet is fostering the superficiality of campaign news coverage, promoting a greater emphasis on personality, rumor, and infotainment. New technology propels campaign coverage at the speed of light. We may long for the days when the television news at least gave the voters seven-second sound bites from the presidential candidates.

Notes

1. Jeffrey L. Pasley, *The Tyranny of Printers: Newspaper Politics in the Early American Republic* (Charlottesville: University Press of Virginia, 2001), 201.
2. John Tebbel, *The Compact History of the American Newspaper* (New York: Hawthorne, 1963), 87.

3. Ibid., 67–68.
4. Jeremy D. Mayer, *American Media Politics in Transition* (New York: McGraw Hill, 2007).
5. Scott Keeter, "The Illusion of Intimacy: Television and the Role of Candidate Personal Qualities in Voter Choice," *Public Opinion Quarterly* 51, no. 3 (1987): 344–358.
6. Thomas E. Patterson, *Out of Order: An Incisive and Boldly Original Critique of the News Media's Domination of America's Political Process* (New York: Vintage, 1994).
7. *State of the News Media 2004,* Project on Excellence in Journalism, stateofthenewsmedia.org (accessed September 13, 2007).
8. Rick Karr, interview with FCC commissioner Jonathan Adelstein, *NOW with Bill Moyers,* PBS, April 3, 2003, pbs.org/now/politics/bigmedia.html (accessed September 14, 2007).
9. Charles Gibson, Paul White Award speech, RTNDA convention, Las Vegas, Nevada, April 24, 2006, journalism.org (accessed September 14, 2007).
10. Reported in *State of the News Media 2007,* Project on Excellence in Journalism (accessed September 14, 2007).
11. Nielsen/Netratings Report, March 2007, netratings.com (accessed September 12, 2007).
12. Jose Antonio Vargas, "Binary America: Split in Two by a Digital Divide," *Washington Post,* July 23, 2007, washingtonpost.com (accessed September 12, 2007).
13. Bob Davis and Jeanne Cummings, "Hot Buttons: A Barrage of E-Mail Helps Candidates Hit Media Fast and Often," *Wall Street Journal,* September 21, 2000.
14. Evgenia Peretz, "Going after Gore," *Vanity Fair,* October 2007 (available online before official release date; accessed at vanityfair.com on September 12, 2007, 4).
15. Andrew Morse, "What Happened in Kerry's Vietnam Battles?" ABC News, October 14, 2004, abcnews.go.com (accessed September 13, 2007).
16. See Ari Shapiro, "Using Hitler to Make a Point," NPR, July 4, 2004, npr.org (accessed September 13, 2007).
17. Larry J. Sabato, *Feeding Frenzy: Attack Journalism and American Politics* (Baltimore, Md.: Lanahan Publishing, 2000).
18. Tom Miller, "Tricky Dick," *New Yorker,* August 30, 2004.
19. Howard Kurtz, "Online Reporter Quits after Liberals' Expose," *Washington Post,* February 10, 2005, C4.
20. Cynthia L. Webb, "The Election That Never Ends . . . Online," *Washington Post,* November 12, 2004, washingtonpost.com (accessed September 14, 2007).
21. "Political Bloggers Lobby against Regulation," Associated Press, September 22, 2005, msnbc.com (accessed September 14, 2007).
22. "FEC Holds Hearing on Regulation of Internet Communications," OMB Watch, July 12, 2005, ombwatch.org (accessed September 14, 2007).
23. "Nielsen Netratings Reports Topline U.S. Data for August 2007," Nielsen Netratings at Nielsen-netratings.org (accessed September 14, 2007).
24. Jeremy D. Mayer, *Running on Race: Racial Politics in Presidential Campaigns 1960–2000* (New York: Random House 2002).
25. "Loathed by Liberals, Falwell Was Force among Right Wing," CNN, May 15, 2007, cnn.com (accessed September 14, 2007).

26. Glen Johnson, "Romney Denies OKing Anti-Thompson Web Site," Associated Press, September 11, 2007.

27. Neil Postman, *Amusing Ourselves to Death: Public Discourse in the Age of Show Business* (New York: Penguin, 1986).

28. The quote is Mencken, but the original source of the quote, newspaper article, book, or other medium is not known.

CHAPTER 10

Campaign Finance Reform— Present and Future

Peter L. Francia, Wesley Y. Joe, and Clyde Wilcox

THE 2008 ELECTIONS PROMISED TO BE the most expensive in American history. By the second quarter of 2007, nearly eight months before the first voting in presidential nomination contests, Hillary Clinton had already raised some $50 million in primary election receipts.[1] This was nearly as much as her husband, President Bill Clinton, had collected in the entire 1995–1996 primary election cycle. Experts expected that total spending in the 2008 elections would be more than $5 billion, not including money spent on state and local campaigns.[2]

A complex set of laws and regulations govern how money is raised and spent in presidential campaigns, and in House and Senate campaigns as well. More than thirty years ago Congress adopted a comprehensive set of campaign finance reforms that created a unified approach to regulation. Over time, however, Congress, the Supreme Court, and bureaucracy incrementally changed the rules, often in the aftermath of scandal. Between bouts of legislation, campaign professionals constantly seek new ways to win under existing rules, which often means stretching regulations and exploring new loopholes.

The rules are also complex because of conflicting values that have led the Supreme Court to create nuanced distinctions that make more sense as constitutional law than as campaign finance regulation. The Court has sought to balance two fundamental values—the need to control government corruption and the importance of free speech. The Court has recognized that large, unregulated contributions to candidates can pose a danger of corruption, as candidates give favors to donors in exchange for campaign cash. However, it has also recognized the value of free speech during an election campaign and on that basis overturned many efforts to limit campaign spending.

Currently federal campaign law regulates how much individuals can give to candidates, parties, and certain types of interest groups. The law also regulates how individuals may spend various types of funds. Tax rules govern what type of groups can raise what types of money, and what they can do with that money in campaigns. Together, these regulations channel money into politics through certain paths that determine which resources campaigns will use in an election. Often the regulations make subtle, sometimes murky, distinctions between different types of contributions and spending.

One example of this complexity is the limits on what individual citizens can do with their money in an election. On the grounds that individuals cannot corrupt themselves, the Supreme Court has prohibited any limits on the amounts of money that candidates can give to their own campaigns for office, although there are limits on the amounts that individuals can contribute to others, including family members who run for office.[3] An individual can give larger but limited sums to political parties and to political action committees (PACs) sponsored by interest groups. However, an individual can give unlimited amounts to a 527 committee because it is an independent expenditure organization, and the 527 can run an ad that attacks a candidate, pass out voter guides, and register voters.[4] These distinctions are the results not of carefully planned regulations, but rather of episodic rulemaking and judicial action.

To elucidate the complexities of the campaign finance system and the factors that will shape its future, this chapter covers several important issues. First, we review the framework of the Federal Election Campaign Act and discuss the events and circumstances that led to its eventual unraveling. Second, we discuss the Bipartisan Campaign Reform Act and consider its initial successes and failures. Third, we review some new and prominent proposals for campaign finance reform and speculate about their prospects of ever becoming law.

The Evolution and Framework of Campaign Finance Reform

Campaign finance legislation originated as a result of the lack of transparency in campaign spending. The first steps were taken in a 1971 law known as the Federal Election Campaign Act. The steps were very modest. The 1972 reelection campaign of President Richard Nixon used unreported campaign funds to pay hush money to the "plumbers" whom the campaign hired to break into Democratic National Committee headquarters at the Watergate hotel in Washington. The subsequent scandal led to Nixon's resignation from office because of his involvement in directing the cover-up of those actions.[5] The Watergate scandal led to significant reforms, which serve as the framework for campaign finance laws today.

The 1974 comprehensive amendments to the Federal Election Campaign Act (FECA) established the fundamental framework for campaign finance regulations. The law originally set out five main elements:

1. *Limits on the amounts of money that individuals, interest groups, and parties could contribute to candidates (and other committees) in national elections.* The

intent of the provision was to limit the possibility of corruption of federal officials, who might provide policy favors for big donors.

2. *Limits on the amounts that individuals, interest groups, parties, and candidates could spend in elections.* The purpose of this provision was to lower the cost of campaigns and decrease the demand for contributions.

3. *Disclosure requirements for both contributions and spending.* The goal of this provision was to allow voters, journalists, and others to see who had supported which candidates, as a way to expose potential corruption.

4. *Public financing in presidential elections.* According to proponents of FECA, a public finance system would eliminate the need for candidates to raise large sums of money.

5. *Enforcement of the law by the Federal Election Commission.* This provision established an independent regulatory commission to enforce the law (instead of allowing the president to enforce the law) to prevent partisan pressure.

All significant actors in national campaigns were required to form committees, which would raise and spend money according to FECA rules and file regular reports. Interest groups formed PACs, which could raise money in limited amounts from members and use it in election campaigns. Candidates were to form campaign committees, which would report all contributions and spending.

During the first years of FECA, campaign donors channeled their money into PACs, which then contributed that money directly to candidates. The number of PACs rapidly increased to nearly 4,000, a number that has remained nearly constant for more than twenty years.[6] PACs were widely criticized for "buying elections," but in hindsight they had two important virtues: they raised money in small contributions from their members, and their fundraising, contributing, and spending were transparent. Over time, however, the FECA regulatory system failed to limit the growth of money in national elections.

FECA Unravels

In 1976, the Supreme Court weakened FECA's restrictions on expenditures. The court ruled in *Buckley v. Valeo* (424 U.S. 1 [1976]) that spending money is a form of free speech protected by the First Amendment.[7] The ruling invalidated most campaign spending limits. Candidates could voluntarily give up their free speech rights in exchange for public funds, but otherwise they could not be limited in the amount they spent on campaigns, including their own funds.

Following the ruling, the law still permitted interest groups (and individuals) to spend unlimited amounts in "independent expenditures" to advocate the election or defeat of candidates, provided that they did so through PACs. Later court rulings have allowed interest groups to spend treasury funds for "issue ads" that do not explicitly endorse a candidate. The law also allowed political parties to collect unlimited amounts of money to advocate the election or defeat of a candidate, if they did not coordinate that activity with the candidate.[8] These provisions signaled the end of any meaningful spending limits for candidates, PACs, and parties.

The Court upheld contribution limits in that decision, but in 1979 Congress allowed individuals and interest groups to give unlimited amounts to political parties, if the money was spent for party-building activities and to help state and local candidates. This "soft money" soon became a way for companies, unions, and wealthy individuals to make very large contributions—often hundreds of thousands of dollars or more. In theory, donors did not give these contributions to any particular federal candidate, but in practice, political parties often earmarked the money for particular races. When the Supreme Court ruled in *Colorado Republican Federal Campaign Committee v. Federal Election Commission* (518 U.S. 604 [1996]) that political parties could make unlimited campaign expenditures provided that they were independent of the candidate, party leaders began aggressively soliciting soft money contributions from businesses and wealthy individuals.[9]

The Court later allowed interest groups to spend unlimited amounts to advocate issues, so long as their advertisements did not include "express advocacy." In practice, this meant that any advertisements that did not use words such as "vote for," "reelect," "help defeat," and other explicit voting instructions could be financed by unlimited contributions from wealthy supporters, from corporate profits, or from membership dues. In practice, issue ads could launch a devastating attack on a candidate, as long as they just said, "Tell candidate X how you feel," instead of "Vote against candidate X." [10] Thus by 2000, groups and individuals could give only limited amounts directly to candidates, but they could give unlimited amounts to parties and interest groups to help elect those same candidates. This development effectively eroded contribution limits.

Because these "issue ads" were not "campaign ads," their sponsors did not have to disclose them as expenditures to the Federal Election Commission (FEC). In general, 527 committees, rather than PACs, financed issue ads. Soon groups with names such as "Citizens for a Better Montana" and "Republicans for Clean Air" were spending large sums that were not transparent to the public.[11] These committees filed tax forms with the IRS, but forms that were neither comprehensive nor timely. This development weakened FECA's goal of ensuring disclosure of campaign expenditures, given that important elements of the campaign were not transparent.

The rising cost of presidential elections was another development that struck at a major FECA provision. The system of public financing, which reformers hailed as a landmark accomplishment when FECA became law in the 1970s, gradually became obsolete roughly a quarter-century later. In 2000, George W. Bush became the first major candidate to refuse federal matching funds in the primary elections, so as to be able to spend without limit, and his campaign broke all spending records.[12] In 2004, Democratic candidates John Kerry and Howard Dean also refused matching funds, and by early 2007 it was clear that most major presidential primary candidates would opt out of public funding.[13] It is possible that one or more candidates will opt out of public funding for the general election as well.

Finally, the FEC was never an aggressive regulatory agency, and its effectiveness eroded as Congress consistently underfunded it and limited its audit powers. The commission is composed of three Democratic and three Republican members. In the 1990s, both parties put forward increasingly partisan choices, so that the commission was frequently deadlocked.

During the late 1980s and 1990s, these rules affected the flow of contributions, with money going increasingly toward political parties in the form of soft money or to 527 groups for issue advocacy campaigns. As FECA eroded, donors increasingly channeled their money to groups trying to help or hurt candidates, not to the candidates themselves. PACs grew during this period, but their portion of all financial activity declined.

The Push for Reform

By the late 1990s, journalists, foundations, and scholars were increasingly vocal in their criticism of federal campaign finance regulation. Soft money was immensely attractive to party leaders because they could raise as much from a few interest groups in an evening as they could from tens of thousands of individuals over several months. In 1992, the national political party committees together collected $86 million in soft money. By 2000, that total had swelled to $495 million—a sixfold increase in just eight years.[14] In 1997, Republicans in Congress held hearings about soft money fundraising by the Clinton White House,[15] at the same time that GOP leaders were busily raising large sums of their own soft money.

Reformers, including members of Congress, criticized the growth of soft money on several grounds. First, because these contributions were often very large, they had the capacity to influence the actions of Congress. If a PAC gave a candidate $5,000 before an election, it was unlikely that the group could expect any favors from that candidate if the candidate won. But interest groups could channel hundreds of thousands of dollars through political parties into the same election, and that amount was substantial enough that many members believed that it affected legislation.

Second, the process of raising soft money became increasingly unseemly. Both political parties held soft money fundraising events the day before major markups of legislation. Interest groups complained that they had no choice but to contribute if they wanted a voice in the negotiations. A number of prominent business leaders criticized soft money fundraisers as a form of extortion, but only a few were willing to make a public pledge not to contribute.[16]

Finally, some argued that soft money distorted the equality of the political process. Even those who give small amounts of money are wealthier than the average American, but those who could afford to give hundreds of thousands were an elite group that already enjoyed numerous advantages in politics. These large soft money contributions, which average citizens could not afford to give, amplified the voices of the wealthiest Americans.

The large sums spent on "issue advocacy" also caught the eye of reformers. Critics charged that issue ads were not transparent because it was difficult, and often impossible, to trace who was funding them. During the 1996 election, for example, Democrat Bill Yellowtail of Montana watched his lead in the polls disappear to Republican Rick Hill when an issue ad alleged that Yellowtail physically abused his wife and failed to pay child support. The group that paid for the ad went by the innocuous name "Citizens for Reform." [17] Ads such as these often dominated local elections in the late 1990s and early twenty-first century and in some cases cost more money than the candidates themselves were able to raise and spend. Because wealthy citizens and interest groups typically financed issue ads, they further contributed to political inequality.

The Bipartisan Campaign Reform Act

In 2002, nearly thirty years after the passage of FECA, Congress passed the Bipartisan Campaign Reform Act (BCRA). Unlike FECA, the new law did not try to create a comprehensive campaign finance regulatory system but instead sought to patch the biggest problems that had developed over time. BCRA banned large soft money contributions to political parties and barred politicians from soliciting soft money for interest groups. BCRA also required state and local parties to fund any federal activities with "hard money" (contributions subject to federal limits) as opposed to "soft money" (contributions not subject to federal limits), although there are limited exceptions for voter registration and get-out-the-vote activities. State and local parties may pay for voter registration and get-out-the-vote efforts with soft money (known as "Levin Amendment" funds) up to $10,000 per source (if allowed under state law). Money raised for Levin Amendment funds must also meet a number of requirements.[18]

The law still allowed large contributions to various interest groups, which could run issue ads, but there were limits on the ads, as well as new standards for identifying campaign ads. Under the new law, "campaign ads" included those that mentioned a candidate by name or appeared on television or radio during the period of intense campaigning before the election. PACs could still fund these ads as independent expenditures, but they could only do so with funds raised through small contributions. Before the campaign's final days, 527 committees could run issue ads, and during the campaign they could mount phone, mail, and door-to-door campaigns, but 527 committees must disclose these contributions to the IRS.[19]

BCRA contained one other important provision, which doubled the amount that individuals could give to candidates for federal office, increased the amount that they could give to political parties, and left in place the limits on how much they could give to PACs. This provision was intended to make it easier for candidates, and to a lesser extent parties, to raise hard money once the ban on soft money took effect.

An eclectic coalition of interest groups immediately challenged BCRA before the U.S. Supreme Court, but the Court upheld the core elements of the law. In 2007, with new justices serving, the Court struck down parts of the issue advocacy ban in a confusing ruling that left campaign activists uncertain about what the law allows. By late summer, Congress was considering legislation to ban all enforcement of issue advocacy regulations, although the fate of this legislation was uncertain.

Expectations for BCRA

In the two election cycles after the enactment of BCRA, parties, candidates, and interest groups adapted their fundraising and campaigning to fit the new law. Critics argued that the bill would starve political parties and candidates of the funds they needed to communicate with voters and would strengthen the role of special interests in federal elections. In a plaintiff's principal brief filed in the Supreme Court case *McConnell v. FEC* (540 U.S. 93 [2003]), litigants led by the Republican National Committee argued, "BCRA will not only weaken political parties in absolute terms; it will weaken them relative to special interest groups like the NRA, the Sierra Club, and NARAL." [20] While the BCRA law did increase the maximum amount that an individual could contribute to a national party committee from $20,000 to $25,000 (with the maximum rising to $26,700 in 2006 to adjust for inflation), most experts doubted that this modest increase would offset the anticipated soft money losses.

There were other dire predictions. Some suggested that BCRA would be especially troubling for Democrats, who had depended more on soft money in past elections. Others, such as the AFL-CIO and the Chamber of Commerce, argued that the issue advocacy ban would limit interest groups' ability to communicate their issues to voters.

Finally, some skeptics argued that the bill would have no effect because money would pour into other channels. The "hydraulic theory" of campaign finance holds that campaign regulations cannot stop those eager to push their money into politics because there are always lawyers and loopholes. Supreme Court justices John Paul Stevens and Ruth Bader Ginsburg observed in the majority's decision in

McConnell v. FEC, "Money like water will always find an outlet." [21] The implication is that large donors would simply contribute to 527s and increase their giving to PACs and parties to replace their soft money contributions.

By contrast, reformers foresaw some clear benefits that would spring from BCRA. One major prediction was that the law would weaken the impact of big donors on politics. In the words of BCRA cosponsor Sen. Russell Feingold, "The point [of BCRA] was to break the connection between the officeholders and the money." [22] Reformers also hoped to rein in issue ads by 527 committees and bring more transparency to their funding. By barring 527s from running ads in the weeks just before the election, they also hoped to stimulate more spending on grassroots mobilization.

Did BCRA Work? Evidence from Recent Elections

There is evidence that in the two elections since BCRA, the law had some of the effects hoped for by its supporters and few of the problems predicted by its critics. The fears of critics that BCRA would starve political parties and stifle political debate did not come true. The Democratic National Committee (DNC) and Republican National Committee (RNC), for example, were able to raise more in hard money alone in 2004 than they previously raised in hard and soft money combined.[23] Expenditures were also up across the board. The most dramatic increases came in the form of independent expenditures, which increased for Democratic Party committees from $2.3 million in 2000 to $176.5 million in 2004, and for Republican Party committees from $1.6 million in 2000 to $88 million in 2004.[24] Democratic Party expenditures further increased for direct contributions and coordinated expenditures from 2000 to 2004. Similar patterns emerged for Republican Party committees during the same period.[25]

Likewise during the 2006 election national party committees raised more than $700 million combined, a 75 percent increase over 2002, offsetting much of their lost soft money revenue.[26] The national parties were able to spend significant sums of money to influence the 2006 election. In the short period from October 1 to October 15, 2006, for example, national party committees spent a combined total of almost $46 million in independent expenditures.[27] These independent expenditures allowed the parties to carry out big advertising campaigns and maintain a strong presence in the elections. The parties targeted the money carefully, spending the lion's share of their resources in the most competitive races of 2006.

National party committees also financed highly sophisticated get-out-the-vote (GOTV) and voter outreach programs during the BCRA period. This is important to note because several political experts predicted that the soft money ban would seriously damage the parties' voter mobilization operations. However, with such great success in raising large sums of hard money, the parties were able to continue their expansive GOTV efforts.

In addition, the national parties set records for the amounts of money they spent on direct candidate support in the presidential election of 2004. BCRA, in short, did not reduce the importance of national parties in federal elections. As political scientist Tony Corrado concluded, "After BCRA, the national party organizations were stronger, not weaker." [28]

National parties also have adapted to the BCRA law by developing successful outreach efforts to small donors, who have helped finance the same extensive party campaign operations that existed during the previous campaign finance regime. Between 2000 and 2004, the amount parties raised in contributions of $200 or less surged from $226 million to $449 million. [29] The national parties raised significantly more money from small donors in 2006 than in 2002. This reflects a major success for BCRA reformers. By banning large soft money donations, BCRA effectively forced national party committees to return to grassroots fundraising.

Moreover, BCRA did not disproportionately harm the Democratic Party. Many experts anticipated that the Democratic Party would struggle to raise money in small amounts, given its past dependence on large soft money donations. However, the DNC not only kept pace, it raised slightly more money than the RNC in 2004 and again in 2006. [30] This was not a failure on the part of the RNC, which outperformed its fundraising totals from the previous cycle. Instead, the party fundraising totals reflected the enormous success of both the DNC and RNC in fundraising during the first election under the new BCRA law.

Similarly, BCRA did not stifle the voices of interest groups in campaigns. Indeed, interest groups spent considerably more in 2004 than in past presidential campaigns, although the close race and the polarizing nature of the candidates may well have inspired the surge. [31] Interest groups also increased their grassroots efforts, especially during the election period, when the law barred many from paying for broadcast advertising with funds from sources other than the group's PAC.

BCRA's Impact on Soft Money

BCRA further reduced the amount of soft money raised by the political parties and interest groups. Between 2002 and 2004, the total soft money raised by parties and 527 organizations declined from $742 million to $318 million. The total declined still further in 2006. [32]

Cynics had predicted that most soft money donors would channel their money to 527 committees and increase their hard money giving through PACs. Although total contributions to 527 organizations in federal elections went up nearly three-fold, from $151 million in 2002 to $424 million in 2004, [33] the overall amount of soft money actually decreased from the previous cycle. In fact, most soft money donors did not even increase their hard money contributions, much less give at a rate to compensate for the loss of soft money. This was especially true in the corporate sector, which had been a reluctant donor of soft money and which seized the opportunity to say no to fundraising appeals. Other interest groups, such as labor unions, did increase their giving to 527 committees, from $54.9 million in 2002 to $94.4 million in 2004.[34]

Yet BCRA did not end large contributions by wealthy donors and interest groups. In 2003, many Democratic strategists worried that their party could not raise enough to compete with George Bush, and many wealthy party patrons increased their giving to 527 committees. A number of large committees such as America Coming Together (which topped all 527 groups by spending more than $78 million in the 2004 election),[35] the Media Fund, and others raised large sums and helped coordinate a pro-Democratic campaign in the media and door to door. Millionaire George Soros gave tens of millions to 527 committees in 2004 and nearly $4 million to various groups in 2006. By 2006, nearly three-fourths of the funds that 527 committees raised came in contributions of $100,000 or more.[36] Clearly, BCRA did not eliminate the ability of wealthy interests to invest in campaigns, but it did provide an excuse for those who had faced intense pressure to give in the past to withdraw.

Regulations on issue ads had some minor impact on the timing of such ads, but the volume of advertising by interest groups was considerably higher in 2004 than in past elections, contrary to the fears of BCRA critics. These ads continued to spark controversy for their negative tone. Perhaps the best example was the series of advertisements sponsored by a 527 organization known as the "Swift Boat Veterans for Truth," which formed in 2004 to oppose the presidential candidacy of Democrat John Kerry.

The group put together its first advertisement on August 4, 2004. The one-minute advertisement entitled, "Any Questions?" ran in several highly competitive states. The advertisement featured thirteen members of the Swift Boat Veterans for Truth, who claimed to have served with John Kerry during the Vietnam War. The thirteen denounced Kerry's military service, and the ad claimed that Kerry had "not been honest about what happened in Vietnam"; that he "lied about his first Purple Heart"; that he "lied to get his bronze star"; that he "lacks the capacity to lead"; that he is "no war hero"; and that he "betrayed the men and women he served with." The group ran similar ads against Kerry on August 20 ("Sellout"), August 26 ("Gunner"), August 31 ("Medals"), September 17 ("Dazed and Confused"), September 21 ("Friends"), September 30 ("Never Forget"), and October 13 ("Why?" and "They Served").[37] The attack ads generated enormous controversy for their shrill content and led to criticisms that 527s lacked accountability and needed further regulation. Democratic 527 committees also ran predominantly attack ads against President Bush.

In 2004 and especially 2006 other types of committees began to engage in electoral activity. Section 501(c) (3) of the tax code allows groups to qualify for tax-exempt status and receive tax-exempt contributions of unlimited size if their purpose is to promote the social welfare of the country. These groups can engage in educating voters on political issues or encouraging their participation in elections. However, all political activities must remain strictly nonpartisan, and 501(c) (3) groups are barred from endorsing candidates or lobbying government. Yet the relatively slow pace of IRS investigations of the tax status of these charities makes them attractive electoral vehicles in the short run. Organizations assuming a new prominence included American Taxpayers Alliance, Common Sense Ohio, Focus on the Family Action, FreedomWorks, and Democracy Alliance.

Prospects for Reform: Near Term

In 2007 many of the problems that had developed in the FECA framework continued. The Supreme Court reiterated its ban on spending limits, and in *Federal Election Commission v. Wisconsin Right to Life* (2007; docket 06-969) the Court appeared to open the door to greater issue advocacy spending by corporations and other groups. Contribution limits remain in effect, but over the past two elections 527 committees have increasingly come to depend on large contributions from wealthy donors, and 501(c) (3) organizations have become more active in elections, presumably also funded by large contributions. Disclosure remains problematic, with 527 committees filing late in the process and the sources of funding for 501(c) (3) and other organizations not disclosed. The public financing system is on the verge of irrelevance, as major-party presidential candidates continue to spurn it.

Yet there is little chance for comprehensive reform in the near future. Major reform of campaign finance regulation probably requires a major scandal, coupled with solid margins for the majority party in Congress.[38] In the short run only minor reforms are possible, and even they are not terribly likely to pass. With the Supreme Court signaling clearly that spending limits are not allowable, and with large contributions to 527 committees and 501(c) (3) groups clearly allowed, reformers have begun to shift their attention to ways to create more equality in the campaign finance process. Some of the near-term proposals for reform are somewhat less overarching than BCRA or FECA.

Reforming the Presidential Nomination Campaign Finance Rules

If any reform will pass in the near future, it is likely to involve the system of presidential public financing. Currently, primary election candidates can receive federal funds to match the first $250 contributed by each donor. However, they have to pledge to abide by nationwide and state-by-state spending limits.

Several members of Congress have introduced their own bills to reform the system, although it is unlikely that any would pass before the 2008 campaign is over.

For many reformers, the public financing system had several important virtues. First, the system provided seed money to many lesser-known presidential candidates, thereby widening the field of candidates and the range of ideas debated during the campaign. Second, the system gave candidates an incentive to approach smaller donors for contributions, instead of flying from one $2,000 a plate dinner to another. Third, the public financing system constituted an endorsement of the idea that elections are a public good.

Although proposed reforms run the gamut from eliminating public funds altogether to tinkering with the allocation of money, reformers believe that more serious changes are necessary. The Campaign Finance Institute's task force on presidential nomination financing recommended a series of changes, including these:

- *Increasing the spending limits, so that candidates could accept public funds and still compete in the process.* The task force recommended doubling the spending limit and allowing candidates to spend as much as any nonparticipating candidate.
- *Increasing the amount of public funds provided to match small contributions.* The task force suggested matching all contributions of $100 or less at a ratio of three to one, making a contribution of $100 worth $400 to the candidate. This should give candidates an incentive to solicit small contributions, especially now that Internet fundraising makes collecting small contributions easier.[39]

Reforming the Disclosure System

U.S. Supreme Court Justice Brandeis wrote, "Publicity is justly commended as a remedy for social and industrial diseases. Sunlight is said to be the best of disinfectants; electric light the most efficient policeman." [40] Voters can only hold policy makers responsible for any special policies or favors they provide donors if they have access to information about who has given to whom. Thus disclosure is clearly a necessary condition for accountability in campaign financing.[41]

Recent developments in campaign finance leave the disclosure system incomplete, however. While there is full disclosure to the FEC of contributions to candidates, political parties, and PACs, it is the IRS that tracks contributions to 527 committees, which results in less complete and timely disclosure. Moreover, there are no disclosure provisions for contributions to various section 501 organizations, leaving a major gap in the ability to trace money in elections.

Reformers have suggested a variety of rules that would force disclosure of all campaign-related spending to the Federal Election Commission. Disclosure is the one part of campaign finance regulation that is widely accepted across the political spectrum, so there might be some chance that this kind of legislation might pass, especially if the 2008 campaign entails a good deal of undisclosed activity.

Possibilities for Reform: Long Term

There is little chance for any immediate, comprehensive reform of campaign finance. In part the reason is that political leaders disagree on what is best policy. It is also attributable to the fact that politicians are interested in their own reelection and the success of their party. Furthermore, this type of legislation is difficult to compromise and requires considerable public support. However, a major scandal in campaign finance might spur considerations of systematic changes in the rules. Political observers have discussed two sets of comprehensive reforms in recent years—full deregulation of campaign finance and full public funding of campaigns.

Public Financing

The collapse of the presidential public financing system has not discouraged some members of Congress and public interest group allies from continuing to press for a system of public financing for congressional elections. By some measures, the idea now enjoys its highest level of congressional support in many years. Yet efforts to enact such legislation have been under way for at least a decade, and they continue to confront formidable obstacles to passage. Supporters may, however, find encouragement from related victories at the state and local levels.

Public financing schemes run the gamut. They include full public funding of major-party candidates in the general election, more limited proposals to provide some subsidies to candidates at the start of their campaign or after they meet a certain threshold, and plans that give incentives to individuals to contribute to candidates (e.g., through tax credits).

Advocates of public funding of congressional elections cite a variety of reasons for promoting such programs. Many justifications arise from the broad goal of increasing the competitiveness of congressional elections.[42] In 2006, for example, nearly three dozen congressional candidates ran without opposition, presenting voters with no choice in the election. Proponents claim that a system of public funding could reduce the need to raise a large sum of money as a barrier to running for office. People who do not easily have access to money, but are otherwise candidate material, might be able to establish their credibility as candidates and attract the support needed to wage a campaign. Such programs could also increase the diversity of the pool of potential candidates by enabling women, members of some minority groups, and others who often lack access to networks of wealthy prospective donors more easily to run for office.[43] Some congressional incumbents think that the money chase consumes too much of legislators' time, diminishing the institution's overall effectiveness. Other supporters of public financing argue that such programs can rein in the cost of elections and have many other potential benefits.[44]

During the 110th Congress, however, the most widely discussed rationale for public financing has been an interest in reducing corruption, or at least the appearance of corruption, in Congress. In particular, exponents of public financing of congressional elections now frame such measures as an important part of Congress's broader current effort to curb lobbyist influence in Washington. Lobbying reform shot up the congressional agenda after several influence-peddling scandals exploded into the national headlines and arguably contributed to the Republican Party's loss of control of both houses of Congress in the 2006 elections. The most notorious produced prison terms for Washington superlobbyist Jack Abramoff, former representative Bob Ney (R-Ohio), former U.S. Department of the Interior deputy secretary J. Steven Griles (the second-highest-ranking official in the agency), and others. As of this writing, the Federal Bureau of Investigation continues to probe connections between many other current or former lawmakers and Abramoff, other significant lobbyist campaign donors, and potential bribers.[45]

Concerns about representation and congressional ethics have led some federal lawmakers to push for a public financing option for congressional elections. Perhaps the most widely discussed of these proposals is Rep. John Tierney's (D-Mass.) Clean Money, Clean Elections Act (H.R. 1614). Explicitly modeled on the public funding programs in Arizona and Tierney's neighboring state of Maine, the act would create a voluntary public funding system. Congressional candidates could choose to finance their campaigns with public money if they could demonstrate sufficient public support for their candidacy. Candidates could raise some private funds at the earliest stage of the campaign. However, these contributions could not exceed $100 from a particular individual. Ultimately, to qualify for public funding a candidate would have to raise a specified number of "qualifying contributions" from residents of the candidate's state. As in Arizona, these contributions would be limited to five dollars. By raising many of these small contributions, a candidate would demonstrate his or her campaign's viability, thereby reducing the possibility that public funds would go to marginal candidates. Candidates receiving public funds would then have to agree to refuse private contributions to the campaign and to abide by voluntary limits on campaign expenditures.

In 2006, some liberal members of the House began to press for an alternative, more radical bill, the Let the People Decide Clean Campaign Act (H.R. 2817), introduced in the 110th Congress by David Obey (D-Wis.). The Obey measure would pay for U.S. House of Representatives elections with money raised through a combination of (1) voluntary contributions from individuals who file federal income tax returns, and (2) a 0.1 percent fee assessed from corporations with profits in excess of $10 million in a given year. The measure would also reduce the role of state and national party spending and impose an outright ban on independent expenditures in campaigns for the House. This proposal, however, has very little support from moderate and conservative members of Congress, who consider it another "big government" program. Its chances of becoming law are therefore very slim, barring perhaps a major campaign finance scandal.

Indeed, in ten years public financing legislation still has yet to receive even one dedicated committee hearing in the House. And although some citizen activist groups may be attempting to build public support for public financing, public opinion on the subject remains volatile and highly sensitive to the wording of survey questions.[46] A majority of Americans typically support the idea of replacing private financing with public funding. However, public support plunges when a survey words a question in a way that emphasizes the use of tax revenue to finance elections and de-emphasizes the objectives of public funding programs. Consequently, one can easily imagine that if the Tierney bill were to approach possible enactment, it might not survive a "public education" campaign aimed at its defeat. Moreover, even if citizens generally favor such a proposal in principle, will they spur Congress to put it on the active legislative agenda? If the Abramoff-era scandals have failed to engender sufficient public pressure for this reform, one wonders what it would take to mobilize sufficient public demand.

Despite the obstacles at the federal level, however, it would be a mistake to conclude that proponents of public financing are engaged in a quixotic quest. During the past decade they have succeeded in establishing such programs in Maine (1996), Vermont (1997), Arizona (1998), Connecticut (2005), and some major U.S. cities. A 2004 pilot program to fund state legislative elections in New Jersey with taxpayer subsidies has produced mixed results, but the state will continue to experiment with public financing. In 2007, governors Bill Richardson (D-N.M.), Eliot Spitzer (D-N.Y.), and Christine Gregoire (D-Wash.) endorsed public financing of elections in their respective states. Certainly one can imagine a long-term scenario in which more states ultimately embrace public financing, and that state legislators who embrace such systems eventually move on to Congress and bolster support for a comparable federal-level system. If, at the same time, the systems garner favorable reviews from citizens, public support for comparable federal legislation could harden. Still, that is a long way off at best.

Deregulation of Campaign Finance

A very different proposal, coming mostly from libertarians and conservative Republicans, is to scrap contribution limits entirely in favor of a regime that depends entirely on disclosure. California representative John Doolittle (R) has sponsored a bill, the Citizen Legislature and Political Freedom Act, to reform the campaign finance system in that manner. In November 1999, he introduced H.R. 1922, to remove all limits on political contributions and end public funding of presidential campaigns. The bill would also strengthen disclosure, requiring more timely and thorough reporting of soft money donations.

The argument for deregulation is sometimes based on principled arguments about free speech and sometimes based on the ineffectiveness of limits.[47] As Doolittle himself has argued, "The goal of effective campaign finance reform is to encourage political speech rather than limit it. It is to promote competition, freedom, and a more informed electorate. . . . Today's system hurts voters in our republic by forcing more contributors and political activists to operate outside of the system where they are unaccountable and, consequently, more irresponsible." [48] Doolittle's legislation, however, received only tepid support in the 106th Congress and stands little chance of passage in the foreseeable future.

Creative Alternatives in Campaign Finance

Barring a significant scandal and a large majority for one party in Congress, major reform of campaign finance is unlikely. Republicans generally oppose public financing schemes (although some support matching fund and tax credit versions), and Democrats generally oppose deregulation. Some campaign finance critics have suggested the utility of thinking in new ways and trying entirely new models of regulation. Such prospects may be very long term, but they do represent cutting-edge thinking on campaign finance reform.

One recent example of this type of thinking is a proposal by Bruce Ackerman and Ian Ayres.[49] These scholars argue that it is time to move past ideas of contribution limits and to create a new paradigm in campaign funding. They propose a voucher plan for all citizens, using what they call "Patriot Dollars," which could be given to candidates for federal office. With no contribution limits, wealthy donors would still be free to contribute large sums, but the total amount available via vouchers from average citizens would force candidates to pay attention to the less affluent.

In addition, they propose an agency to "anonymize" contributions by holding them and then releasing them in a block to candidates. They argue that when candidates ask for contributions, many important groups feel that they cannot refuse, but if all contributions were anonymous, then everyone would claim that they had already "given at the office," and thus the direct link between contributions and access would be broken. Policy makers would be powerless to determine which of the various interests and individuals actually made contributions and would therefore have few incentives to do favors for donors.

Conclusion

To regulate the influence of money in U.S. elections has proved to be a difficult task. As FECA demonstrated, campaign finance regulations often succeed initially in curbing the dominance of big money but then fail to keep pace with the latest methods of fundraising. The new BCRA has attempted to correct the excesses that developed in the campaign finance system during the late 1990s, and to this point, although not perfect, it has been successful in at least some important respects, notably in forcing political parties to rely less on excessively wealthy donors and return to grassroots fundraising.

However, BCRA has certainly not solved every problem, nor has it completely shut out the influence of wealthy donors, who continue to spend large sums financing the activities of 527 organizations. These and other challenges remain for reformers, who face an uncertain future, particularly given that the U.S. Supreme Court's ideological leanings have moved in a more conservative direction following the retirement of Justice Sandra Day O'Connor, who was replaced by Samuel Alito in 2006. The recent 5–4 ruling in *Federal Election Commission v. Wisconsin Right to Life,* which saw the Court relax BCRA's restrictions on issue advocacy advertisements, hints at potentially bleak future for more restrictive campaign finance provisions.

As campaigns constantly evolve and discover new and creative ways to raise money, the reaction on Capitol Hill is likely to follow a familiar pattern. Reformers will argue the need for additional restrictions, while opponents will cite the current law's failures as further evidence that restrictions are fruitless and threaten political speech. Although the direction that campaign finance reform will take is difficult to predict, the debate surrounding it is likely to sound very familiar.

Notes

1. "Race for the White House: Banking on Becoming President," Center for Responsive Politics, www.opensecrets.org/pres08/index.asp (accessed September 1, 2007).
2. Paul Bedard, "2008 Shocker: It Will Cost $5 Billion," *U.S. News & World Report,* April 23, 2007.
3. For more information, please refer to the U.S. Supreme Court case *Buckley v. Valeo,* 424 U.S. 1 (1976), at www.campaignfinancesite.org/court/buckley1.html (accessed July 15, 2007).
4. The name "527 organizations" comes from the fact that they fall under Section 527 of the Internal Revenue Code. They are exempt from taxation, but contributions to them are not tax deductible. The groups can accept unlimited soft money donations from various sources, including individuals, unions, and corporations, and can spend the donations on issue advocacy advertisements and get-out-the-vote efforts.
5. For a thorough account of the Watergate scandal, see Stanley I. Kutler, *The Wars of Watergate* (New York: Norton, 1992).
6. Peter L. Francia, "Interest Groups," in *Guide to Political Campaigns in America* (Washington, D.C.: CQ Press, 2005), 200–201.
7. For more information, see *Buckley v. Valeo,* www.campaignfinancesite.org/court/buckley1.html.

8. Anthony Corrado, "Party Finances," in *The New Campaign Finance Sourcebook* (Washington, D.C.: Brookings Institution Press, 2005), 169.

9. Ibid.

10. For more information, see Anthony Corrado, "Money and Politics: A History of Federal Campaign Finance Law," in *The New Campaign Finance Sourcebook*, 33.

11. "Republicans for Clean Air" generated significant controversy in the 2000 presidential election. See "McCain Files FEC Complaint over TV Ad Run by Bush Supporters," CNN, http://archives.cnn.com/2000/ALLPOLITICS/stories/03/06/mccain.ads/index .html (accessed September 1, 2007).

12. "Improving the Basic Tradeoff: Spending Limits in Return for Public Funds," Campaign Finance Institute, www.cfinst.org/president/pdf/CFI_Chapter2.pdf (accessed September 1, 2007).

13. David B. Magleby, J. Quin Monson, and Kelly D. Patterson, *Dancing without Partners* (Lanham, Md.: Rowman and Littlefield, 2006), 57.

14. "Campaign Finance eGuide," Campaign Finance Institute, www.cfinst.org/legacy/ eguide/basics.html (accessed July 15, 2007).

15. For more information, see John F. Harris, "Clinton Defends Fundraising," *Washington Post*, September 23, 1997, A01.

16. Bradley A. Smith, "Faulty Assumptions and Undemocratic Consequences of Campaign Finance Reform," *Yale Law Journal* 105, no.4 (1996): 1049–1091.

17. Viveca Novak and Michael Weisskopf, "The Secret G.O.P. Campaign," *Time*, November 3, 1997, www.time.com/time/magazine/article/0,9171,987280,00.html (accessed July 15, 2007).

18. Levin Amendment funds must meet the following conditions: (1) federal officeholders and national parties may not receive Levin Amendment funds; (2) all receipts and disbursements of Levin Amendment funds must be disclosed; (3) party committees in two or more states, or two or more party committees in the same state, are prohibited from jointly raising Levin Amendment funds; (4) a state party committee cannot raise the money for use in other states; (5) Levin Amendment funds cannot be used for federal-candidate specific or generic advertising; (6) Levin Amendment activities must be funded consistent with FEC hard money or soft money allocation rules; (7) the state or local party must raise its own matching hard money; and (8) Levin Amendment funds cannot be transferred between party committees.

19. Francia, "Interest Groups."

20. "McConnell v. FEC: Supreme Court: Plaintiff's Briefs," Campaign Legal Center, www.campaignlegalcenter.org/McConnell-99.html (accessed July 15, 2007).

21. "Highlights of the McCain-Feingold Decision," Center for Responsive Politics, www.opensecrets.org/news/BCRAdecisionquotes.asp (accessed July 15, 2007).

22. Eliza Newlin Carney, Peter H. Stone, and James A. Barnes, "New Rules of the Game," *National Journal*, December 20, 2003.

23. Anthony Corrado and Katie Varney, "Party Money in the 2006 Elections," Campaign Finance Institute, www.cfinst.org/books_reports/pdf/Corrado_Party-2006_Final.pdf (accessed September 1, 2007).

24. Robin Kolodny and Diana Dwyre, "A New Rule Book: Party Money after BCRA," in *Financing the 2004 Election,* edited by David B. Magleby, Anthony Corrado, and Kelly D. Patterson (Washington, D.C.: Brookings Institution Press, 2006), 198.

25. Ibid.

26. Anthony Corrado, "Parties Playing a Major Role in Election '06," Campaign Finance Institute, www.cfinst.org/books_reports/pdf/Parties_Corrado_102606.pdf (accessed July 15, 2007).

27. Ibid.

28. Anthony Corrado, "Party Finance in the Wake of BCRA: An Overview," in *The Election after Reform: Money, Politics, and the Bipartisan Campaign Reform Act,* edited by Michael J. Malbin (Lanham, Md.: Rowman and Littlefield, 2006), 19–37.

29. Corrado, "Parties Playing a Major Role in Election '06."

30. Kolodny and Dwyre, "A New Rule Book," 184.

31. Gary C. Jacobson, *A Divider, Not a Uniter: George W. Bush and the American People* (New York: Longman, 2006).

32. Stephen R. Weissman and Kara D. Ryan, "Soft Money in the 2006 Election and the Outlook for 2008," Campaign Finance Institute, www.cfinst.org/books_reports/pdf/NP_Softmoney_06-08.pdf (accessed July 15, 2007).

33. Stephen R. Weissman and Ruth Hassan, "BCRA and the 527 Groups," in *The Election after Reform: Money, Politics, and the Bipartisan Campaign Reform Act,* 81.

34. "Labor Union Donations to Federal 527s in the 2002 and 2004 Cycles," Campaign Finance Institute, www.cfinst.org/books_reports/TablesFigures/EAR_Tables5-7.pdf (accessed July 15, 2007).

35. "Federal 527 Organizations in the 2004 Election Cycle," Campaign Finance Institute, www.cfinst.org/books_reports/TablesFigures/EAR_Tables5-4.pdf (accessed July 15, 2007).

36. Weissman and Ryan, "Soft Money in the 2006 Election and the Outlook for 2008."

37. Swift Boat Veterans for Truth, www.swiftvets.com (accessed July 15, 2007).

38. Diana Dwyer and Victoria A. Farrar-Myers, *Legislative Labyrinth: Congress and Campaign Finance Reform* (Washington, D.C.: CQ Press, 2000).

39. "So the Voters May Choose. . . Reviving the Presidential Matching Fund System," Campaign Finance Institute Task Force on Financing Presidential Nominations, 2005, 6–8.

40. Brandeis University, see www.brandeis.edu/investigate/sunlight (accessed September 1, 2007).

41. Herbert E. Alexander, Janet M. Box-Steffensmeier, Anthony J. Corrado, Ruth S. Jones, Jonathan S. Krasno, Michael J. Malbin, Gary Moncrief, Frank J. Sorauf, and John R. Wright, *New Realities, New Thinking* (Los Angeles: Citizen's Research Foundation, 1997), 9.

42. Kenneth R. Mayer, Timothy Werner, and Amanda Williams, "Do Public Funding Programs Enhance Electoral Competition?" paper presented at the Fourth Annual Conference on State Politics and Policy Laboratories of Democracy: Public Policy in the American States, Kent State University, April 30–May 1, 2004.

43. Timothy Werner and Kenneth R. Mayer, "The Impact of Public Election Funding on Women Candidates: Comparative Evidence from State Elections," paper presented at the 2005 Annual Meeting of the Midwest Political Science Association, Chicago, April 7–10, 2005.

44. Nolan L. Reichl, "What We Know and What We Don't: A Review of the Literature Empirically Analyzing the Effects of State Campaign Finance Reform Laws," senior thesis, Stanford University Law School, April 21, 2006.

45. Philip Shenon, "Federal Lawmakers from Coast to Coast Are under Investigation," *New York Times,* July 26, 2007.

46. Stephen R. Weissman and Ruth A. Hassan, *Public Opinion Polls Concerning Public Financing of Federal Elections 1972–2000: A Critical Analysis and Proposed Future Directions* (Washington, D.C.: Campaign Finance Institute, 2005), www.cfinst.org/president/pdf/PublicFunding_Surveys.pdf.

47. Bradley A. Smith, *Unfree Speech: The Folly of Campaign Finance Reform* (Princeton: Princeton University Press, 2001); see also John Curtis Samples, *Welfare for Politicians? Taxpayer Financing of Campaigns* (Washington, D.C.: Cato Institute, 2005).

48. "The Case for Campaign Finance Reform," Hoover Institution, www.campaignfinance-site.org/book/html/307.html (accessed July 15, 2007).

49. Bruce Ackerman and Ian Ayres, *Voting with Dollars* (New Haven: Yale University Press, 2002).

CHAPTER 11

Election Administration — Trends in the Twenty-First Century

Tari Renner

PRIOR TO THE DISPUTED PRESIDENTIAL ELECTION OF 2000, no one would have believed that problems with scraps from ballot paper, known as "chads," would have a dramatic impact on election reform in America. In that year, the question of how ballots were counted in the state of Florida determined who won the presidency. A variety of voting standards were used by different Florida counties for counting the "hanging chads," or perforations, in the statewide recount process. In the end, the U.S. Supreme Court cut short the recount process by a 5–4 vote, and George Bush won the Sunshine State—and the presidency—by 537 votes.

The impact that the Florida results had on the process of ballot counting was profound. The results led to passage of the Help America Vote Act (HAVA) of 2002 and ushered in a new era of reforms to improve technology to count votes and improve American citizens' access to the ballot box. Sen. Christopher Dodd (D-Conn.), one of the law's authors said, "The Help America Vote Act is appropriately the first civil rights act of the twenty-first century." [1] New electronic technology is to supplant older voting methods that in some instances were less than reliable. HAVA has been complemented by an explosion of new technologies to count ballots more accurately and efficiently. Moreover, many states are moving to alternative means of voting such as early voting and "no-excuse" absentee or mail ballots. The U.S. military and some states have either seriously considered or experimented with the use of Internet or online voting

The purpose of this chapter is to examine election administration in America and contemporary controversies in regard to it. The chapter begins with an overview of the political environment in which election administration occurs and its basic processes and technologies. Next, I examine the consequences of recent federal laws such as HAVA on state and local government practices and voter turnout. Finally, I analyze contemporary controversies in election administration and speculate about possible reforms and challenges in both the near and the long term.

The Political Environment

There are fifty states and thousands of local jurisdictions responsible for administering U.S. elections from dogcatcher to president. Some states (such as California) have large, diverse, and highly transient populations that are widely dispersed geographically. Others (such as Vermont) have small, homogeneous, and stable populations residing in less-expansive areas. All of these variables affect the jurisdiction's task of administering the electoral function. The greater the size and diversity of a community's population (including the proportion of racial and linguistic minorities), for example, the greater the complexity of its task of planning and implementing elections.

Given the nature of America's state-centered federalism, states are the core units of political culture differences and constitutional policy making. They are the only constitutionally independent governments. Local governments are their legal creatures. We see consistency in city and county election practices in some states but not others. Shortly after the 2000 elections in Pennsylvania, for example, local election officials told General Accounting Office (GAO) researchers that the state had sixty-seven counties and, therefore, there were sixty-seven ways of conducting elections in the Keystone State.[2]

Efforts at national reform must take these empirical realities into account. The impact of different rules and procedures, as well as technologies, will be different across the widely divergent jurisdictions that administer elections in their communities. Some states and communities will respond more sluggishly than others to national trends and legislative policy shifts. Furthermore, despite the waves of nationalization of practices and procedures, election administration in Loving County, Texas, with a homogeneous population of a few hundred, will be fundamentally different from Los Angeles County, California, with nearly ten million residents with a wide variety of demographic characteristics.

The effects of possible future reforms in election procedures and technologies will be further complicated by the realities of our national political party system, in which the balance of power between Democrats and Republicans is extremely tight. In fact, we have recently experienced the five closest consecutive presidential elections (1988–2004) since the end of the Civil War party system (1876–1892). Changes in election administration policies or practices rarely have neutral consequences. Debates on possible reform consistently strike political and ideological chords.

The Process of Election Administration

The goal of election administration is presumably to make voting as easy and transparent as possible. The American electoral process comprises four core tasks, each of which has attracted controversy and proposals for reform in recent years. The core tasks are the following:

1. *The development and maintenance of voter lists and registration.* Local election officials have responsibility to register eligible voters and maintain their jurisdiction's voter registration lists. That includes updating voter information and purging the names of voters who are no longer eligible.

2. *The implementation of absentee, early, or mail voting.* The number of people who vote prior to the actual election day, either by mail or in person, has increased in recent years as states have made it easier to do so.[3] The process of implementing pre–election day voting may include the design of special ballots, as well as educating the public about the availability of these forms of voting.

3. *The administration of election day voting.* Officials must arrange for polling places for each precinct, design ballots, recruit and train the temporary poll workers in each precinct, and prepare and possibly test the equipment used for casting and tabulating votes. The election administrators focus on election day procedures such as the opening and closing of polling places, helping voters to cast their ballots, and whether and how provisional ballots will be used, among many other activities. Their plan must be in place well before election day.

4. *Vote counting and certification.* Following the election, officials must tabulate the ballots cast. They must determine what ballots might be "spoiled" or ineligible to be counted and how to count eligible ballots that cannot be read by the mechanical equipment. They must audit and certify the final vote count and conduct recounts where necessary.

Tens of thousands of elected, appointed, and civil service officials work full-time administering elections. In addition, recent estimates are that there are over one million poll workers who are hired as temporary employees to actually make election day happen. Jeanette Senecal reports that they are "responsible for organizing the polling place, managing the equipment, assisting voters with new machines, ensuring the proper handling of provisional ballots, [and] dealing with sometimes confusing check-in and verification procedures" [4] among many other critical tasks. Senecal found that although the requirements for hiring poll workers and their training, compensation, and working conditions vary substantially across states and localities, common problems affect the majority of communities. The most active cohort of poll workers in the past is aging, and that will affect how full-time officials handle their recruitment, training, and retention in the future. In addition, two very real constraints affect both full-time officials and temporary employees—they generally have shoestring budgets and limited permanent staff.

The rules and procedures for election administration vary widely throughout the United States. The inequities in standards for ballot counting from county to county within the same state, for example, became painfully apparent during the infamous Florida recount of 2000. There are also critical differences in procedures for purging voter lists and in identification requirements for voting. It is much easier to register and participate in some states and communities than in others. Minnesota, Wisconsin, and Montana, for example, have same-day voter registration, and in North Dakota there is no statewide voter registration.

Voting Systems Technologies

Different technologies are also used throughout the nation. Standardization of precise technologies is not mandated nationally because that is traditionally the domain of the states. Thus, states are not always consistent with each other. Even among localities within a state (depending on state laws) voting system technologies can be different. The most important distinction is between older technologies and the newer electronic voting systems. The former include paper ballots, mechanical lever voting machines, and punch card equipment (which came under particular scrutiny after the Florida recounts of 2000).

The newer, electronic technologies include two primary types: optical scan and direct recording electronic (DRE) systems. Optical scanning electronically tabulates paper ballots on which voters have darkened ovals (much as in standardized tests). They are counted using optical-mark-recognition equipment. The actual ballots can be tabulated at the individual polling places (precinct count optical scan) or at a central location.

DREs tabulate votes electronically without the use of paper ballots. There are two basic types of DREs: pushbutton and touch screens. Pushbutton DREs are the older technology and are larger and heavier than touch screen systems. The two also differ in ballot presentation. Pushbutton machines typically present the voter with all the choices on a single ballot, whereas touch screens typically require voters to page through the ballot choices.

Both types of DREs are designed to prevent a common voter problem and source of invalid ballots—"over voting," or casting more votes than are legally permitted. If a voter adds a second choice in an election for a single position, for example, then only the second vote is counted. Other presumed benefits from both DREs include visual enhancements to highlight ballot choices; easy accommodations for voters with disabilities, such as Braille keyboards and audio interfaces; and a review feature that requires voters to review their choices before pushing the final, "Vote" button. The major criticism of DRE systems is their lack of an official paper trail. Defenders of DRE technology assert that they do retain electronic images of all ballots, which can be used for auditing and recounts. A variety of critics, including computer scientists, citizen groups, and elected legislators, remain unconvinced about the security and accuracy of DREs.[5]

Despite their concerns, between the 2000 and 2004 elections, following the Florida recount fiasco, there was a clear movement toward DRE systems and away from the old voting technologies. Table 11.1 shows the use of the major old and new technologies for casting ballots in the last two presidential elections. Use of both major forms of old technologies declined, while the use of newer electronic technologies increased. The data show the percentages of American registered voters who used each technology in each election. Punch card systems declined from 31 percent in 2000 to 19 percent in 2004; mechanical levers decreased from 17 percent to 14 percent during the same period. Optical scans increased slightly, from 31 percent to 32 percent, between the two elections, and DREs increased from 12 percent to 29 percent.

TABLE 11.1 Use of Major Voting System Technologies in the 2000 and 2004 Presidential Elections

	Percentages of registered voters using the technology	
	2000 election	*2004 election*
Older technologies		
Punch cards	31	19
Mechanical levers	17	14
Newer technologies		
Optical scan	31	32
Direct recording electronic systems (DREs)	12	29

Source: Tabulated by the author from testimony by Randolph C. Hite before the Subcommittee on Technology, Information Policy, Intergovernmental Relations and the Census, Committee on Government Reform, U.S. House of Representatives, July 20, 2004.

Recent National Reforms: Motor Voter and HAVA

Two major pieces of legislation have somewhat reduced the variation in voting policies and practices among U.S. states and communities. In 1993, the National Voter Registration Act (NVRA), the so-called Motor Voter law, was passed by Congress and signed by President Bill Clinton (it did not take effect until 1995). NVRA's main goal was accessibility. The 2002 Help America Vote Act (HAVA), cited in the opening of this chapter, brought the principles of accuracy and accountability to the forefront of election administration.

NVRA: The Motor Voter Law

The Motor Voter law was designed to make the process of registering to vote easier and more accessible. It required states to allow citizens to register by mail and also required them to accept a universal mail-in voter registration form designed by the Federal Election Commission (FEC). States were free to mail voters a state-specific form, but they were required to honor the FEC form as a valid application for registration. The law requires voter registration forms to be available in public places. The critical policy departure from the past is that government agencies take a direct and proactive role in registering citizens to vote (as is common in other western democracies). The popular name comes from its provision requiring departments of motor vehicles to incorporate voter registration materials into the process of applying for or renewing a driver's license or nondriver's identification. Agencies responsible for public assistance programs must also offer voter registration. These include the agencies administering Temporary Assistance for Needy Families (TANF), Medicaid, Food Stamps, and the Women, Infants and Children (WIC) program.

The precise impact of the Motor Voter law is unclear. As with all legislation in the real world, we cannot know what would have happened in the absence of the stimulus. It probably added voters to the registration rolls but not the nine million cited by the Web site devoted to the legislation. It appeared to do little to increase aggregate national voter turnout. Turnout in the two presidential elections following Motor Voter (1996 and 2000) was lower than in the election before its passage (1992). In a recent statistical analysis over several elections, Brown and Wedeking found that although NVRA increased voter registration rolls, it had little direct effect on increased turnout among the states. They concluded, "By encouraging lower income citizens to register, NVRA has helped create a pool of registered citizens less likely to vote." [6]

Help America Vote Act (HAVA)

The policy goals of the Help America Vote Act of 2002 (HAVA) were quite different from those of the Motor Voter law. HAVA was passed in reaction to the problems that became apparent in the disputed presidential election of 2000. A key component of HAVA is federal grants to states and localities to replace old voting technologies such as punch cards and lever machines. HAVA also contains requirements for "second chance voting," meaning that voters can privately check for and correct ballot errors when there may be a machine error or malfunction. It requires that at least one voting device per polling place be accessible to disabled voters. These provisions meant that jurisdictions would need advanced technology to be able to handle the requirements of HAVA, providing impetus for more jurisdictions and states to buy DREs.

Other important requirements of HAVA, such as the use of provisional ballots, have generated considerable controversy. An individual whose name does not appear on the official voter registration list must be allowed to cast a ballot subject to verification that they are duly registered. The idea behind this reform was that no voter would be turned away at the polls. A recent example shows the impact of this provision: In Ohio in 2004, 158,642 provisional ballots were counted in the close presidential race, in a state that Bush won by 118,601 votes.

Another area in which state and local variation in response to HAVA has produced considerable controversy is voter identification requirements. HAVA requires only that all first-time registrants who register by mail must provide some identification at the time they vote, unless the individuals have already provided such identification with their voting application.

The law also established a new federal Election Assistance Commission (EAC) as a national clearinghouse for election system data; it is also to promote the study and evaluation of election procedures to highlight methods of voting and administration that are the most convenient, accessible, and easy to use. The commission received no formal rulemaking authority but can issue voluntary guidelines for voting systems and for HAVA requirements. The EAC was to have two Republican and two Democratic appointees. The first commissioners were appointed in December 2003, and the commission began to operate in January 2004. The EAC also has a separate Standards Board composed of a state election official and a local election official from each state representing different political parties. The Standards Board reviews voting systems and develops voluntary guidelines. The commission is responsible for the testing, certification, decertification, and recertification of voting system hardware and software. It uses the data to develop and adopt voting system guidelines. It also administers a variety of types of grant programs including disability access, voting technology research, computerized statewide voter registration lists, provisional voting, and a variety of pilot programs.

States Making the Act of Voting Easier: Absentee, Early, and Mail Voting

All states permit some form of voting prior to election day, by mail or in person. Traditional so-called absentee voting has historically been through the mail and has generally required a reason or "excuse" why the voter would be unavailable to cast their ballot on election day. Traditional absentee voting was cumbersome for both voters and election administrators (the former had to explain themselves and the latter had to judge whether the excuses were valid). States have been moving away from the excuse requirements in recent years, and as of 2006 a majority (twenty-eight) now have "no-excuse" absentee voting through the mail.[7]

Early voting allows many voters to cast their ballots in person or through the mail before election day.[8] The use of "non–election day" franchise options, such as absentee and early voting, makes voting easier and reduces the likelihood of congestion problems on election day. These reforms have spread to the point that in 2006 only fourteen states permitted neither early nor absentee in-person voting.[9] Paul Gronke and his colleagues examined the impact of the reforms and found statistically significant increases in voter turnout only in those states that have adopted no-excuse absentee voting combined with in-person early voting. Regardless, the effects on turnout were relatively minor.[10]

Voting by mail systems (VBM) involve sending every registered voter in a jurisdiction a ballot up to three weeks before election day.[11] Voters can mail them back or drop them off to election officials. VBM systems give voters time to cast ballots at their convenience. The state of Oregon has conducted all of its elections by mail since a special U.S. Senate election in early 1998. More recently, King County, Washington, including the city of Seattle and its immediate suburbs, has announced that it will move to a VBM system in 2008. King County will become the largest local jurisdiction in the country to use all-mail voting. Officials there expect approximately one million ballots in the 2008 presidential election.[12]

Controversies in the Short-Term Future

Throughout U.S. history, controversy has surrounded how governments count votes, particularly in high-profile national races. In this section I examine some of the most pertinent issues that will affect the process of voting in the next several years.

Quality of Election Data

"Reliable data is the mother's milk for studying election reform. . . . Without reliable data, we cannot intelligently assess the results of election laws like HAVA, much less determine what changes should be made prospectively." [13] Thad Hall and Daniel Tokaji found a lack of common standards and definitions among jurisdictions for collecting and reporting data. The problems extend to the most basic types of information, such as the number of ballots cast in a particular election—ten states could not report that simple statistic. Thus, a necessary first step for reforming election administration in America is to improve the reliability and validity of the public record election data. The inconsistencies in data collection practices and data availability are dramatic among the fifty states and thousands of local governments involved in election administration.

Many academic researchers and organizations committed to improving the electoral process have bemoaned the lack of accurate and easily available information. To remedy the data quality problem, Hall and Tokaji propose developing common standards and interoperability of data sets through a money-for-data federal grant program: "States that provide quality precinct-level data get paid. Those that provide incomplete or inaccurate data would not get paid." [14]

In its most recent biennial report to Congress, the Election Assistance Commission described the difficulty it encounters in obtaining accurate and consistent data from many states and local jurisdictions. The data quality problems make it difficult for the agency to monitor compliance with the requirements of federal legislation. The EAC recommended that the states work with the agency to establish consistent standards and to achieve interoperability of voter databases. The agency's report stressed the importance of having databases capable of tracking voter registration and voting history accurately, as those data are important for purging names from voter lists and implementing ID requirements.[15] The absence of such quality data could lead to problems not only in the presidential elections in 2008 and 2012, but also in subsequent midterm elections.

The problem of improving the quality of election data in America may not have the partisan cast of other contemporary controversies, but the fiscal and jurisdictional obstacles may be just as great. Any reforms will require a monetary commitment from governments at all levels, but experience suggests that they are unlikely to be given the highest budgetary priority by elected officials. Experience also suggests that the existing standard operating procedures of state and local election bureaucracies are likely to change very slowly. Florida was put on the cutting edge of change by necessity; Georgia was not.

Provisional Ballots

To prevent voters' being turned away at the polls because their names do not appear on the list of registered voters, Section 302 of HAVA requires provisional or "failsafe" voting. This is an attempt to reduce disfranchisement of voters as a result of administrative or clerical errors. Specifically, if a voter believes that they are eligible to vote even though their name is not on the registration list, they may cast a provisional ballot. If election officials later determine that the voter is eligible under state law, then the provisional ballot will be counted. To cast a provisional ballot at the polling place, the voter must sign an affirmation that he or she is a registered voter in the jurisdiction and eligible to vote in the election.

Provisional voting has further complicated the tasks of election administration and produced a wide variety of problems. Election officials are required to have a notification system in which individual voters can check to find out whether or not their vote was counted, and if not, the reason it was denied. On-site poll workers must provide people who seek to cast a provisional ballot written information about the notification system. Furthermore, as one would expect in America's state-centered system of election administration, the states have responded very differently to the HAVA requirements. Some, for example, count provisional ballots as long as they are cast in the correct county; others require them to be cast in the correct precinct. In West Virginia, voters are directed to cast provisional ballots if they fail to provide adequate identification. In the state of Maryland voters were required to cast provisional ballots when polling places extended their hours. Consequently, the rates at which provisional ballots were counted in the last presidential election varied dramatically from a high of 96 percent in Alaska to 6 percent in Delaware.[16]

Voter List Maintenance

The accuracy of voter lists is obviously critical to U.S. elections, but the specific ways to ensure accuracy are not so obvious. The difficulties and problems in list maintenance have led to suggested reforms that include the provisional voting discussed above.

HAVA mandates that names be removed as a result of death, mental incompetence, felony conviction, or change of residence. In the process, however, states are supposed to ensure that eligible voters are not removed from the voting rolls in error. The purging process of removing names from the statewide list is supposed to be completed no later than ninety days before a federal election.

The purging process at the statewide level has created substantial challenges for state election officials. Purging often involves computerized database matching against official records of felony convictions and deaths (when the data sets match names and birthdates, the voter's name is removed or purged from the rolls). Although the likelihood that different individuals will share the same name and date of birth is low at the individual level, large data sets can produce high absolute numbers of errors. Some databases may be incompatible because variables such as race may be coded in different ways. Given these methodological problems, election reformers have advocated using multiple criteria, in addition to name and date of birth, for purging through database matching, as well as requiring formal notification to the voter.[17]

Because voters eliminated through purging are disproportionately members of racial minorities and the poor, Democrats and Republicans have differed on the processes and zeal for administering these requirements. The Bush administration's Justice Department has come under fire for pushing states to purge their voter registration lists more aggressively. In 2005, for example, the Justice Department sued Missouri's Democratic secretary of state, Robin Carnahan, for failing to eliminate ineligible voters from the state's registration rolls. A federal judge threw out the suit this past spring, citing several reasons including the absence of any evidence of voter fraud. As Joseph Rich, a former chief of the Voting Rights Section of the Justice Department states, "Aggressive purging of the voter rolls tends to have a disproportionate impact on voters who move frequently, live in cities and have names that are more likely to be incorrectly entered into databases. . . . [T]his means poor, minority voters." [18] If the least affluent and racial minorities are the most likely to be removed by aggressive purging of voter rolls, then the partisan consequences of such actions would benefit Republicans.

Voter Identification Requirements

The debate over requiring voter identification at the polling place has a similarly partisan cast. The only identification requirement specified in HAVA is that all first-time voters who registered by mail must provide some ID at the time they vote, unless they already provided it with their registration application. The specific forms of acceptable ID enumerated in HAVA include valid photo identification, a copy of a current utility bill, a bank statement, a government check, a paycheck, or other government document that shows the name and address of the voter. Given the exigencies of 9/11, official identification has become even more important to voting officials to ensure that the integrity of the voting process is maintained.

Currently, 26 states and the District of Columbia do not have identification requirements greater than those mandated in HAVA; 24 states go further by requiring identification prior to casting a ballot.[19] Of the latter group, 17 accept a range of documents that do not necessarily have to include a photo. Seven states have adopted photo identification requirements at the polling place. However, the future of these requirements is questionable because of their potential discriminatory effect on racial minorities and the least-affluent voters, especially in states covered by the Voting Rights Act (mostly in the South), since empirical evidence indicates that such requirements disproportionately affect racial minorities.

A recent study commissioned by the EAC on the impact of state voter identification laws found significantly lower turnout in states that required documentary identification at the polls, compared to those who did not have such a requirement.[20] The gap was the greatest for African Americans, Asian Americans, and Hispanics. Voter identification policies are similar to the aggressive purging of voter lists in that the primary motivation for pursuing each must be to gain political partisan advantage, since there are few incidents nationally of actual vote fraud. The EAC itself has been accused of buckling under partisan pressure from the Bush White House in its handling of the findings of a study that has reinforced the existing academic literature to the effect that vote fraud is not a major problem in America.[21] These issues are thus almost assuredly short term, since there appears to be no systemic problem in election administration that proponents are attempting to resolve.

Disfranchisement of Convicted Felons

HAVA authorizes the purging of voter names for felony conviction, but predictably, the states vary tremendously in their policies and practices on whether and how voting rights can be restored. The offenses for which one might lose one's voting rights, perhaps for life, range from writing a bad check or possession of marijuana to armed robbery or murder. In fact, five states disfranchise people for some categories of misdemeanors, as well as felonies.[22] In thirty-five states, the voting rights of felons are automatically restored after the completion of their sentences (although the individuals must register to vote again). In the other states, disproportionately southern, felons are disfranchised for life unless they receive a pardon or go through some special approval process.

The large number of incarcerated people in the United States means that millions of Americans are disfranchised in any given election. Disproportionate shares of the disfranchised are racial and ethnic minorities or whites who come from the least-affluent segment of society. Approximately 13 percent of African American males cannot vote because of felony disfranchisement.

The restoration of voting rights to former offenders is a highly charged political issue. The chairman of the House Judiciary Committee, John Conyers (D-Mich.), has made the issue a personal mission. Some conservative Republicans, however, argue that voting is a privilege whose loss is the price of breaking the law when the crime is serious (a felony). In a highly polarized and evenly balanced partisan environment, slight changes in the eligible electorate could potentially tip the political scales.

Voter-Verifiable Paper Audit Trails (VVPAT)

Concerns about ballot security generally and the lack of a paper trail in direct recording electronic voting systems (DREs) have led Congress to consider a variety of legislation to amend HAVA's ballot verification procedures and requirements in favor of a mandatory paper trail audit capacity for voting equipment. Although the timetables for compliance vary, the proposed changes would require all voting equipment to produce a voter-verifiable paper audit trail (VVPAT). Voters could use the paper record to verify their choices, and it would serve as the official ballot in possible recounts.

The problems of not having a so-called paper trail were dramatized by the disputed election in Florida's thirteenth congressional district in 2006. In an ironic twist, the contest to succeed Katherine Harris in the House of Representatives produced controversy and calls for electoral reform. Democrat Christine Jennings apparently lost to Republican Vern Buchanan by less than 400 votes on election day. However, an unusually large number of voters in Sarasota County did not record a vote for either candidate in the congressional race. The total number of "under votes" was more than 18,000—far more than the winner's narrow margin of victory. But because Sarasota County used touch screen voting, without a paper trail, there were questions about how to determine definitively whether or not the ballots were properly counted.

The incident led Florida to eliminate so-called paperless voting systems throughout the state. Immediately after Republican governor Charlie Crist signed the legislation, Jennings hailed the reform saying, "By eliminating the paperless voting system, Florida can now be a national model for fair and accurate elections." [23]

Recent Developments in Voting Verification

The disputed Florida contest was one of many catalysts for reform at the federal level as well. In the House, the leading expert on voting technology in Congress, Rep. Rush Holt (D-N.J.), introduced H.R. 811, the Voter Confidence and Increased Accountability Act of 2007.[24] In the upper chamber, Sen. Dianne Feinstein (D-Calif.) introduced similar legislation, the Ballot Integrity Act (S. 1487). At this writing, the Feinstein proposal appears to have broader support, at least in part because the deadline for voter-verified paper ballots is two years later than the one in H.R. 811 (2010 as opposed to 2008). The proposed legislation includes requirements that every polling place have emergency paper ballots to offer voters in case voting machines break down or other problems arise that cause long delays. The Feinstein bill also includes provisions for increased grant programs to help states purchase voting equipment; sets purging, no-excuse absentee voting, and poll worker training requirements; mandates that states develop guidelines for timely counting of provisional ballots; and prohibits states from rejecting military and overseas ballots because of nonessential requirements.[25] After an election, localities would be required to conduct rigorous audits of most federal contests to ensure that the machines had functioned properly.[26]

A variety of obstacles have prevented either bill from passing in the current Congress. The National Association of Counties (NACO) and other groups representing the interests of state and local election administrators have lobbied heavily against the proposals. NACO and others are concerned that one-size-fits-all federal legislation will require them to "junk most of the voting equipment" [27] that has been recently purchased. NACO maintains further that the proposed timetables are unrealistic and would result in a rush to new technologies, which need adequate time for testing, poll worker training, and voter education.[28] A statement from the Elections Technology Council (ETC), the voting system manufacturers' industry trade association, reinforced the timetable concerns. The ETC supports the VVPAT concept but maintained last spring that it was too late to implement changes for the 2008 federal elections. The organization estimated that it would take from eighteen months to more than four years to fully deploy the proposed changes.[29] Another obstacle is that advocates for the blind and disabled are concerned that touch screen machines will be phased out before optical scanners are made easier to use. They fear that the handicapped will not be able to use the optical ballots without help.

The results of a recent Georgia pilot project support the legitimacy of some of these concerns. The project was conducted in three precincts in three Georgia counties in the 2006 general and runoff elections. The study found technical challenges with VVPAT technology, including paper jams and ballot tape layout; increased voting time; and a lack of ensured anonymity. The manual audits were costly, time-consuming, and prone to human error. However, exit polls indicated an increase in voter confidence in accuracy and security with the use of VVPAT. Overall, more than 80 percent of voters surveyed supported a verifiable paper trail.[30]

The latter finding reflects the strong support that people express when asked if they favor a paper trail for voting. There appears to be widespread suspicion of machines without a paper trail. The combination of mass support and elite-level support from computer scientists and other activists suggests that the movement toward elimination of DRE systems without a paper trail will not go away in the immediate future. However, the cost and logistical difficulties of switching to machines with printed records may slow the spread of the change.

Online or Internet Voting

No other reform or technology has as much potential to revolutionize the administration of U.S. elections as online or Internet voting. It has the promise to alter fundamentally every aspect of the process and address many contemporary problems, such as the aging of our nation's poll workers and the training of new ones, accessibility for the disabled, provisional ballots, voter purging, voter identification, and the multimillion-dollar cost of new voting machines. Indeed, the broad vision articulated by supporters of Internet voting could make virtually every task of election administration easier, if not automatic. In the future, Internet voting might reduce the variation and confusion in election administration among states and localities more dramatically than any piece of federal legislation. Even the traditional physical precinct or polling place might become a relic of the past. However, as with "blind" e-mails offering to share large sums of money from a foreign bank, the promise is probably too good to be true, at least in the short run.

The primary concerns about online or Internet voting are security, access, and legitimacy. Of these security is probably the most serious. Although vote fraud and election tampering are feasible with other voting systems, they are particularly worrisome in Internet voting. Internet voting leaves open the possibility that someone other than the eligible voter could actually cast the ballot or that the results could be technologically altered. Many critics, including prominent computer scientists such as Ronald Rivest, maintain that the outcome of an election could be altered by computer viruses or hackers. According to Rivest, the biggest challenges are to prove that votes are recorded as cast and are tallied accurately.[31] It was the concern over precisely those issues that led the Pentagon to cancel a program for the 2004 presidential election that would have permitted as many as 100,000 military and overseas citizens to vote through the Internet.

The access issues result from the so-called digital divide in the United States. Great inequities exist in people's access to the Internet and their comfort with using a computer. These problems could be addressed by effective election administration. Remote site systems, in which people could vote from any computer connected to the Internet, are only one of the many options. It is possible, for example, to have computers available at each polling place or at a variety of public places, such as libraries or city halls, instead of traditional voting machines, with trained poll workers to assist voters with the new technology. The latter options would, however, negate some of the presumed advantages of Internet voting, such as reducing the costs of voting for individuals and governments.

A variety of public elections in recent years have included experiments with Internet voting. They include the Arizona Democratic primary in 2000, the Michigan Democratic caucus in 2004, and the national elections in Estonia in 2007. The results of these limited exercises suggest that any movement toward Internet or online voting in the short run is unlikely to increase voter participation. In the most recent example, in the eastern European nation of Estonia, only 30,243 voters, or 5.4 percent of the total, cast their ballots online.[32]

Brian Krueger challenges the emerging conventional wisdom among scholars that patterns of Internet political participation will replicate the existing patterns of participatory inequality in America because the most advantaged in society access the Internet at much higher rates than the least advantaged. Kruger maintains that the focus on access has important theoretical limitations. "If one accepts the possibility of near equal access, then explorations of the Internet's potential should include theoretical guidance about what types of individuals would most likely participate if equal access were achieved." His empirical test concludes that "the Internet shows genuine potential to bring new individuals into the political process." [33]

Internet voting may someday revolutionize election administration in America and throughout the globe. But the prospects for its widespread use are not bright in the short term, as the access, security, and legitimacy concerns are too great at this point. The intensity of voter reaction to the lack of a verifiable paper trail in DRE systems is likely to pale in comparison to the concerns over Internet voting. There will, of course, continue to be pilot projects in states and communities and with military and overseas voting. Many companies and universities are using online voting successfully for a variety of types of elections. However, the nature and scale of their operations are fundamentally different from the administration of government elections with legal and constitutional consequences.

Conclusion

The broad trends in American election administration have been toward national standards and reduced variation in policies and procedures among the states and their localities. The national movements have generally been aimed at improving voter access to the ballot box and broadening popular participation (the trends in disfranchising felons, purging lists, and voter identification requirements notwithstanding). But despite the nationalizing effects of Supreme Court decisions, the Voting Rights Act, Motor Voter, and HAVA, there continue to be very substantial differences in the conduct of elections among the fifty states and thousands of local jurisdictions. (In fact, as this book goes to press, the Supreme Court is examining the constitutionality of an Indiana law that requires voters to produce a government-issued photo ID at the polls as proof of identity.)

Our country's immediate future challenges in election administration involve election systems and technology. The security and accuracy of how we count ballots are the most critical issues to be resolved. The problem of dangling chads is being replaced by the problem of absence of a paper trail with the new technology of DREs. Regardless of whether bills before Congress to require voter-verified paper audit trails become law, the central concerns of ballot verification and accuracy will not be resolved in the short term but rather far beyond the end of the decade. Furthermore, the movement toward paper trails will likely slow as the costs and complications of the change become more apparent.

The American Enterprise Institute–Brookings Institution Election Reform Project contends that verifiable paper trails may not be enough. Researcher Timothy Ryan of the Election Reform Project claims that paper ballots can be "modified, counterfeited or destroyed." He also claims that machines that produce paper ballots "are susceptible to mechanical failure." Ryan proposes two alternative systems: One, known as Prime III, developed by researchers at Auburn University, employs a "separate electronic witness" in the polling booth that acts independently of the voting machine to double-check how votes are counted. The second type of machine, designed by a team at the University of Maryland, is known as Punchscan. The most prominent feature of Punchscan is that it enables voters to go to a "computer and use a receipt to review their individual ballots online." But current legislative proposals, according to Ryan, do not consider either technology because neither produces a verifiable paper audit.[34] It is likely that in the short term verifiable systems to count votes will continue to rely on paper and not on cutting-edge technology.

The myriad controversies, litigation, and legislative reforms since the 2000 presidential election have placed election administration in a state of instability and uncertainty that will likely continue for the foreseeable future. Constant change and turmoil have made it difficult for administrators to plan and budget for elections with any degree of confidence. There is uncertainty about voting equipment, audit requirements, the personnel skills and training that may be necessary, and rigid or unrealistic deadlines set by policy makers.[35] There may be another wave of federal election reform in the next year or two, with new voting system technologies, new deadlines, and more unfunded or underfunded mandates. The contemporary controversies discussed here, over provisional voting, improvements in voter list maintenance, voting rights for felons, and so forth, have yet to be resolved. Resolving them will necessarily involve more changes for election administrators.

The act of voting will become easier in the near future as a result of the diffusion of reforms in no-excuse absentee, early, and mail voting and same-day voter registration. These changes, however, are unlikely to affect the socioeconomic bias of the participating electorate. People in society with the most education and money tend to have the highest levels of political interest and engagement—the core factors that drive citizens to vote.[36] Reforms to make it easier for registered voters to cast ballots may actually increase, rather than decrease, socioeconomic bias in the composition of the voting public, since it is the most "engaged citizens who take advantage of liberal voting rules. Those lacking political interest remain nonvoters." [37] The research by Krueger, however, suggests that broad-based Internet voting might be an exception to the conventional wisdom about the impact of electoral reforms.[38]

In the long run, advances in technology may dramatically improve all aspects of election administration, including broadening mass participation. That could ultimately increase the legitimacy of, and public confidence in, American elections. As part of this process it is likely that voter access to and interest in Internet voting will increase as the digital divide narrows. As a nation, however, we are unlikely to pursue Internet voting beyond the pilot project phase until we can be sure that it is at least as secure and accurate as our current voting systems.

Notes

1. Sen. Christopher Dodd (D-Conn.), statement, Hearing on Nominations for the Election Assistance Commission, Rules Committee, U.S. Senate, October 28, 2003.
2. Randolph C. Hite, "Electronic Voting Offers Opportunities and Presents Challenges," release by the General Accounting Office prior to testimony before the Subcommittee on Technology, Information Policy, Intergovernmental Relations and the Census, Committee on Governmental Reform, U.S. House of Representatives, July 20, 2004.
3. Adam J. Berinsky, "The Perverse Consequences of Electoral Reform in the United States," *American Politics Research* 33 (2005): 471–491.
4. Jeanette Senecal, "Election Day Front Line: Poll Workers," *National Voter* 56 (2007): 6.
5. Hite, "Electronic Voting Offers Opportunities."
6. Robert D. Brown and Justin Wedeking, "People Who Have Their Tickets but Do Not Use Them," *American Politics Research* 34 (2006): 479.

7. Berinsky, "The Perverse Consequences of Electoral Reform"; see www.electionline.org.

8. Berinsky, "The Perverse Consequences of Electoral Reform."

9. See www.electionline.org.

10. Paul Gromke et al. "Early Voting and Turnout," paper presented at 2008 and Beyond: The Future of Elections and Ethics Reform in the States, conference at Kent State University, Columbus, Ohio, January 2007.

11. Berinsky, "The Perverse Consequences of Electoral Reform."

12. Richard Smolka, editor, "King County Plans to Allow Voters to Track Absentee Ballots on Web," *Election Administration Reports,* June 11, 2007.

13. Thad Hall and Daniel Tokaji, "Money for Data: Funding the Oldest Unfunded Mandate," www.equalvote.blogspot.com, June 5, 2007.

14. Ibid.

15. Richard Smolka, editor, "EAC Report to Congress on NVRA Recommends That States Standardize Registration Data," *Election Administration Reports,* July 9, 2007.

16. See "Maximizing the Effectiveness of Provisional Voting," www.projectvote.org.

17. See "Maintaining Current and Accurate Voter Lists" at www.projectvote.org.

18. Greg Gordon, "Vote Law Drive Questioned," *Miami Herald,* International Edition, June 5, 2007, 2A.

19. See the National Conference of State Legislatures Web site, www.ncsl.org.

20. Eagleton Institute of Politics, "Best Practices to Improve the Help America Vote Act of 2002," Rutgers University, 2005.

21. Alec Ewald, *A Crazy Quilt of Tiny Pieces: State and Local Administration of American Criminal Justice Disfranchisement Law* (Washington, D.C.: Sentencing Project, 2005).

22. Ibid.

23. Stacey Edison, "End of Screen Voting Lauded," *Bradenton Herald,* May 22, 2007, A1.

24. Christopher Drew, "Overhaul Plan for Vote System Will Be Delayed," *New York Times,* July 20, 2007.

25. Richard Smolka, "Senator Feinstein Introduces Comprehensive Election Reform Bill," *Election Administration Reports,* May 29, 2007.

26. Drew, "Overhaul Plan for Vote System Will Be Delayed."

27. Alyson McLaughlin, "Standardized Voting Bill Fast-Tracked despite County Objections," *County News* 39, p. 2 (May 21, 2007).

28. Richard Smolka, "NACO Opposes Holt Bill, Asks for 2–3 Year Delay before Implementation of Any New Standards," *Election Administration Reports,* March 19, 2007.

29. Richard Smolka, "House Plans to Mark Up Holt Bill after Returning from Spring Recess," *Election Administration Reports,* April 2, 2007.

30. Richard Smolka, "Georgia Secretary of State Issues Report Finding Significant Challenges with VVPAT Technology," *Election Administration Reports,* April 16, 2007.

31. Tim Greene, "Don't Trust Online Voting, Speaker Says," *Network World,* www.computerworld.com, April 13, 2007.

32. See www.osce.org.

33. Brian S. Krueger, "Assessing the Potential of Internet Political Participation in the United States," *American Politics Research* 30(2002): 476.

34. Timothy Ryan, "A Damaging Paper Chase in Voting," *Washington Post,* September 8, 2007, A15.

35. Richard Smolka, telephone interview, July 12, 2007.
36. Steven J. Rosenstone and John M. Hansen, *Mobilization, Participation and Democracy in America* (New York: Macmillan, 1993).
37. Berinsky, "The Perverse Consequences of Electoral Reform," 484.
38. Krueger, "Assessing the Potential of Internet Political Participation."

CHAPTER 12

Campaigns and Democracy— Into a New Era

Dick Simpson

WHEN HE WAS A STATE LEGISLATOR IN ILLINOIS, Abraham Lincoln said that there are three basic tasks in a political campaign: Canvass the district, identify your voters, and get them to the polls. Nothing much has changed, except for the technology. To win elections you still have to talk to the voters, find out who supports your candidate, and get them to vote on election day. The fact that we use computers, e-mail, Web sites, paid media ads, public opinion polls, microtargeting, automatic phone calls to potential voters, and direct-mail appeals does not change the fundamentals of campaigning. Yet technology in new political campaigns does make a difference. It provides the opportunity to increase democratic participation in elections. It also provides Orwellian opportunities to manipulate voters and citizens.

The Cost of Modern Political Campaigns

Because of new technology and the cost of staff and campaign consultants, new political campaigns have gotten very expensive. In local campaigns for city council in large cities, as well as for county board, state legislature, and citywide offices in smaller towns or suburbs, there are usually at least three paid staff members. There is also the need to buy paid campaign ads at least on cable TV and radio and in local newspapers. Direct-mail and phone campaigns and a candidate Web site, in addition to the traditional precinct operations, are also expensive. These kinds of local campaigns now often cost from $100,000 to $250,000. Compare that to the focus of this book, national political campaigns. Even congressional campaigns will often require as many as five or six paid staff members and paid public relations, advertising, and campaign consultants. The need to have Web sites and sophisticated Internet technology adds to the costs. Successful congressional campaigns usually cost over $1 million to run. Campaigns for statewide office, at least in the larger states, cost more than $10 million. Presidential campaigns cost hundreds of millions of dollars, with more than $40 million raised before the first primary or caucus vote is cast. In the 2004 presidential campaign, George W. Bush spent $5.92 for each of his 62 million votes. In 2006, it cost winning congressional candidates an average of $11.19 per vote to win their seat in the House of Representatives.[1]

These expensive campaigns cannot be funded just by the candidate, a few modestly wealthy friends, and excited volunteers. Professional fundraising and larger campaign contributions by interest groups, political parties, and political action committees are required. So, in addition to general campaign electioneering plans, a campaign has to develop specific, serious fundraising plans from the beginning. In short, high-tech, candidate-centered, multimedia, new technology campaigns are too expensive for just a good candidate running on good issues to win regularly. The danger of high-cost campaigns is that they will undermine democracy, because it is often the candidates with the most money, not the best character and the best ideas, who win. Candidates without personal wealth or the ability to raise large campaign donations are often eliminated.

Sometimes political parties seek out prominent individuals to run and can provide the candidate the necessary resources to get started. Most of the time, however, the candidate who wants to run must assemble the resources first before any political organization will accept him or her as a viable candidate. That wealthy individuals and powerful groups control the recruitment and election of most successful candidates is a threat to our representative democracy. Those candidates, once elected, then can potentially skew government policies to favor their largest contributors.

Raising these massive amounts of campaign funds requires both wealthy groups and individuals. As Boatright points out in chapter 2, 40 percent of congressional campaign funds in the past four elections have come from political action committees (PACs). Moreover, campaign fundraising both in presidential and in many congressional campaigns depends heavily on influential contributors who solicit and bundle $50,000 to $100,000 or more in campaign contributions. This dependence on PACs and large contributors has to some extent begun to be offset by new Web site and e-mail solicitations, which serve to broaden the base of these campaigns. However business interest groups, such as Goldman Sachs, which contributed $3.4 million in 2006, and unions, such as the National Education Association, which contributed $2.4 million, remain critical to funding national and statewide campaigns; so do wealthy individuals who solicit contributions, like the 221 "Rangers" and 327 "Pioneers" who together raised $77 million for President George W. Bush's reelection campaign in 2004 (data from chapters 8 and 2).

Candidate Image

In any campaign, a candidate's image is important. In the 2004 presidential election, President Bush attempted to project the image of a successful "war president," who led the country after the terrorist attacks of September 11, 2001, and led the war on terror in Afghanistan and Iraq. His Democratic opponent, Sen. John Kerry (D-Mass.), pushed his image as a genuine war hero who had the courage to protest the Vietnam War and as a U.S. senator who was particularly knowledgeable about foreign affairs and national security. Thus, despite concerns about the economy and domestic issues such as gay marriage or dealing with pollution, the 2004 presidential election was fought and won over who would be the best leader in wartime. As subsequent events have shown, it is not clear that President Bush was actually the best leader to fight the war. However, he clearly won the image war in the 2004 campaign.

So even before the issues of the campaign are joined, a positive image for the candidate must be created. Shaping that image is the task of the candidate, the campaign manager, and public relations consultants. Allowing an opponent's portrayal of the candidate to go unanswered will surely lose the election.

In the new campaign era, a candidate's persona can be manipulated more easily to influence voters, particularly those who are undecided. Campaigns, candidates, reporters, and citizens must be aware of such dangers. New technologies give campaigns more filters for candidate image presentation than in the past, when citizens were more likely to know their representatives personally. How those images are altered may be more sophisticated today, but the phenomenon traces at least as far back as Joe McGinniss's book *The Selling of the President 1968*, which told the story of Richard Nixon's successful campaign makeover.[2] Since then campaigns have used public opinion polls and focus groups to determine the most positive image of candidates and which negative attack ads best discredit their opponents. Then campaigns simply choose the most effective media to deliver those messages forcefully. These techniques, so highly developed in presidential campaigns, are now available to any candidate for state, local, and congressional office with the money to pay for the consultants and experts who know how to use them.

The changes in the techniques of public opinion polling and focus groups—from random digit dialing to calling from voter files, and now to online Internet surveys—do not change the basic use of polls and focus groups, according to Candice J. Nelson in chapter 5. Polls and focus groups, however conducted, are still used to determine the views of potential voters on issues and the candidate's image and to test both positive and negative advertising. Certainly public opinion polling provides useful information to candidates, the news media, and public officials, whether obtained by phone interviews, Internet surveys, or focus groups, and that information can illuminate a concern they are unaware of. Unfortunately, it also has the potential to undermine democracy itself. There are no simple legislative cures for the evils that poll information can cause when it is misused by those in the political process, most especially candidates. The only safeguards are capable opposing candidates, independent journalists and bloggers, and a wise and sophisticated electorate.

Delivering the Message

Publicity and communicating through the media are used to recruit volunteers, attract campaign donors, and win votes. The best campaigns have a single, unified theme. "Free media" is not really free because it has to be exploited by professional public relations staffers and highly paid political consultants, but it is cheaper than many other ways of delivering the message. Consultants call it "earned media" because the candidate has to take action and controversial stands, using the proper public relations techniques, to "earn" media coverage.

Few if any campaigns anymore are solely won by press conferences and staged campaign events covered by the media. There are other methods by which a good campaign delivers its message. One method is paid advertising. Others include personal campaigning by the candidate, precinct work by campaign supporters, direct-mail and phone campaigns, and creative use of the Internet. Although the use of new techniques such as Internet Web sites has greatly increased in the twenty-first century, with even major aldermanic and school board campaigns beginning to employ them, a mix of campaign techniques must be used to deliver a candidate's message to the voters.

On the Internet: Money and Video

For a number of campaign cycles now, candidates have been developing the Internet as a means of winning elections. Before the 2000 elections no campaign had been won simply through the use of the Internet, and it is still impossible to win elections by use of the Internet alone. Yet the Internet is playing a bigger role. It is relatively cheap, and in its various forms it can be used to recruit and coordinate volunteers, provide background campaign information to reporters and bloggers, raise significant sums of money, reach important opinion and community leaders, and of course, convince some voters to vote for candidates. For instance, direct-mail fundraising costs forty cents for every dollar raised; Internet appeals cost less than a penny for every dollar a campaign receives in contributions.

Presidential campaigns have developed the techniques of Internet campaigning most extensively. In the primary elections in 2000, Democratic presidential candidate Sen. Bill Bradley (D-N.J.) used the Internet to rally scattered volunteers to meetings and inspire them to open home headquarters and organize in their local communities. Bradley also raised money successfully on the Internet, as did

Republican presidential candidate Sen. John McCain (R-Ariz.), who was the most successful candidate up to then in Internet fundraising. McCain raised more than a million dollars in less than forty-eight hours in the 2000 election.[3] Successful Internet campaign efforts in the 2000 election have forced all presidential candidates since to have extensive Internet sites listing their press releases, campaign platforms, and speeches. They have also used them to recruit volunteers and, most important, raise money.

By the 2004 Democratic primary elections, former Vermont governor Howard Dean almost won the nomination through his enormously successful Internet fundraising. He raised $7.5 million in the period from April to June 2003, $1.5 million more than John Kerry in the same period. Two-thirds of his contributions came via the Internet.[4] What was even more impressive, and later widely copied, was his mobilization of volunteers through "meetups" in communities throughout the primary states.

The 2004 campaigns of Sen. John Kerry and President Bush soon followed the Dean example with innovative Web sites and special e-mail lists to stimulate supporters to attend campaign rallies, sign nominating petitions, send letters to the editor of the local newspaper, and of course, give ever-greater sums of money in the first campaign in the nation's history to raise and spend over a billion dollars. Non–candidate organizations like MoveOn and ACT (America Coming Together), in support of Kerry, and Christian conservative organizations in support of Bush made extensive use of similar Internet techniques. By late 2007, the 2008 campaigns had already broken all fundraising records, in large part through the Internet. Sen. Barack Obama (D-Ill.) received $10.3 million through Internet contributions in the second quarter of 2007 and recruited an amazing 258,000 contributors in the first six months of the year.[5] Local congressional candidates now also use the Internet. Virtually all of them have Web sites, as do all seated congressmen. In the 2006 midterm elections, 31 percent of the voters used the Internet to get political news and e-mailed others to discuss the races.

Among the latest techniques are e-videos on such sites as YouTube and Facebook. The most famous YouTube videos thus far have been the "macaca" comment of defeated senator George Allen (R-Va.), Barack Obama's "Obama Girl," and Hillary and Bill Clinton's "Sopranos" ad. In the 2008 presidential campaign, CNN sponsored the first presidential debate, in which Democratic candidates gathered at the Citadel, in Charleston, South Carolina, to answer questions submitted by video on YouTube. The videotaped questions were selected from among 3,000 entries.[6]

In addition to Web sites and e-videos, many congressional candidates and presidential campaigns at the state level coordinate their volunteers using e-mail lists, which allow the campaign staff to send an e-mail letter to all volunteers at once, at no cost. They use e-mail appeals in addition to the candidate Web page, to which constituents, supporters, and potential supporters can be referred, to raise money as well as to encourage them to attend political events.

As with all communication methods, it takes money and expertise to set up campaign Web sites and Internet operations. They have to be updated as often as several times a day. There is also danger in the use of Internet technology. As Philip Howard describes it, "Political communication technologies have become so advanced that it is possible for campaign managers to send significantly different messages to potential supporters. . . . [P]olitical campaigns in the United States are increasingly manipulative, as managers find new ways to distribute propaganda, mine data, mark political interests, and mislead people unfamiliar with computing technologies." Howard argues that what he calls "hypermedia campaigns" have succeeded "mass media campaigns" through these new technologies.[7] Joseph Graf, in chapter 4, takes the position instead that the Internet and other new media do not supplant older media such as television ads in mobilizing support and fundraising, but complement the older media. Either way, there are positive and negative aspects to campaigning on the Internet.

Using the Internet to campaign certainly has democratizing potential. It costs less to use than expensive mass media advertising. It can mobilize large numbers of citizens to participate in the election. It allows hundreds or thousands of small financial contributors to become more significant to a campaign than a few wealthy individuals or powerful interest groups, freeing elected officials to represent "the people" rather than particular interests. Anyone can support a candidate by e-mail, on a blog, or in a chat room, building the buzz for a candidate and the momentum of a campaign. The Internet is not a passive medium because it requires some form of engagement by the user. Yet it is not a form of direct democracy because the campaigns establish the medium being used, and the implications can be deleterious to citizens and governance.

Advertising

Political advertising is undergoing a technological revolution unimaginable a decade ago. Ads are not only appearing on television and radio but also on the Web, in Web videos, and in e-mail videos. Most often, as Tad Devine points out in chapter 3, ads are filmed using digital technology, so that modified versions of the same ad appear on television, the Internet, and even cell phone screens. The mix depends primarily on the money each campaign has to spend and on the audience the campaign seeks to reach.

Advertising on cable television can be very inexpensive and cost-effective for candidates. As Devine has shown, cable ads reach down even to the local level. For instance, in Calabasas, California, a community of only 20,000 residents, councilman James Bozajian was able to secure his reelection by a landslide, when other incumbents were defeated, with a series of thirty-second cable TV spots purchased for as little as $17 a spot. Rather than purchase ads during only the last two weeks of an election, as candidates tend to do on high-priced broadcast TV channels, candidates advertising on cable TV purchase ads three months before the election, giving voters enough time to see them. Cable TV ads must have the same quality, or "production values," as commercials seen on regular TV channels—they cannot be made at home by an amateur on his computer and still be effective in swaying voters. A campaign needs voters to remember an ad, to be persuaded by it. Campaigns cannot show the same spot for twelve weeks, with rare exceptions. Rather they create a series of spots to introduce the candidate, present her platform and issues, and give a final pitch with endorsements from newspapers and other media. Generally a campaign focuses ad buys on the four or five most popularly watched channels, concentrating on local news channels that are watched by the most interested voters.

Although congressional and presidential campaigns have the funds to concentrate mainly on traditional ads on television, the cheaper costs of cable TV and the growing number of viewers of cable programs mean that we can expect candidates for national office to make much greater use of this medium in 2008 and beyond.

Still newer for candidates are Web videos or e-videos, which can be downloaded from a candidate's Web site, or better still e-mailed to family, friends, supporters, and other e-mail lists that a campaign can obtain. According to interviews by the *Dallas Morning News,* local candidates say that "e-mailing the videos is more immediate and cost-effective than traditional campaign ads, especially if the recipients forward the video to friends and family." [8]

All advertising, from the most old-fashioned to the latest high-tech, highlights and reinforces (1) the candidate's name (and image), (2) the office for which they are running, and (3) the reason to vote for the candidate (which echoes the campaign theme). In major campaigns, advertising can consume as much as 70 percent of the budget. The newer techniques allow campaigns to find a less expensive way of reaching voters with ads, but they do not guarantee truthfulness or a full discussion of the issues.

Advertising, especially unfair, negative ads attacking opponents late in the campaign in ways that cannot be countered effectively, can undermine the democratic process. One cannot forget the advertisement run against Sen. Max Cleland (D-Ga.) in 2002, during his Senate reelection campaign. Cleland is a bona fide war hero, a triple amputee by virtue of his wounds suffered in the Vietnam War. His opponent, Saxby Chambliss, accused the Georgia senator of being soft on national security through a television ad that showed a picture of Cleland in tandem with pictures of Osama bin Laden and Saddam Hussein.[9] Whereas ads can tell us about candidates and issues, inform and educate, they can also distort the service and destroy the careers of valued public servants.

Personal Campaigning in Decline: The Lost Art of Persuasion?

In political films like *Blaze,* in which Paul Newman portrays Earl Long running for governor of Louisiana, or in *The Last Hurrah,* in which an old party boss attends political rallies, torchlight parades, and funerals, we see the most common image of political campaigns. Campaigning is about the candidates themselves, meeting the voters, shaking their hands, being seen in parades and meetings, and speaking at large rallies of political supporters. Even in this modern era of mass media, targeted direct mail, and the Internet, a candidate still must make, or appear to make, personal appearances to be elected. Of course, direct personal campaigning is insufficient in most presidential, statewide, and even most congressional campaigns. What must be used instead to convey information to the voters are media reports of candidates campaigning directly to some voters and groups. Most voters will not personally meet or hear the candidate. Samuel Popkin, in his book *The Reasoning Voter,* argues that not only is more campaign information good for voters, but even more important, campaigns best serve when candidates personally connect with citizens. In other words, technology at its best can facilitate, but not substitute for, candidates' personally educating voters.[10]

Modern Field Organizations and Voter Mobilization

In high-tech, candidate-centered, modern campaigns, sometimes money, professional political consultants, and paid advertising, along with specialized direct-mail and phone campaigns, may defeat the best precinct work. It is harder and harder, in an economy that demands that everyone work, often at more than one job, to find enough people to volunteer to cover all the precincts and reach all the voters. But precinct work can also make a significant contribution to citywide, statewide, congressional, and presidential campaigns. Of course, precinct work must be adapted to recent changes in elections, such as the fact that as many as 50 percent of the voters vote absentee long before election day in states such as Oregon, Florida, and Washington.[11] Since thirty-five states allow "no-excuse" absentee voting, it is a problem for all campaigns to adapt both their precinct work and marketing strategies to influence these earlier voters.

Campaign precinct work can take on new forms and be combined with the Internet and other forms of high-tech campaigning. For instance, in the 2004 campaign, MoveOn mounted a massive attempt to register student supporters of John Kerry in their dorms and on campus and then mobilize them to vote. Information and instructions were sent by e-mail to all MoveOn student volunteers. They were told how to register other students to vote and how to obtain absentee ballots from their home precinct or in the precinct where the school dorm was located. Equally important to getting more students to vote for MoveOn candidates was sending e-mails reminding students to register, to vote, and to go door to door in the dorms to get their fellow student voters to the polls. Similar techniques are being adapted today, where the Internet and shoe leather combine to register voters, find voters who favor particular candidates, and get them to the polls on election day.

Modern technology, however, cannot substitute for shoe leather. Staffing a field operation with trained workers able to carry out petition and voter registration drives, a door-to-door canvass, and poll watching on election day is still the secret to winning elections. Precinct work provides a personal and inexpensive way to reach voters, register them, deliver a campaign message, and get voters to the polls. It is still the best way to carry out Abe Lincoln's electioneering advice to canvass the district, identify your voters, and get them to the polls. It is key for effective get-out-the-vote (GOTV) campaigns at the state and national levels. A campaign can have the best candidate, get the best publicity, raise money, and hold the most successful campaign rallies, but if it doesn't have the workers to go door to door convincing voters, it is often doomed. Even national presidential campaigns depend more than many realize on door-to-door contacts.

Of course, precinct work is only one form of voter mobilization. In the high-tech, new campaigns of the twenty-first century, microtargeting, direct mail, phone campaigns, Internet advertising, and e-mail voting reminders are all part of the process. By 2006, both the Republicans and the Democrats had developed sophisticated seventy-two-hour plans, using political parties, interest groups, and volunteers to deliver "their" voters to the polls. Blogs, e-mails, and Web sites are pressed into service, creating a "virtual community" and an online campaign to supplement the traditional precinct worker ground wars in reaching voters.

Yet all of this has some disturbing aspects for our democracy. Consumer and lifestyle orientation data, in addition to demographic information and voter profiles from electronic databases, are used to microtarget voters in ways that can undermine citizen privacy. Political parties and campaigns are gaining access to information that was private and using it for political purposes. Although microtargeting and data collection have not yet reached the intrusive, "Big Brother" level, in the brave new political world campaign workers and political officials potentially could gain too much private information about individuals and use it to manipulate citizens' political decisions. As Semiatin points out in chapter 6, today the business world and the political world share information about voter history, issue salience, consumer choices, and the lifestyle behavior of individual citizens without their knowing.

We should consider enacting new privacy laws to prevent private companies, governments, and political campaigns from obtaining too much information about us individually. Citizens have a responsibility to educate themselves and their lawmakers.

From Party-Centered, to Candidate-Centered, to Interest Group Election Campaigns?

For at least the last fifty years, elections have been changing from party centered to candidate centered. Candidates have had to raise more of their own money, define the issues on which they are running, and deliver their message to the voters with less and less help from the political parties. As Kasniunas and Rozell spell out in chapter 8, interest groups, both in the traditional form and as 527 committees, are having an ever-greater impact on campaign fundraising, issue advocacy, endorsements, and voter mobilization. Group campaign contributions through PACs are critical to all major campaigns. Sometimes their separate political ads, like those by the "Swift Vote Veterans for Truth" against John Kerry in 2004, directly affect election outcomes. It is too much to declare that all political campaigns have become interest group centered. But it is now clear that there is a three-way alliance among the candidate, the political party, and interest groups. When they work well together, the candidates supported by their party and the interest groups usually win.

Interest groups are invaluable in articulating the concerns of their members and in mobilizing voters on election day. Yet interest group–controlled campaigns are also a threat to democracy. As James Madison warned in the *Federalist*, No. 10, interest groups, which he called "factions," promote the self-interest and ideological passions of some citizens over the rights of other citizens and the public interest.[12] Interest group mobilization is good because it organizes individuals and gives a voice to their concerns. It amplifies their voices so that they are heard in government decision making. But whereas interest articulation is important, society also requires interest aggregation. That is best done by political parties, which bring together different interests and force groups to compromise to create a single political platform, which will be supported by a majority of voters. Interest groups do not play this critical function.

Are Parties Vital Enough to Check Interest Groups?

As candidate-centered, interest group–based campaigns become stronger, are political parties too weak to play their role successfully? Current campaign funding laws have the effect of further limiting political parties.

But as Shaiko demonstrates in chapter 7, political parties have not yet been overwhelmed by interest groups and in many ways have been revitalized. The "party service" model that Shaiko refers to has enabled national committees to modernize themselves to assist candidates and mobilize voters. They have been able to raise money more effectively than was expected when large soft money contributions were eliminated by campaign finance reform legislation. They have embarked on new membership campaigns to compete in all fifty states, particularly under Democratic Party chairman Howard Dean. However, candidate-centered, interest group–based campaigns are still strong enough to undermine political party contributions to representative democracy.

Accountability Diminishes: Reporting Politics in the Twenty-First Century

Technology can facilitate political participation, but it can also facilitate distortion. Jeremy D. Mayer points out in chapter 9 that the new political reporter may be masquerading as a legitimate journalist, when in fact that individual is a partisan. In fact, campaigns have their own reporters today, putting information on Web sites and blogs. The result is that accountability is lost because there is no filter of journalistic standards. The information may or may not be accurate, but Internet and mobile technology accelerate the reporting of "news" as fact, when it might be rumor. This is no different from what partisan newspapers did in the early nineteenth century, with one exception—then the reportage was not instantaneous, and there was time for reflection. Today that reflection time is lost, and that injures both the citizenry and the profession of public service. When fact and rumor cannot be distinguished, then constitutional values we hold dear are at risk. Truthfulness is not a commodity for trade.

Are Voters Customers?

The book began with the premise that elections are becoming more customer driven in the new century. Earlier we referred to campaigns being more interest group centered, although we acknowledge that parties are still vital. Is there a connection? And if so, what implication does it have for democracy? In both cases, campaigns and interests are seeking to entice voters (or members) and to satisfy their wants. There is no problem when a group, party, or candidate uses research to seek a greater understanding of the people whom they wish to represent. However, treating democracy as a commodity has a corrosive effect on the meaning of citizenship. When citizens are thought of as customers, they are usually offered choices between the Democratic and Republican brands. Is a citizen's civic duty simply to choose the "better" brand? And even if the brands have value, as commodities, can they be replaced, discarded, or devalued? As implied earlier, when candidates connect personally with citizens, and a bond is forged between them, it is not based on customer satisfaction but on shared values. That is at the heart of democracy and representation.

Winning Elections

Campaigns for elected office are exciting, demanding, and rewarding if they are well run. They are indispensable to democracy. New campaign techniques for the most part simply modernize the basic campaign strategies that Lincoln articulated. The new campaigns and new campaign technologies have the potential to allow "the little guy" to participate more effectively and to better inform the electorate. However, they also have a dark side—the possibility of manipulation, disinformation, and unfair, negative tactics, which defeat good candidates and create greater voter apathy and antipathy. There is also the danger that our privacy is endangered when campaigns acquire so much information about our personal lives, as they micro-target us as potential supporters.

The ideal model of election communication is a debate in which the voters can hear all the candidates at the same time and carefully weigh the strengths and weaknesses of each and their stands on issues. New laws can achieve public financing of elections, require greater transparency, and provide better privacy protections. All of these contribute to candidates' being better able to communicate to voters and disclose their financial contributors. As Francia, Joe, and Wilcox argue in chapter 10, if there are to be new laws that provide for public funding of campaigns or term limits on officeholders, they will be passed by the states, not the national government. Neither national leaders nor the citizens are demanding more changes at the national level at the moment.

In the end, modern campaign techniques will not be controlled by new laws alone. Nor can the potential evils of new political campaigns be curbed by protests from political scientists and editorial writers. The new campaigns with their modern technology can be made to serve and not subvert democracy only if the public uses the additional information available and the possibilities of the Internet to elect the best possible candidates. Voters must reject candidates who misuse new technology to spread disinformation about themselves or their opponents.

If the democratic ideal remains a public debate, then all candidates must have the opportunity to present themselves and their message to the public as unfiltered as possible. With public financing, full campaign contribution disclosure, and guaranteed voter privacy, candidates will have an equal chance to present their case. With greater candidate information presented by cable television and the Internet, careful campaign scrutiny by political reporters and bloggers, and neutral voter information pamphlets published by the government, voters will have the opportunity to cast informed votes that best reflect their beliefs and best promote the public interest. All of these changes need to occur if we are to have free and fair elections in the twenty-first century. Of all the necessary changes in law, probably the most important is some type of public financing, to even the playing field and allow candidates the funds to send their message to the voters without being unduly beholden either to wealthy individuals who bundle contributions or to interest groups through their political action committees. But no single silver bullet will guarantee fair and free elections.

New political campaigns using advanced technology and new methods can promote or undermine democracy. To make sure that democracy is promoted, we need campaign laws that ensure free and fair elections, as Renner suggests in chapter 11. Most of all, we need an aware and informed electorate that will elect candidates who use the new techniques to increase democracy and defeat those who would subvert it.

Notes

1. Brittney Pescatore, "Hey Big Spender: Here Is What It Costs to Buy These Votes," *Campaigns and Elections,* September 2007, 13.
2. Joe McGinniss, *The Selling of the President 1968* (New York: Simon and Schuster, 1969).
3. Campaign Finance Institute, *Small Donors and Online Giving: A Study of Donors to the 2004 Presidential Campaigns* (Washington, D.C.: Campaign Finance Institute, 2006).
4. Chris Taylor, "How Dean Is Winning the Web," *Time Magazine,* July 14, 2003.
5. Jeff Zeleny, "Obama Campaign Raises $32.5 Million," *New York Times,* July 2, 2007.
6. Richard Auxier and Alex Tyson, *Uploading Democracy: Candidates Field YouTube Questions,* Pew Research Center Publications, July 24, 2007.
7. Philip N. Howard, *New Media Campaigns and the Managed Citizen* (Cambridge: Cambridge University Press, 2006), 3.
8. Jake Batsell, "In Plano Mayor's Race Web Ads Are a Sure Hit: Candidates Put a Little Cash and a Lot of Faith in Efficient E-Videos," *Dallas Morning News,* May 11, 2006.
9. Andrea Stone, "Cleland Defeated by Conservative," *USA Today,* November 6, 2002.
10. Samuel L. Popkin, *The Reasoning Voter* (Chicago: University of Chicago Press, 1991).
11. "Election Day Ain't What It Used to Be . . . Political Campaigns Have Changed Their Strategies to Target Early Voters," editorial, *Denver Post,* July 18, 2004, 6.
12. Alexander Hamilton, James Madison, and John Jay, *The Federalist Papers,* any edition. In *Federalist* No. 10, James Madison defined a "faction" or what we would call today an interest group as follows: "By a faction, I understand a number of citizens, whether amounting to a majority or minority of the whole, who are united and actuated by some common impulse of passion, or of interest, adverse to the rights of other citizens, or to the permanent and aggregate interests of the community."

Index